ROUTLEDGE LIBRARY EDITIONS: POLICE AND POLICING

Volume 11

POLICE POWERS AND ACCOUNTABILITY

POLICE POWERS AND ACCOUNTABILITY

JOHN L. LAMBERT

LONDON AND NEW YORK

First published in 1986 by Croom Helm Ltd.

This edition first published in 2023
by Routledge
4 Park Square, Milton Park, Abingdon, Oxon OX14 4RN

and by Routledge
605 Third Avenue, New York, NY 10158

Routledge is an imprint of the Taylor & Francis Group, an informa business

© 1986 J. L. Lambert

All rights reserved. No part of this book may be reprinted or reproduced or utilised in any form or by any electronic, mechanical, or other means, now known or hereafter invented, including photocopying and recording, or in any information storage or retrieval system, without permission in writing from the publishers.

Trademark notice: Product or corporate names may be trademarks or registered trademarks, and are used only for identification and explanation without intent to infringe.

British Library Cataloguing in Publication Data
A catalogue record for this book is available from the British Library

ISBN: 978-1-032-41114-9 (Set)
ISBN: 978-1-032-41898-8 (Volume 11) (hbk)
ISBN: 978-1-032-41905-3 (Volume 11) (pbk)
ISBN: 978-1-003-36030-8 (Volume 11) (ebk)

DOI: 10.4324/9781003360308

Publisher's Note
The publisher has gone to great lengths to ensure the quality of this reprint but points out that some imperfections in the original copies may be apparent.

Disclaimer
The publisher has made every effort to trace copyright holders and would welcome correspondence from those they have been unable to trace.

POLICE POWERS AND ACCOUNTABILITY

JOHN L. LAMBERT

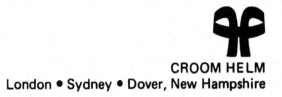

CROOM HELM
London • Sydney • Dover, New Hampshire

© 1986 J.L. Lambert
Croom Helm Ltd, Provident House, Burrell Row,
Beckenham, Kent BR3 1AT
Croom Helm Australia Pty Ltd, Suite 4, 6th Floor
64-76 Kippax Street, Surry Hills, NSW 2010, Australia

British Library Cataloguing in Publication Data

Lambert, J.L.
   Police powers and accountability.
   1. Police – Great Britain – Complaints against
   I. Title
   363.2'0941   HV7936.C6

   ISBN 0-7099-1660-4

Croom Helm, 51 Washington Street, Dover,
New Hampshire 03820, USA

Library of Congress Cataloging in Publication Data

Lambert, J.L. (John L.)
   Police powers and accountability.

   Includes index.
   1. Police–England. 2. Police–Wales. 3. Police–
England–complaints against. 4. Police–Wales–
complaints against. I. Title.
HV8196.A3L35   1986   363.2'3'0942   85-21282
ISBN 0-7099-1660-4

Printed and bound in Great Britain
by Billing & Sons Limited, Worcester.

CONTENTS

Table of Cases
Table of Statutes
Preface

1.	THE POLICING DEBATE	1

2.	THE ACCOUNTABILITY OF THE POLICE	18

Introduction 18
The Historical Background 19
   (a)   The early history 20
   (b)   The 'new police' 23
   (c)   The 1962 Royal Commission 29
The Institutions of Accountability and
   their Effectiveness 30
   (i)   The office of constable 30
   (ii)   Police Authorities 36
   (iii) Chief Constables 44
   (iv)   Central Government 50

3.	THE POLICE COMPLAINTS PROCEDURE	61

Introduction 61
The Police Act 1976 63
The Movement for Reform 68
The Police Complaints Authority 75
Conclusions 81

4.	ARREST AND DETENTION	92

Introduction 92
Arrest 94
   (a)   Arrest without warrant for breach
         of the peace 95
   (b)   Arrest without warrant for
         arrestable offences 98

CONTENTS

(c) General arrest powers 100
(d) Requirements of a valid arrest
     without warrant 102
Detention 111
(i) Custody officers and their duties 112
(ii) Review of Detention 113
(iii) Detention for serious arrestable
      offences 114
(iv) Treatment of Detained suspects .. 117
(v) Criticism of the Detention
    provisions 122

5. STOP AND SEARCH AND RELATED PROVISIONS   137

The Common Law 137
Specific Statutory Authority 142
Road-blocks 149

6. SEARCH AND SEIZURE   156

Introduction 156
Entry onto Private Premises 158
Search 160
(a) On Arrest 160
(b) Under Warrant 172
Seizure 178
Unlawfully Obtained Evidence and
Admissibility 183

7. POLICE QUESTIONING AND SURREPTITIOUS
    SURVEILLANCE   194

Police Questioning 194
The Right of Silence 197
The 1984 Act and Code Procedures 199
(a) The procedural framework 199
(b) Admissibility 203
Tape-Recording 205
Surreptitious Surveillance 207

APPENDIX   220

Table 1 221
Table 2 223

INDEX   226

TABLE OF CASES

Adair v McGarry (1933) 188.
Albert v Lavin (1982) 131.
Alderson v Booth (1969) 94.
Allen v London & SW Ry Co. (1859) 130.
Attorney General for New South Wales v Perpetual
    Trustee Company (1952) 32, 47.

Baker v Oxford (1980) 105.
Barnard v Gorman (1941) 128, 129.
Barnett & Grant v Campbell (1902) 188.
Baynes v Brewster (1802) 128.
Bessel v Wilson (1853) 188.
Bird v Jones (1845) 94.
Brazil v Chief Constable of Surrey (1983) 162.
Burdett v Abbott (1811) 186

Callis v Gunn (1964) 193, 197.
Chic Fashions (W. Wales) Ltd v Jones (1968) 179,
    186, 187, 191.
Christie v Leachinsky (1947) 103, 109, 130, 162,
Clubb v Wimpey & Co (1936) 129.
Cohen v Huskisson (1838) 128.
Conway v Hotten (1976) 215.
Conway v Rimmer (1968) 56.
Crozier v Cundy (1827) 191.

Dallison v Caffery (1965) 131.
Davis v Lisle (1936) 186.
DPP v Ping Lin (1976) 197.
Donnelly v Jackman (1970) 138, 139.
Dumbell v Roberts (1944) 130.

Elias v Pasmore (1934) 188.
Elkins v United States (1960) 193.
Entick v Carrington (1765) 157, 158, 167.

TABLE OF CASES

Farrow v Tunnicliffe (1976)   153.
Fisher v Oldham Corporation (1930)   31, 47.
Frank Truman Export Ltd v Metropolitan Police
    Commissioner (1977)   192.
Fraser v Evans (1969)   218.

Garfunkel v Metropolitan Police Commissioner (1972)
    192.
Gelberg v Miller (1961)   109.
Genner v Sparkes (1704)   186.
Ghani v Jones (1969)   163, 173, 179-180, 181, 182,
    186, 189.
GH Photography v McGarrigle (1974) (Australia)   192.

Hoffman v Thomas (1974)   154.
Humphries v Connor (1864)   97, 98, 128, 186.

Inland Revenue Commissioners v Rossminster (1980)
    187.
Isaacs v Keech (1925)   129.

Jeffrey v Black (1978)   163, 164, 171, 193.
John Lewis & Co v Tims (1952)   131.

Katz v United States (1967)   209.
Kay v Hibbert (1977)   186.
Kenlin v Gardner (1967)   131.
King v Hodges (1974)   128.
King v R (1969)   193.
Klass v Federal Republic of Germany (1978)   218.
Kuruma v R (1955)   57, 193.

Lavrock v Brown (1819)   187.
Leach v Money (1765)   186.
Leigh v Cole (1853)   188.
Lewis v Cattle (1938)   56.
Lindley v Rutter (1980)   162, 165.
Ludlow v Burgess (1971)   139.

McArdle v Egan (1934)   130.
McBride v United States   128.
McFarlane v Sharp (1972)   192.
McGovern v HM Advocate (1950)   188, 193.
Malone v Commissioner of Police for the Metropolis
    (no 2)(1979)   208-210.
Malone v United Kingdom (1984)   211.
Mapp v Ohio (1961)   193.
Mohammed-Holgate v Duke (1984)   151, 214.
Morris v Beardmore (1980)   160, 185, 186.

Park v United States   129.

TABLE OF CASES

Pedro v Diss (1981) 152.
Piddington v Bates (1960) 128.
Price v Messenger (1800) 191.
Pringle v Bremmer & Stirling (1867) 191.

R v Allen (1977) 215.
R v Birtles (1969) 130.
R v Brown (1841) 128.
R v Brown (1977) 140-142.
R v Chief Constable of Devon and Cornwall ex p CEGB
    (1981) 14, 48.
R v Cleary (1964) 215, 216.
R v Corr (1968) 216.
R v Elliott (1977) 215.
R v Fennell (1970) 131.
R v Flynn and Leonard (1972) 216.
R v Gavin (1885) 194.
R v Gilham (1828) 215.
R v Houghton and Franciosy (1977) 137, 138.
R v Howell (1978) 128.
R v Hudson (1980) 132.
R v Ibrahim (1914) 194, 197.
R v Inwood (1973) 94, 95, 151.
R v Jones (1978) 136.
R v Kulynycz (1970) 130.
R v Leathem (1861) 183.
R v Lemsatef (1977) 151, 215.
R v G. Light (1857) 128.
R v Marsden (1868) 186.
R v McGrath (1980) 216.
R v Metropolitan Police Commissioner ex p Blackburn
    (1968) 14, 32, 46, 47, 56, 59.
R v Metropolitan Police Commissioner ex p Blackburn
    (No 3)(1973) 14, 47, 59.
R v Middleton (1975) 215.
R v Naylor (1979) 188.
R v Osbourne and Virtue (1973) 216.
R v Police Complaints Board ex p Madden (1983) 66,
    67.
R v Prager (1972) 215, 216.
R v Priestly (1964) 204.
R v Reeve and Hancock (1872) 215, 216.
R v Rennie (1982) 215.
R v Sang (1979) 35, 36, 57, 183-184, 185, 193, 197.
R v Sherman and Apps (1980) 123, 132.
R v Smith (1959) 215.
R v Taylor (1967) 131.
R v Thompson (1978) 215.
R v Tooley (1780) 106.
R v Walker (1854) 128, 186.
R v Waterfield (1963) 186.

TABLE OF CASES

R v Zaveckas (1970) 215
Rice v Connolly (1966) 129, 137, 138, 151, 194, 215.
Ridge v Baldwin (1963) 55.
Robson v Hallett (1967) 186.
Rochin v California (1952) 187.

Shaabin Bin Hussein v Chong Fook Kam (1970) 108,
    130.
Squires v Botwright (1972) 139.
State v McCloud 128.
Steel v Goacher (1983) 154.

Thomas v Sawkins (1935) 186.

United States v Calundra (1974) 193.
United States v Janis (1976) 193.

Walters v WH Smith Ltd (1914) 129.
Weeks v United States (1914) 192.
Wershof v Metropolitan Police Commissioner (1978)
    180, 192.
Wheatley v Lodge (1971) 128, 131.
Wills v Bowley (1982) 105, 129.
Wiltshire v Barrett (1965) 105, 130.

TABLE OF STATUTES

Airports Authority Act 1975   142, 152.
Aviation Security Act 1982   133.

Badgers Act 1973   152.

City of London Police Act 1839   24, 55.
County and Borough Police Act 1856   26, 27.
Conservation of Seals Act 1970   142.
Criminal Attempts Act 1981   5, 15, 145, 153.
Criminal Justice (Scotland) Act 1980   136.
Criminal Law Act 1967   96, 98, 99, 109, 209.
Criminal Law Act 1977   118, 187.
Customs Amendment Act (Australia) 1979   189.
Customs and Excise Management Act 1979   129.

Dangerous Drugs Act 1967   144.
Deer Act 1963   152.
Deer Act 1980   152.

Explosive Substances Act 1883   133.

Firearms Act 1968   133, 152.

Legal Aid Act 1982   135
Local Government Act 1888   25, 55.

Magistrates' Courts Act 1952   112, 121, 132, 136.
Magistrates' Courts Act 1980   112, 121, 132, 136.
Metropolitan Police Act 1829   24, 47, 55.
Metropolitan Police Act 1839   143.
Misuse of Drugs Act 1971   142, 143, 144, 152.
Municipal Corporations Act 1835   25, 26, 27, 31.

Official Secrets Act 1911   56.

Poaching Prevention Act 1862   142.

LIST OF STATUTES

Police Act 1919   28.
Police Act 1946   28, 55.
Police Act 1964   30, 35, 37, 38, 45, 46, 51, 52, 62,
     151.
Police Act 1969   60.
Police Act 1976   9, 63-68.
Police and Criminal Evidence Act 1984   2, 7, 8, 9,
     15, 54, 75, 76-81, 92, 96, 99-102, 104, 108-
     127, 139, 142, 143-151, 158, 160, 165-178, 181,
     194, 196, 199-205, 206.
     s. 1   145, 146, 153, 155.
     s. 2   146, 153.
     s. 3   146, 153.
     s. 4   150, 154.
     s. 5   149, 150, 154.
     s. 7   143, 152.
     s. 8   160, 175, 178, 182, 187, 191.
     s. 9   176, 177, 181, 182.
     S.10   176, 191.
     s.11   177, 191.
     s.12   177, 191.
     s.13   177, 191.
     s.14   177, 191.
     s.15   174, 190, 191.
     s.16   174, 191.
     s.17   151, 154, 159, 160, 187.
     s.18   160, 171, 172, 187, 190.
     s.19   171, 175, 181, 182, 191, 192.
     s.22   188, 189.
     s.24   99, 129.
     s.25   101, 129.
     s.28   108, 109, 130, 131.
     s.29   95, 151.
     s.30   110, 111, 130.
     s.32   147, 154, 165, 170, 171, 188, 190.
     s.35   110, 131.
     s.36   112, 132.
     s.37   112, 113, 132.
     s.38   113, 133.
     s.39   112, 132, 134.
     s.40   114, 133.
     s.41   113, 132.
     s.42   113, 115, 132, 133.
     s.43   116, 134.
     s.44   116, 117, 134.
     s.46   113, 133.
     s.54   166, 167, 189.
     s.55   168, 189.
     s.56   118, 119, 134.
     s.58   119, 135.
     s.59   120, 135.

LIST OF STATUTES

```
s.60   206.
s.61   121, 136.
s.62   169, 170, 190.
s.64   122, 136.
s.65   169, 189, 190.
s.66   117, 134.
s.67   126, 136.
s.76   203, 204.
s.78   185.
s.84   76, 77, 78, 80, 90.
s.85   76, 79, 80, 90,
s.86   78, 90.
s.87   77, 89.
s.88   77, 89.
s.89   76, 77, 78, 89, 90.
s.90   79, 90.
s.92   80, 90.
s.93   80, 90.
s.95   81, 90.
s.99   89.
s.106  15, 54, 222.
s.116  115, 123, 133, 136.
s.117  165, 174, 188, 191.
```
Police Pensions Act 1948   28, 55.
Post Office Act 1953   208, 217.
Post Office Act 1969   208, 217.
Prevention of Crime Act 1953   153.
Prevention of Terrorism (Temporary Provisions) Act
    1976   136, 138.
Prevention of Terrorism (Temporary Provisions) Act
    1984   135, 152.
Public Order Act 1936   187.

Road Traffic Act 1960   139.
Road Traffic Act 1972   105, 133, 140, 149, 151, 190.
Rural Constabulary Act 1839   25.

Sexual Offences Act 1956   129, 133.
Statute of Winchester 1285   55.

Taking of Hostages Act 1972   133.
Telecommunications Act 1984   217.
Theft Act 1968   129, 146, 153, 159.
Town Police Clauses Act 1847   105, 129.

Vagrancy Act 1824   145.

Wildlife and Countryside Act 1981   152.

PREFACE

In the last few years much excellent work has been done on the subject of the police and policing, some of which has been cited in this volume. At the same time, the study of aspects of policing at degree level has become commonplace. This book has been written primarily with the needs of students studying the police in the context of law and law related courses in mind. It attempts to address those issues which most usually feature in such courses - the constitutional framework within which the police operate, the police complaints procedure and police powers - against the background of the considerable public and political debate about policing which has taken place in recent years. While the Police and Criminal Evidence Act, 1984, has been discussed in what is hoped is sufficient detail to fulfil the purpose set out above, this book does not purport to be a comprehensive guide to that legislation. A number of such specialist guides have, however, been published to which reference can be made as appropriate. It should also be noted that the discussion is limited to the forty three police forces established in England and Wales: it does not deal with policing in Scotland, where the arrangements differ significantly, neither does it deal with the private police forces employed by, for example, the statutory undertakers.

A number of people have assisted during the preparation of this work and I would like to take this opportunity to acknowledge with gratitude my debt to them: those police officers, Home Office officials and police authority clerks who took the time and trouble to respond courteously and speedily to my enquiries; my colleague, Alan Parkin, for his helpful comments on a number of the chapters; the publishers and editors of Public Law and the Modern

PREFACE

Law Review for permission to use some material first
published in those journals; Betty Kleckham for
typing the manuscript; my publishers for their
great forbearance; and finally, my family for their
support. The responsibility for any errors or
omissions remains, of course, entirely my own.

John Lambert,
Hull.

Chapter I

THE POLICING DEBATE

The traditional formulation of the nature of the
police role emphasises impartial enforcement of the
law and accountability. The existence of local
constabularies, democratically accountable to local
police authorities, has been seen as a safeguard
against a national government controlled force and
has helped to foster the idea that the police role
somehow stands outside politics. The enforcement of
the law is a duty owed ultimately to the law itself
and the task of enforcement is carried out impartially and even-handedly. In this way civil liberties
are protected and society is reassured that the
police are not its masters, but its servants.
    This comfortable analysis has been increasingly
under attack in recent years. Indeed, the present
decade has witnessed a public debate about policing,
the intensity of which is virtually unprecedented.
The most immediate cause of the debate was undoubtedly the riots which took place in the early summer of
1981. The setting up of the Scarman Inquiry into the
Brixton disorders[1] received enormous publicity and
culminated in a lengthy and controversial Report,[2]
which recommended changes across the whole ambit of
policing matters. The riots were also significant,
however, in that they provided the catalyst by which
longstanding and deep-seated causes of dissatisfact-
ion with the police were highlighted.
    There has, for example, been a growing realisa-
tion that the traditional formulation of the nature
of the police role masks its true nature. The
policing function inevitably involves the formulation
of policies, the setting of standards, the assessment
of priorities and the efficient utilisation of
limited resources. The police, notwithstanding the
image that they like to project, do not simply
enforce the law. They make policy about what law to

1

THE POLICING DEBATE

enforce, how much to enforce it, when to enforce it and against whom to enforce it. Consequently, the policies they adopt are likely to be elaborate, and one might add, largely publicly unarticulated (despite the higher priority now given to community involvement) and beyond the reach of judicial review.[3] At the heart of the policing debate, therefore, lies the issue of the control of discretionary power.

The myth that the police are simply objective agents of the law has also been exposed by the overt and unmistakeable movement of the police into the political arena. Among chief officers, the movement probably began with Sir Robert Mark, former Metropolitan Police Commissioner, who adopted the role of police publicist in the early seventies. Others followed his example[4] - the "media cop" had arrived. A clutch of highly articulate chief constables, assisted with vigour by the Association of Chief Police Officers (ACPO) expressed clear opinions on the conditions of the times and the police role in the governmental process. A number of them lobbied unashamedly for greater police powers while at the same time, usually denying the need for greater accountability.[5] The success of the lobby can be judged by reference to the Police and Criminal Evidence Act, 1984, which eventually found its way onto the statute book after a three year political battle. Apart from ACPO, the police staff organisations generally have become political pressure groups as was made very evident by, for instance, the unsuccessful campaign waged by the Police Federation, in the media as well as in the lobbies, to persuade Parliament to vote in favour of the reintroduction of capital punishment.

When prolonged and bitter industrial disputes occur, the police role is particularly susceptible to analysis in political terms. Violent confrontation between police and pickets captures headlines and polarises political attitudes. To some, the police are agents of a repressive state, over-reacting and thus provoking violence: others, including the police themselves, argue that they are simply preserving the peace and maintaining law and order, though the question-begging nature of that assertion is perhaps not fully appreciated by those who make it. One thing, however, is clear in such situations; the police will be criticised whatever tactics they employ. As John Alderson, former chief constable of Devon and Cornwall, has commented:

2

THE POLICING DEBATE

> The control of pickets during industrial
> disputes places the police in a
> particularly sensitive situation...The
> police must perforce apply the law with
> great skill and discretion. The clumsy
> use of excessive force would undoubtedly
> be counter-productive. On the other hand,
> weakness would result in exploitation by
> those prone to violence...Drawing lines in
> highly emotional political situations is
> probably the most complex problem facing
> the police in the whole field of public
> order.[6]

The radical shift in the organisation and
character of routine policing which has taken place
over the last twenty years, is discussed particularly
in Chapter Two. The reduction in the number of
forces and the trend towards both regionalisation
and centralisation of policing has distanced the
police from local communities and raised fears about
the movement towards a national or state police
force controlled from the centre and carrying out
policies dictated by the government of the day.
During the miners' strike of 1984/85, the deployment
of large numbers of officers drawn from virtually all
forces in England and Wales to the trouble-spots was
overseen by the National Reporting Centre, set up in
London, under the direction of the President of ACPO.
It effectively replaced the pre-existing "mutual
aid" system under which individual chief constables
requested their chief officer colleagues for a
supply of men as and when the situation demanded and
it is not surprising that questions about the
accountability of the National Reporting Centre
should have been raised by, among others, local
police authorities, some of whom felt that they were
losing contact with the policing arrangements
operating in their own areas. It is against this
background, for example, that South Yorkshire Police
Authority's refusal to pay the bill for feeding and
housing officers drafted into the area to police the
Orgreave Steel Plant must be understood. South
Yorkshire, along with a number of other police
authorities faced additional policing costs of tens
of millions of pounds as a result of the miners'
strike. The financial burden was only one of the
factors behind their decision: another was almost
certainly that the crucial operational decisions
affecting their area were being strongly influenced
by the National Reporting Centre, which gave every

3

THE POLICING DEBATE

appearance of being a law unto itself.[7]

Another recurrent theme in the policing debate has been that of policing styles. The development of the personal radio and the increase in the provision of police vehicles facilitated in the sixties, the introduction of Unit Beat Policing.[8] It was a system under which a Force area was broken down into divisions and sub-divisions and each sub-division further broken down into a number of "areas". Two "areas" would make up one panda car beat patrolled twenty four hours a day. Each area would have an area constable with overall responsibility for the policing of his area and each car-beat was also covered by a detective. As a result of this system, response times to emergency calls were significantly reduced - usually to two or three minutes. In the longer term, however, improved "efficiency" fundamentally changed public demands and increased workloads placed the system under considerable strain. The unit beat teams found it increasingly difficult to act as teams and this aspect of the system virtually collapsed. It was the concentration on the "rapid response" which characterised policing in the sixties and seventies. The police provided a "fire-brigade" or "reactive" service and became preoccupied with response times and law enforcement generally. This concentration on efficiency led to the use of performance indicators to measure the law enforcement aspects of police work - "clear up" rates, response times and so on. By their very nature, the preventive and social welfare aspects of the police role are not susceptible to this form of statistical analysis and were consequently neglected. Law enforcement thus became the major focus of policing policy.

In 1968, the first police "Command and Control" computer was introduced in Birmingham and since that time, a large number of forces have installed computer systems, designed to assist in the best use of available manpower. Baldwin and Kinsey explain how they work:[9]

> At its simplest, the computer is used to keep track of all resources and to plot their availability to respond to calls. When an incident is reported, a VDU operator in the control room will type into the computer all details as they are received - the name and address of the complainant, the locus, the nature of the incident etc. The computer will then

THE POLICING DEBATE

automatically display all details of
traffic patrols, pandas and foot patrols
in the vicinity. The VDU operator then
selects and despatches the appropriate
resource forthwith. The computer is
informed of the action taken and the
system is ready for the next call.

Under such a system, incidents cannot be forgotten
or overlooked and an accurate record of demand and
resource is available for management purposes. At
the heart of the system again, however, is the
concentration on response times.

Reactive policing and the adoption of "hard"
policing methods are closely connected and the
creation of special squads to deal with emergencies
has been especially attacked. The best-known of
these squads is, of course, the Special Patrol Group
of the Metropolitan Police Force, which was set up
in 1965 to aid the local divisions and provide
saturation policing in high crime areas. Since
1965, other Forces have created their own groups,
often named Tactical Support Groups or Force Support
Units. Available evidence suggests that there are
twenty seven such groups in existence in various
parts of the country.[10] Their use in the policing
of inner city areas has been seen by many as a cause
for particular concern.[11] Throughout the seventies,
the evidence that a widening gap was developing
between the police and the ethnic communities
mounted. Saturation policing in such areas, widespread and allegedly discriminatory use of the "sus"
laws and stop and search provisions, were constantly
suggested as major causes of this alienation.
Indeed, when in 1980, the Home Affairs Committee of
the House of Commons examined these issues, one of
their central recommendations was the abolition of
the "sus" laws,[12] a step effected by the Criminal
Attempts Act, 1981.[13]

In Brixton, the SPG were used on four
occasions between January 1978 and September 1980.
Lord Scarman's conclusion was unequivocal: "They
provoked the hostility of young black people who
felt that they were being hunted irrespective of
their guilt or innocence. And their hostility
infected older members of the community..."[14] The
riots in Brixton began on April 10th 1981.
"Operation Swamp" began on April 6th and was sched-
uled to last until April 11th. It involved 112
officers (not from the SPG on this occasion). The
Commander of the operation's written instructions to

5

THE POLICING DEBATE

his men ran as follows:

> The purpose of this operation is to flood
> identified areas...to detect burglars and
> robbers. The essence of the exercise,
> therefore, is to ensure that all officers
> remain on the streets and success will
> depend on a concentrated effort of stops
> based on powers of surveillance and
> suspicion proceeded by persistent and astute
> questioning.[15]

The success of such operations in law enforcement
terms is a matter of conjecture - they may diminish
street crime in the target area only at the expense
of driving it elsewhere. The harm that they can do
to police/public relationships, however, is now a
matter of history.

The riots and their aftermath[16] exposed the
relative inability of the police to handle such
situations effectively and restore law and order to
the streets rapidly and caused the police to take
stock of the situation. An immediate consequence
was increased emphasis on riot training and a comprehensive review of riot control equipment - from
protective clothing to C.S. gas and plastic bullets.
More generally, however, the reception given to the
Scarman Report by the police evidenced a significant
polarisation of attitudes amongst senior officers.
Probably in the majority, are those who see the main
thrust of policing as being summed up in the "holy
trinity" of policing - more men, more powers and
more equipment,[17] thus emphasising law enforcement
and police professionalism. Opposed to this view is
that which sees the police role as at the same time,
more diverse and more marginal. Law enforcement as
such occupies no more than fifty per cent of police
time and the control of crime cannot be achieved by
the police acting alone. To this extent, concentration on enforcement of the law and the police role
in that process, obscures the fact that society as a
whole has a crucially important role to play in
policing. Those who advocate this view, therefore,
see community involvement as central to effective
policing, and it is in this context that community
or "communal" policing must be examined.

Both the concept and the terminology of community policing have in recent years been most closely
associated with John Alderson.[18] At its heart, it
revives the idea of "policing by consent" through
the medium of police officers who are a part of and

THE POLICING DEBATE

responsive to the communities they serve. The aim is preventive or "proactive", as opposed to "reactive", policing. Critics of the idea are to be found outside[19] as well as within the police service. Nevertheless, most forces, since the Scarman Report, have been more active on this front, in part stimulated by the Government who first, through ministerial circular[20] and then, through legislation,[21] have adopted Lord Scarman's recommendations concerning increased police/community liaison and consultation.[22] One of the problems is, of course, that community policing is a label, which like that of police accountability, means all things to all men.

The rift which appears to have developed between the public and the police in the seventies was not just a consequence of the style of policing adopted. The issue of what powers the police should be given has been central to the policing debate, though the link between function and powers is not always clearly made. "Reactive" policing depends mainly on the use of coercive powers, particularly those sanctioning "stop and search". An enduring dilemma is thus highlighted - how can the police be accountable to those upon whom they impose their authority? The damage that can be done to police/community relationships by the arbitrary and insensitive use of undesirably opaque or wide powers is insidious. The uncertain and haphazard nature of some such powers made abuse easy: internal monitoring of their use was inefficient and central supervision, through for example, the Inspectorate of Constabulary, virtually non-existent. The argument that stop and search powers should be abolished, as being both unnecessary and a major contributory course of public unease, was rejected by the government, which chose instead to extend them but control their use more carefully by the provision of more effective safeguards. In addition, the Police and Criminal Evidence Act, 1984, provides increased police powers of arrest, detention, search and seizure. This important and highly controversial legislation, which will provide the framework for policing into the next century, was based upon the recommendations of the Royal Commission on Criminal Procedure, which themselves were highly criticised.[23] Although it is true that the legislation provides some increased protection for the rights of suspects, the balance has been tipped very firmly in favour of the police and the law enforcement aspect of the policing function.

Public confidence in its police forces can, of

7

THE POLICING DEBATE

course, be damaged in a more dramatic manner, as the Metropolitan Police Force found to its cost in the aftermath of the revelations of wholesale corruption in its vice squad in the early seventies,[24] while later in the same decade, the failure of "Operation Countryman" to identify and bring to justice more than a handful of corrupt London officers further damaged the credibility of the police. Allegations of police brutality and mistreatment of suspects in detention also became more prevalent (or perhaps simply more highly publicised) during this period and there were a number of causes celebres. The most widely publicised was the death of the teacher Blair Peach during the policing of a demonstration in Southall in 1978 by the SPG. The allegation that he was killed by a blow from a police weapon has never been satisfactorily refuted, despite considerable evidence that some SPG members were carrying unauthorised weapons, because the Home Secretary refused to set up a public inquiry into the death.[25] The deaths of Jimmy Kelly and Liddle Towers after being held in police custody similarly provoked controversy about the police treatment of them. In 1980, it was revealed that between 1970 and 1979, some 274 people had died while in police custody.[26] In the overwhelming majority of the cases, death resulted from natural causes and the police were in no way responsible. Nevertheless, such statistics, when made publicly known, inevitably engender public concern.

In 1977, the Fisher Inquiry into the Maxwell Confait murder case,[27] which was set up following the quashing of the murder convictions of three youths who had "confessed" to the killing, raised serious questions about the way in which the police had handled the investigation, particularly in relation to the treatment of juveniles and mentally handicapped suspects. It also found, and this was extremely worrying, that experienced Metropolitan Police officers either ignored, or were ignorant of, some of the provisions of the Judges' Rules, particularly those dealing with the "right"[28] of a suspect to make telephone calls. That the rather tighter control of the treatment of suspects in detention introduced by the Police and Criminal Evidence Act, 1984, and the associated Codes of Practice is a consequence of the Confait case, cannot be doubted.

Public disquiet about the events and incidents outlined above was exacerbated by the strongly held feeling in some parts of the community that the police could not be relied upon to investigate

THE POLICING DEBATE

abuses of power and wrongdoing by the police themselves sufficiently rigorously and impartially. The procedures for investigating complaints against the police are examined in detail in Chapter Three, and it is not intended to rehearse again here that discussion. A number of general points can be made, however. The Police Act, 1976 was enacted, against a background of substantial opposition from within the police service, to introduce an independent element, the Police Complaints Board, into the procedures. The Board signally failed to allay public unease that justice was not being seen to be done, if indeed it was being done. Critics of the scheme, among them as we shall see, Lord Scarman, argued that independent investigation of complaints by non-police investigators was crucial if public confidence in the complaints procedures was to be restored. As the "policing debate" intensified in the eighties, the complaints procedures became a major political issue and were scrutinised by a number of official bodies. The need for reform became manifest: the direction that the reforms should take was hotly contested. In the event, the Police and Criminal Evidence Act 1984, reformed the procedures by creating a new Police Complaints Authority with extended powers to supervise investigations. Independent investigation of complaints however, has been rejected, with the result that the police complaints controversy is likely to continue unabated.

The final trend which became apparent in the latter half of the seventies was the re-thinking by the police authorities of their role. The rift between the police authorities and chief constables came to a head as we have seen in 1984 against a background of the controversy over the policing of the miners' strike. Previously, however, there had been some notable public disputes between certain authorities and their chief constables. The Chairman of the South Yorkshire Police Authority went on record in 1977 as saying that the only function of the police authority was to rubber stamp decisions of the police. Relationships between the police and the authority became so strained that when the authority set up a working party to investigate the relationships between the police and the public in South Yorkshire, the chief constable refused to co-operate with it.[29] At about the same time, the chief constable of West Mercia was reported as saying that he was not prepared to be accountable to a local government committee for his actions.[30] Perhaps the most publicised disagreement at the

THE POLICING DEBATE

time, however, was that which involved the Merseyside Police authority. The chief constable refused to reveal to the authority the substance of the police inquiry into the death of Jimmy Kelly, who had died in police custody. This precipitated a row in which the chief constable told members of the authority to "keep out of my Force's business." In response, the authority set up a Working Party to examine the role and responsibilities of the police authority. In its Report, the authority reasserted the independence of police authorities and their ability to require chief constables to account for their actions.[31]
It is important to make the point that the most assertive police authorities have been those controlled by Socialists. Their disputes may not be mirrored in the relationship between chief constables and police authorities over the country as a whole. It is the persistence of authorities like Merseyside and South Yorkshire, however, which has highlighted the relative weakness of police authorities' powers and the virtually complete autonomy of chief constables in operational matters. They argue that local police forces should be locally accountable and that this requires that it should be the police authorities and not chief constables who should control policing policies by requiring the police to operate within a policy framework laid down by the authority.[32] The conventional response to this is that it would lead to politically motivated policing, but in so far as this view is based on the assumption that we presently do not have politically motivated policing, it is highly debatable. It is argued in Chapter Two that the operational autonomy of chief constables gives them enormous power to dictate the style and form of policing in their areas and their decisions cannot but be related to their attitudes and opinions. And can it seriously be argued that a policy of community policing, predicated as it is on community participation, is not a political choice?
Chief constables, as one might expect, are opposed to any extension of police authorities' powers and even John Alderson, often regarded as the thinking man's policeman, denied under his system of communal policing the need for police authorities to play a more meaningful role in the policing of their areas. His police, he said, should contribute to "the common good" and not be "the servant or tool of the majority."[33] Of course, not all police forces are subject to the police authority system in the

THE POLICING DEBATE

sense outlined. The police authority for the Metropolitan Police Force is the Home Secretary and in the seventies there developed a strong lobby to subject the Metropolitan Police to the same kind of police authority system which exists in the provinces. The lobby was spearheaded by the Greater London Council, which pointed to the anomaly that London is policed by two separate police forces (the Metropolitan Police and the City of London Police) and urged that a police authority, exercising extended powers, should be drawn from the elected members of the London Boroughs. The GLC even set up its own (non-statutory) police committee with its own staff to monitor policing in London. While the proposed abolition of the Metropolitan Counties might be thought to give the Home Office an opportunity to re-think the police authority system generally, it is clear that there are no proposals to reform the police authority system except in so far as is strictly necessary. The Home Secretary will remain the police authority for the Metropolitan Police; the other Metropolitan police authorities will vanish and be replaced by Joint Boards drawn from the District and County Councils.

Conclusions

In this chapter, an attempt has been made to discuss some of the trends and developments in policing which have taken place over the last fifteen to twenty years. While the survey does not purport to be comprehensive, all of the issues highlighted challenged the classic formulation of the police role set out at the beginning and reopened fundamental questions about the nature of policing and the relationship of the police with the public. That the police and policing generally, have been going through a difficult and perhaps transitional phase, should be self evident. The governmental response has been four-fold: considerably expanded coercive powers, limited changes in the procedures for investigating complaints against the police, modest innovation in police/community liaison and proposals to set up an independent prosecution system.[34]

The policing debate, however, will continue because the changes are ad hoc responses to what are largely perceived to be current policing problems. There has been little or no attempt at an official level to take a long-term view of the changes that might be necessary in policing in England and Wales.

THE POLICING DEBATE

The last fifty years have seen three Royal Commissions dealing with the police. The first was mainly concerned with police powers.[35] The second, with structure and organisaion.[36] The most recent with pre-trial criminal procedure.[37] By their terms of reference, all three have been confined. The Royal Commission on Criminal Procedure suggested wide-ranging reforms in the law relating to police powers and the prosecution of offences. As will become apparent in Chapter Two, the adoption of a system of independent crown prosecutors has important implications for police accountability. In narrow terms, the Commission was aware of that[38] but it nowhere assesses the impact of its recommendations upon the general arrangements for securing police accountability. On police powers, it argued that law enforcement procedures should be open, fair and workable,[39] but it did not consider what functions society wishes the police to perform and how police powers and the conditions of their exercise are related to the performance of those functions.

In any consideration of policing, the first question to be asked must be, what role do we want the police to perform in society? The answer given to that question has implications for everything else. If the main role is seen as law enforcement, then the police must be organised and equipped, both physically and in terms of the powers they possess, to enable them efficiently to enforce the law. This style of policing, however, is likely to create a permanent hostility between police and public as they will meet only in situations of stress and in the long term be inefficient, therefore, as the lack of public co-operation hampers police effectiveness. It must be remembered that most police activity is initiated by members of the public; the police, by and large, do not detect crime acting on their own. Rapid response times thus become largely irrelevant if the initial contact is either not made at all or made so late as to frustrate the investigation. If, on the other hand, the main role is seen as preventing crime and preserving the peace, this equally has implications for police organisation and powers. The preventive role, for instance, will depend on securing the active co-operation of the community and community involvement in policing must inevitably raise questions about community involvement in monitoring and controlling police activities. A further point is that the police have taken on a number of roles beyond crime prevention, peace-keeping and law enforcement. In particular, they

THE POLICING DEBATE

have entered upon a significant "helping and referral" role. As a disciplined, organised body, operating with good communications twenty four hours a day, the police have proved useful as general providers of assistance - dealing with domestic disputes, lost and found property, missing persons, information giving, the chronically alcoholic and so on. It has been estimated that up to half the time of the police is spent on activities largely unconnected with the prevention and detection of crime. This vast area of activity must be taken into account when examining the nature of the policing function. Law enforcement, as such, may well be hindered and complicated by the fact that so much police effort is expended on non law enforcement activities. Preventive policing, on the other hand, may well be assisted by this helping and referral role.

It is the extent to which all of these functions are compatible which is the real nub of the problem. The truth is that we expect the police to do all of the things set out above - to combine the rapid response with caring, sensitive policing, to apply uniform standards at the same time as responding to local policing needs, to prevent crime as well as to detect it, to remain cool and courteous in the face, sometimes, of extreme provocation and to respect civil liberties at the same time as infringing them. The conundrum for the policy makers, as well as for society as a whole, is how to balance them.

Some of the ways in which policing could be improved are examined in this book: improved opportunities for community liaison and consultation with the police; independent investigation of complaints and an independent prosecuting service; clear, acceptable and understandable policing policies. Others, for example, more rigorous selection procedures and improved training for the police,[40] are beyond its scope. The essential interrelationship of all of these issues, however, will not be considered at an official level if we continue to institute investigations, whether at the level of Royal Commission or Departmental Working Party which by their terms of reference are forbidden to explore the wider issues. The kind of inquiry needed would be expensive in terms of time and resources, but until it takes place, fundamental questions about policing are not going to be satisfactorily answered.

THE POLICING DEBATE

<u>Notes</u>

1.   Lord Scarman was appointed on 14th April 1981 to hold a local inquiry under section 32 of the Police Act, 1964 by the Home Secretary. The terms of reference were "to inquire urgently into the serious disorder in Brixton on 10-12 April 1981 and to report, with the power to make recommendations."

2.   The Report was published in November 1981, Cmnd. 8427.

3.   The courts have consistently taken the view that policing policy and the control of prosecution discretion will be the subject of review only in exceptional cases. See R v Metropolitan Police Commissioner ex p. Blackburn [1968] 2 QB 118 and R v Metropolitan Police Commissioner ex p. Blackburn (No 3) [1973] QB 241, in which Lord Denning M.R. said: "...in the carrying out of their duty of enforcing the law, the police have a discretion with which the courts will not interfere" (p. 254). For a more recent example, see R v Chief Constable of Devon and Cornwall ex p. CEGB [1981] 3 ALL ER 826.

4.   Among the most notable were Mark's successor as Metropolitan Police Commissioner, Sir David McNee, James Anderton, Barry Pain and John Alderson.

5.   The best example is provided by the famous "shopping list" of powers submitted by Sir David McNee to the Royal Commission on Criminal Procedure. See, Written Evidence of the Commissioner of Police of the Metropolis.

6.   See J.C. Alderson, The Principles and Practices of the British Police, in Alderson (ed.) The Police we Deserve, (Wolfe) p. 48.

7.   Some observers would also suggest an overtly political motive for this decision. It was challenged in the Divisional Court by the Attorney General. The proceedings were adjourned on the understanding that the chief constable be allowed to meet the costs involved out of the police budget - see The Times, 5.7.84 and 7.7.84. Merseyside Police Authority was also very unhappy about the role of the National Reporting Centre and at one time was on the verge of challenging its chief constable, Mr. Kenneth Oxford, in the courts. The Authority's chairman, Margaret Simey is reported to have said "We want this to be a test case. Who authorised Oxford to spend the money. We did not." In similar vein, Edwin Shore, chairman of the police committee of the Association of Metropolitan Authorities said: "In the policing of the miners' dispute, the police

THE POLICING DEBATE

authorities have been ignored, yet over £30 million has been spent." - see generally The Observer, 3.6.84. See also, The Guardian, 1.6.84. In the late summer of 1984, the Home Office announced that it would meet virtually all additional policing costs arising from the miners' strike.

8. I am indebted to the excellent discussion of this and related policing styles in Baldwin and Kinsey, Police Powers and Politics, (Quartet Books, London, 1984), Chapter 2.

9. Ibid., p. 53.

10. Details of these Groups are included in Policing the Eighties, State Research Bulletin (Vol. 3) No. 19, September 1980.

11. See e.g. Rollo, The Special Patrol Group in Hain (Ed.) Policing the Police, Vol. 2, pp. 153-208.

12. Race Relations and the 'Sus' Law, Second Report from the Home Affairs Committee, Session 1979-80, H.C. 559 (1980).

13. See s.8. Note, however, that it was thought necessary in view of the abolition of 'sus' to create a new offence of interfering with vehicles - see s.9.

14. Report of the Scarman Inquiry into the Brixton Disorders, op. cit., para. 4.22.

15. The instructions are quoted in the Scarman Report, ibid., at para. 4.39.

16. The Brixton disorders are given prominence because (a) they occurred in London and (b) they were the subject of Lord Scarman's inquiry. They were followed by riots of a similar kind in other parts of the country, most particularly Toxteth in Liverpool and Moss-Side in Manchester. They were preceded, and this is often overlooked, by riots in Bristol in 1980.

17. This, particularly apt, phrase is used by Baldwin and Kinsey, Police Powers and Politics, op. cit.

18. He develops his ideas most systematically in his book Policing Freedom, (MacDonald and Evans, 1979). See also by the same author The Case for Community Policing, in Cowell et al., Policing the Riots, (Junction Books 1982).

19. As a good example, see Waddington, Community Policing : A Sceptical Appraisal, in Norton, (ed.) Law and Order and British Politics, (Gower, 1984) at pp.84-99.

20. See H.O. Circular 54/1982.

21. Police and Criminal Evidence Act, 1984, s.106.

15

THE POLICING DEBATE

     22. These issues are discussed in greater detail in Chapter 2.

     23. See e.g. Baldwin and Kinsey, Police Powers and Politics, op. cit., McBarnet [1981] Crim. L.R. 445, Lidstone, [1981] Crim. L.R. 454, Inman [1981] Crim. L.R. 469.

     24. Sir Robert Mark provides an account of his efforts to eradicate corruption in his autobiography, In the Office of Constable, (Collins, 1978). An interesting and detailed account of the nature and scale of the corruption is provided by B. Cox et al. in The Fall of Scotland Yard, (Penguin, 1979).

     25. A clear precedent for this was the Inquiry conducted by Lord Scarman into the death of the student Kevin Gately during the Red Lion Square demonstration in London in 1974. See Cmnd. 5919 (1975).

     26. See Deaths in Police Custody, Third Report from the Select Committee on Home Affairs, Session 1979/80, HC 631 (1980).

     27. The Confait Case, Report by the Hon. Sir Henry Fisher, HC 90 (December 1977).

     28. The independent Policy Studies Institute Report on the Metropolitan Police, commissioned by Sir David McNee when Metropolitan Police Commissioner, found widespread departure from procedural rules - e.g. failure to tell people that they have been arrested, bullying tactics in interrogation, no records of informal interviews with suspects, breaches of the Judges' Rules and so on.

     29. See Working Together, A Report on Relationships between the Police and the Public in South Yorkshire, South Yorkshire County Council, March 1977.

     30. Worcester Evening News, 12.12.79. Reported in State Research Bulletin, (vol. 4) No. 23, May 1981.

     31. See Role and Responsibilities of the Police Authority, Merseyside Police Authority, 1979.

     32. In the autumn of 1979, Jack Straw, M.P. introduced into Parliament a Private Members Bill (the Police Authorities (Powers) Bill 1979) designed inter alia to give police authorities power to determine general policing policy. The Labour party has committed itself to legislation on similar lines.

     33. See J.C. Alderson, Policing Freedom, op. cit.

     34. At the time of writing, the Government's Prosecution of Offences Bill is going through Parliament. It is based upon legislative proposals set out in a White Paper in 1983 and discussed in

THE POLICING DEBATE

Chapter Two.

35. Royal Commission on Police Powers, Cmd 3297 (1929). Its terms of reference were "...to consider the general powers and duties of police in England and Wales, in the investigation of crimes and offences."

36. Royal Commission on the Police, Cmnd 1728 (1962). Its terms of reference were "to review the constitutional position of the police...the arrangements for their control and administration and in particular to consider (1) the constitution and functions of local police authorities; (2) the status and accountability of members of police forces..."

37. Royal Commission on Criminal Procedure, Cmnd. 8092 (1981). Its terms of reference were "...to examine...whether changes are needed in England and Wales in (i) the powers and duties of the police in respect of the investigation of offences and the rights and duties of suspect and accused persons, including the means by which these are secured; (ii) the process of and responsibility for the prosecution of criminal offences; and (iii) such other features of criminal procedure as relate to the above..."

38. Ibid. See particularly the discussion at paras. 6.48-6.60.

39. Ibid., at para. 2.18.

40. In recent years, the police recruit has received approximately twelve weeks initial training followed by a period (usually two years) as a probationary constable. Lord Scarman in his Report, supra., recommended a substantially longer period of initial training followed by improved supervision during probation. The Policy Studies Institute Report, supra, found that entry standards into the Metropolitan Police were too low, selection interviews too short, and that too few graduates were recruited and that the period of initial training needs to be extended and made more effective. On this latter point, for example, the Institute found that racial prejudice in the Met. was pervasive (though it was not normally carried over into action). The Met. has taken some measures to respond to these criticisms by e.g. extending as from April 1985, the period of initial training to twenty four weeks and introducing more effective Human Awareness courses.

Chapter 2

THE ACCOUNTABILITY OF THE POLICE

Introduction

The widespread public and political debate about
policing which has taken place over the last few
years has focused, *inter alia*, upon the issue 'of
police accountability. There are those who argue
(for example, chief constables, the Home Office),
that the police are fully accountable for their
actions, through internal disciplinary procedures,
police authorities, Parliament and that the concept
of "policing by consent" could not be applied to
policing in the United Kingdom were things otherwise. Others, (for example, The National Council
for Civil Liberties, some police authorities, Lord
Scarman) take the view that the institutions by
which accountability is said to be achieved are
incapable of providing it. In consequence, they
argue, the police have retreated more and more into
their specialised and increasingly technological
world of law enforcement and crime control, becoming
remote from the communities they serve and promul-
gating policing policies and styles which suit only
their own purposes. One difficulty in the way of
understanding, let alone, reconciling, these oppos-
ing views is that "police accountability" has become a slogan whose meaning is only imprecisely
defined. Accountability, in its narrow sense, is
an *ex post facto* process by which actions are scrutinised after they have occurred. In this sense, the
police may be said to be accountable to the law for
the exercise of their powers. An unlawful exercise
of police power can be challenged through the
courts and civil remedies obtained where the
challenge is successful. In this way, courts are
given an opportunity, albeit rarely exercised, to
give a ruling on the extent of police powers which

18

THE ACCOUNTABILITY OF THE POLICE

in a loose sense, may then be seen as controlling future police action to the extent that the police are prepared to adhere to the limits thus imposed by the courts. Where they do not, further challenges will be necessary before redress can be obtained and it is inevitable under this system that the judicial role in securing accountability in this sense, will be peripheral. The judicial role could be made more dynamic by the adoption into English law of an exclusionary rule along American lines, whereby evidence obtained by unlawful police behaviour would automatically be excluded from a trial, but the process would still remain essentially one of ex post facto review.

Those who argue most vociferously in favour of greater police accountability, however, are arguing not solely in terms of extending the obligation of the police to justify their actions, but are seeking the introduction of mechanisms by which prior control over policing policies and actions can be achieved, either by extending the power of central authorities to determine police actions or, (more usually), by extending the ability of local communities to determine policing policies for their areas. In this way, the police will be compelled to operate within a framework of policies and rules devised to control directly what they do and how they do it. The difference between these approaches is partly a matter of emphasis - in a sense, today's ex post facto review becomes tomorrow's prior control - but there is also a fundamental difference between, on the one hand, imposing limits on unlawful police actions and, on the other, imposing limits on what policies the police should employ within the law. The impact of either system is crucially determined by the structure and organisation of the institutions created for the purposes of securing accountability.

In this chapter, the effectiveness of the institutions which form the basis of police organisation will be examined in detail, but their development and significance can only properly be understood against the background of the historical events which have helped shape them.

The Historical Background

On the face of it, policing in England and Wales today has little in common with policing in the nineteenth century or in earlier times. And yet, some of the essential features of modern policing

19

THE ACCOUNTABILITY OF THE POLICE

are the products of centuries of historical development. The continuing importance of the status and office of constable, the autonomy of chief officers, the existence of local police forces and the balance between central and local control of policing, are features which have long existed. Modern police forces have evolved from institutions created centuries ago to serve different purposes and totally different communities. Even the far-reaching reforms introduced in the nineteenth century did not fundamentally alter the character of policing in the country. The "new police" were better organised, better trained, better qualified and better suited to the policing of a newly industrialised and complex society, but the local nature of policing and the primary responsibility placed upon the constable as the guardian of the peace, both features perpetuated by these reforms, could demonstrate a pedigree stretching back to Saxon times.

An awareness of the impact of this evolutionary process upon modern policing is essential for an understanding of the institutional mechanisms by which the police are said to be accountable for their actions. The existence of local constabularies, accountable to local police authorities, has been seen as a safeguard against a national, government controlled force. The organisation of policing, therefore, is said to ensure that the police are responsive to the needs of the local community and are impartial, in the sense that policing policies cannot be controlled by the political party in power nationally. In the same way, the legal status of the office of constable is said to deny the possibility of political control of policing. The police constable is not an employee subject to the direction of his employer, but an office holder exercising original authority. His powers are conferred upon him directly by the law and it is the law to which he is responsible for the exercise of those powers. The implications of these aspects of the organisation of policing, in the context of accountability, are legion and will be examined later in this chapter. First, however, it is necessary briefly to survey the influences and pressures which have helped shape the structure and direction of modern policing.

(a) The early history

Most police historians trace the origins of the

THE ACCOUNTABILITY OF THE POLICE

modern police constable to the tythingman of Saxon times.[1] He was elected by his peers in the local community and exercised wide responsibilities for all aspects of local government on their behalf. Among his many duties was the duty of maintaining the peace. He was not, however, a royal officer, as his authority derived from the community he served rather than from the sovereign. By the same token, the peace which he was responsible for maintaining was not the King's peace but a "local" peace which attached to the community and its members. Consequently, if the peace of the community was broken, the community as a whole was responsible for restoring it and apprehending the offender. Thus, the "hue and cry" required everyone to join in the pursuit of the wrongdoer.[2] After the Norman Conquest, this system continued unchanged in its essentials, though the tythingman was no longer elected but appointed by the local lord of the manor. Also, as the Saxons were now a conquered people, the Normans could not entirely rely on Saxons to enforce a Norman conception of peace and order. Accordingly, the sheriff, the royal representative, was given augmented authority to supervise the maintenance of the peace and the administration of the law. The authority of the tythingman was thereby diminished.

By about the middle of the thirteenth century, the term "constable" came to be applied to the tythingman and at about the same time, the system of "watch and ward" was introduced in towns and cities.[3] This was a system by which all the able bodied men of a town served regularly, under the control of the constable, as watchmen at the town or city gates between the hours of sunset and sunrise. Strangers approaching the gates were liable to be arrested by the watchmen and detained until morning when they would be handed over to the constable. "Watch and ward" was an extremely significant development. Not only did it reassert the Saxon principles of "policing" - local communities policing themselves - but also marked the emergence of a distinction between town and rural policing,[4] a distinction which was to continue for the next seven centuries. Another distinction which had emerged by the end of the thirteenth century and which has had an equally lengthy history, was that between the policing of London and the rest of the country. London was divided into twenty-four wards, each with six watchmen controlled by a constable responsible to an alderman. The aldermen, together with the Mayor,

21

THE ACCOUNTABILITY OF THE POLICE

formed the Common Council of the City and were responsible for its government.[5] Again, these arrangements, although different, reaffirmed policing as a local government matter.

With the emergence of the office of justice of the peace in the fourteenth century, the constables soon found themselves in a position of subservience to them. In 1378, the holding of the offices of sheriff and justice of the peace simultaneously was prohibited and from that time on, the authority of the sheriff waned at the expense of the phenomenal growth in importance of the justices of the peace. Throughout the fifteenth and sixteenth centuries, the magistrates were given ever more responsibility and it was probably inevitable that the unpaid parish constables should become their subordinate, executive officers. The practice began of constables being sworn in before the justices and by the seventeenth century, the justices had acquired the power of appointing constables. As the duties of the magistracy expanded, so did those of the constables. The office, which was compulsory (every householder being liable to serve as constable for a specified period), became more and more onerous and time-consuming. It lost much of its traditional status, and in response, the practice emerged of householders appointing and paying deputies (who themselves often deputed the duties further) rather than accepting the office themselves. Inefficiency and incompetence became widespread as illiterate men of low intelligence were recruited in this manner to perform the duties of the office.

When large-scale or widespread public disorder occurred, it was usual to turn to the military to supplement the constabulary: parish constables, even when augmented by the swearing in of special constables, simply were not capable of dealing with riots and mob violence. By the beginning of the eighteenth century, however, there was often considerable reluctance on the part of the magistrates to employ the military to quell disturbances, as their brutality and lack of discipline had made them extremely unpopular. In many places, the wealthy middle classes began to turn to private voluntary associations to protect their property and catch offenders. These private police forces were funded by subscriptions and usually policed only on behalf of their subscribers. It has been estimated that by the 1830s, there were over five hundred of them.[6]

However, it was not just the inability of the

THE ACCOUNTABILITY OF THE POLICE

parish constables and town watchmen to deal with riots and other large-scale disturbances which gave the impetus to the movement for reform. A system of policing which had evolved primarily to provide a degree of protection for small, rural communities, was fundamentally unsuited to cope with the new law and order role occasioned by the consequences of the industrial revolution, the expansion of the population and the growth of towns. The nineteenth century reforms introduced full-time, remunerated officers who were bureaucratically organised to facilitate their specialisation in police work. They undoubtedly marked a new era in policing. But the process of reform was protracted and controversial and demonstrated that although, ultimately, old institutions were adapted rather than new ones created, that was by no means inevitable.

(b) The "new police"

It was in London that the need for reform was most clearly manifested. In addition to the constables and watchmen of the City of London, over the years the London boroughs had acquired the authority to appoint constables and their control was vested in a variety of parish and municipal authorities. They took their orders from the bodies which had appointed them. Indeed, such was the totally ad hoc nature of policing in London that it was not thought improper for individual magistrates themselves to organise groups of constables who acted under their immediate direction. Particularly associated with this form of policing were the famous Fielding brothers, Henry and John, who succeeded each other as Chief Metropolitan Magistrate in the years between 1750 and 1780. The Fieldings' Bow Street runners, so named after the location of the offices occupied by the Chief Metropolitan Magistrate, not only became the best-known of these magistrate sponsored constabularies, but also were eventually made the responsibility of the Home Secretary.[7]
As in the rest of the country, however, the quality of the constabulary was low - the men appointed were frequently illiterate and corrupt. Lawlessness was widespread and the enforcement of the law totally inefficient. It was the inability of the constabulary to deal with mob violence, however, which precipitated the demands for reform. During the Gordon Riots of 1780, for example, London was taken over by the mob and even the military were

23

THE ACCOUNTABILITY OF THE POLICE

powerless to intervene. Recognising a growing problem was one thing, however, dealing with it was quite another. In the forty year period prior to the establishment of the Metropolitan Police Force in 1829, no fewer than seventeen Parliamentary committees examined the problem of maintaining law and order. Opposition to the establishment of an organised, salaried, full-time police force was widespread and those who sometimes argue that the establishment of the "new police" was simply a political expediency designed to keep the lower classes in their place overlook the fact that the opposition was voiced as loudly by the wealthy middle-classes as by any other group. In 1822, a Parliamentary Select Committee, in a much quoted passage, commented:

> ...It is difficult to reconcile an effective system of police, with that perfect freedom of action and exemption from interference, which are the great privileges and blessings of society in this country; ...the forfeiture or curtailment of such advantages would be too great a sacrifice for improvements in police or facilities in detection of crime...[8]

Nevertheless, in the face of this opposition, the Metropolitan Police Act was passed in 1829 and its provisions were the model upon which the later reforms were based. In particular, the legislation recognised and maintained the common law office of constable together with the traditional principle of the constable's subordination to the justices. Accordingly, the Act granted power to appoint two justices of the peace to set up a police force for the Metropolitan area composed of a "sufficient number of fit and able men" who would be sworn in as constables and exercise all the common law powers of that office. Under the Act, the justices[9] were given the power to direct the force so created, but were themselves subjected to the authority of the Secretary of State. Thus, a degree of external supervision was imposed through the Secretary of State and ultimately thereby, to Parliament. The City of London successfully resisted attempts in 1829 and 1839 to amalgamate the City of London force with the newly created Metropolitan Police. Although it remained separate, it was, however, reorganised in 1839.[10]

THE ACCOUNTABILITY OF THE POLICE

1829 was notable not only for the establishment of the Metropolitan Police. In that year, also, Edwin Chadwick, who had long been involved in police reform, published his famous essay, <u>Preventive Police</u>, in the London Review.[11] Its principal conclusion was that the temptations of a career of crime "arise from the absence of appropriate and practical arrangements by means of a constabulary"[12] and urged a commission of inquiry. This proposal was duly adopted some years later when the inquiry was set up in the form of a Royal Commission under the chairmanship of Chadwick himself. It reported in 1839.[13] In the light of the previous history of policing, the Chadwick Report proposals were radical. It recommended the creation of a national, centrally organised police force under the direct control of Police Commissioners responsible to the Home Secretary and based on and recruited from the Metropolitan Police. Underlying this proposal was the widely held contemporary belief that much of the criminal problem was of a migratory nature in that criminals residing in the towns committed crimes in the inadequately policed countryside and then returned to the towns undetected. Central co-ordination was a precondition of dealing efficiently with this problem but Chadwick also realised that the proliferation of local, separate forces, operating independently of each other in their own areas was likely to lead to inefficiency, rivalry and interforce jealousy.

The Report evoked a storm of criticism in which the principle of local control over policing was vociferously defended. In the forefront of the attack upon the proposals were the Municipal Boroughs who, by the Municipal Corporations Act, 1835, had acquired the responsibility of making adequate arrangements for the policing of their towns and who were unwilling to yield up any of their powers. The government of the day caved in under the weight of this criticism and presented a compromise measure to Parliament. The Chadwick Report's central recommendation, the establishment of a national police force, was dropped. The result was the Rural Constabulary Act, 1839, which facilitated the provision of county police forces. However, because the 1839 Act pre-dated by nearly fifty years the establishment of County Councils as administrative organs of local government,[14] the responsibility for maintaining county police forces was placed upon the justices. The legislation, however, did not apply uniformly. All boroughs

25

THE ACCOUNTABILITY OF THE POLICE

incorporated under the 1835 Act were exempted from it, as were towns which had a separate Court of Quarter Sessions and the Metropolitan Police District. Also, any town or parish which had a population of over 10,000 in 1831 and which had a local Act for watch and ward was similarly exempted. In 1840, the government acceded to the demands that police reform should be confined to those parts of counties thought by the local magistracy to need it.

The result of this tentative and piecemeal reform was a patchwork of constabularies, some reformed and some unreformed. Even in those counties where the 1839 Act was adopted, the "new police" faced initial hostility and as late as 1856, when the County and Borough Police Act of that year imposed upon all counties and boroughs the obligation to maintain professional police forces, some twenty two counties had failed to adopt the 1839 Act, preferring instead to retain the traditional parish constable system. Similarly, thirteen boroughs had ignored the 1835 Act. By 1856, there were 239 separate police forces in England and Wales. Even the 1856 legislation, which was designed to bring a degree of unity to the policing arrangements (largely through the appointment of Crown Inspectors of Constabulary who were required to inspect all forces and by the introduction of an annual grant from the Exchequer towards the cost of pay and clothing, the payment of which was conditional upon whether the force was efficient), was unable to alter the piecemeal nature of much that had gone on before. After 1857, some borough and county forces voluntarily amalgamated and the 1888 Local Government Act accelerated this process by requiring all boroughs with a population of under 10,000 to merge their police forces with the surrounding counties. In this way, by the end of the century, the number of police forces had been reduced to 183.

At this point, it is worthwhile to assess the impact of these reforms. They mark the beginning of the modern policing era and there is no doubt that the country was policed more effectively as a result of them. The policing emphasis throughout the nineteenth century, however, continued to be the preservation of the peace. Police work from then on, was no longer an unremunerated, part-time occupation carried out by ill-qualified men: it became the specialist occupation of far better qualified constables who were organised and trained more effectively. The nineteenth century,

26

THE ACCOUNTABILITY OF THE POLICE

therefore, heralded the beginnings of the professionalisation of the police force. It is the way in which these changes were achieved, however, which is significant. The battle between local or national organisation, though it has recurred since, was fought and won in the 1830s. Despite the attractions of the Chadwick Report's logic - that efficiency, adequate deployment of men, the free flow of information and common rules and regulations, demanded the establishment of a national force - the ancient tradition of local policing was far too firmly engrained into the nation. And at a time when local government was constantly expanding, it should come as no surprise that the nineteenth century confirmed policing as a local function. The office of constable was preserved, as was the traditional subordination of the constable to the justices, although the constitutional implications of this latter aspect of the arrangements were not squarely faced. By the end of the century, police committees had been established for all the provincial forces. In the boroughs, these were the Watch Committees created by the Municipal Corporations Act, 1835 and composed of not more than one third of the borough council; in the counties, they were standing joint committees composed of equal numbers of justices and county councillors. The traditional distinction between town and rural policing was also preserved, a distinction which was to continue to be important until as late as 1974. Indeed, the very durability of the nineteenth century reforms hampered the development of the police service, particularly in the present century. Standardisation and centralisation, as we have seen, were totally inimical to the spirit of the nineteenth century reforms and were, in any event, prevented by the administrative realities of police organisation. By definition, the initiative had to come from central government.

As has been noted, the process began with the County and Borough Police Act, 1856, but it was not until the twentieth century that central government began to play a significant role in the policing function. In 1918, some parts of the Metropolitan Police went on strike, discontented with their pay, their status and their conditions of service. The government's response was immediately to introduce new pay scales and in March, 1919, to institute the Desborough Committee.[15] The two reports of the Committee, published in 1919 and 1920, were accepted by the government almost in their entirety and the

27

THE ACCOUNTABILITY OF THE POLICE

impact of their recommendations was enormous. The Police Act, 1919 and the regulations made under it in 1920 not only raised the social and economic status of the police, but also laid the framework within which governmental moves to standardise and centralise policing could be successfully initiated. The Home Office was given far greater powers to regulate individual forces. The basis upon which the central government grant was paid to police forces was changed. It would now only be payable where the Home Secretary was satisfied that the force was fully and properly administered and for the first time, the Home Secretary was empowered to withhold all or part of the grant for any length of time. In addition, the Act empowered the Minister to draw up regulations relating to the organisation of forces, pay and allowances, clothing and conditions of service. Compliance with the regulations was ensured by making it a condition of the award of the government grant. It was the Police Act 1919, also, which set up the Police Advisory Council and the Police Federation. The dangers of suppressing grievances had been well illustrated by the 1918 police strike and the Council and Federation were the government's response. The Home Secretary's powers were further strengthened in 1946, when he acquired the power to approve voluntary schemes or initiate compulsory schemes for the amalgamation of police forces[16] and again in 1948, when he received additional powers in respect of police pensions.[17] Apart from these statutory duties, over the years the Home Office became more and more involved with the provision of central or regional services and facilities to the police, such as forensic science laboratories, the supply and maintenance of communications equipment, criminal records, mutual aid schemes and police training schools.

By the late 1950's, there were 125 police forces in England and Wales. The growing influence of central government had ensured a degree of uniformity, but there were still significant differences between them, not least in terms of size. Some city forces had an establishment five times greater than forces policing quite large counties. The City of Liverpool force, for instance, had an establishment of 2048 officers; the county of Northamptonshire had a police establishment of 398. The largest force outside London, was Lancashire's with an establishment of 3293; the smallest, in Dewsbury, had a strength of just 94. The situation was complicated by the fact that where a county

28

THE ACCOUNTABILITY OF THE POLICE

contained a large number of boroughs, the latter would have their own forces in addition to the county force. Again, the prime example was Lancashire, which had seventeen totally separate forces within its area.[18] In addition, the relationship between the police and the various bodies exercising statutory powers over them was vague and ill-defined. For instance, the nineteenth century legislation had meticulously preserved the subordination of the police to the magistracy, but this was a form of control which by the twentieth century had become virtually moribund and both police authorities and chief constables claimed to be the heirs of those powers.

This fragmented system was ripe for reform but, as so often happens, the review when it came was a response to a series of controversial incidents which had caused public concern. In 1956, disciplinary action was taken against the chief constable of Cardigan after complaints that his force was not being properly administered. A year later, criminal charges were brought against the chief constable of Brighton and some of his senior officers. The chief constable was acquitted but subsequently dismissed by his Watch Committee;[19] two of his officers were convicted of corruption and sent to prison. Not long after that episode, the chief constable of Worcester was convicted of fraud and imprisoned. In 1959, the chief constable of Nottingham was suspended by the Watch Committee after he had refused to submit a report requested by the Committee and this dispute was only resolved when the Home Secretary intervened. The government's response to these and other incidents[20] was to appoint a Royal Commission charged with the task, _inter alia_, of reviewing "the constitutional position of the police throughout Great Britain."

(c) The 1962 Royal Commission

The Commission's Report was a disappointing document in which the forces of tradition and conservatism combined to defeat any suggestion that radical changes in the organisation of policing were necessary. This attitude, which pervaded the Report, is well summed up in the following statement:

> ...we have borne in mind that it is in the tradition of this country to allow institutions to evolve and change gradually encouraged, guided and supported by public

THE ACCOUNTABILITY OF THE POLICE

opinion. We think that this tradition
is sound, particularly in relation to
the police.[21]

Thus, while recognising that "the structure of the
police system today and its legal basis echo not
only the requirements of policing a century ago but
also the fears and prejudices as well as the
political wisdom of the Victorian age,"[22] the
Commission dismissed "the strong case for bringing
the police under complete central control"[23] on the
ground that any necessary changes could be achieved
"without seriously disturbing the local basis on
which the present police service rests."[24] Nowhere
was this unwillingness to take positive action more
evident than in the approach of the Commission to
the powers of chief officers. In a famous statement,
the Commission commented: "The problem of controlling the police can...be restated as the problem of
controlling chief constables"[25] and yet, the Report
assiduously refrained from imposing greater control
over them.

In many respects, therefore, the Report of the
Royal Commission, which was adopted virtually in its
entirety by the Police Act, 1964, represented a
watershed in policing. The local policing tradition
was once again preserved, but the amalgamation
process, endorsed by the Commission, which continued
in the sixties and seventies, ensured the relative
demise of local community involvement in policing and
the relative increase in the power and authority of
chief constables as police forces became fewer and
much larger. At the same time, the influence of
central government continued to grow but because the
constitutional foundations of the relationship
between chief constable, police authority and Home
Office were not firmly laid by the Royal Commission,
its legal basis has become dangerously ambiguous when
looked at in the context of policing developments
over the last twenty years, as will become apparent
in the next section.

The Institutions of Accountability and their effectiveness

(i) The office of constable

The ancient origins of the office of constable
have already been set out in detail but it is
difficult even today to state with precision the
legal status of that office and this is a limitation

THE ACCOUNTABILITY OF THE POLICE

which has important implications for the issue of accountability.

It has become trite law that the constable is an officer whose authority in legal terms is original, not delegated, and which is exercised at his own discretion by virtue of his office. The history of the office, however, does not support this proposition. We have seen how, from very early times, the constable gradually became subservient to the magistracy and carried out his duties subject to magisterial direction. We have also seen how subservience to the magistracy was formally adopted in the legislation establishing the "new police" in the nineteenth century. In addition, there is substantial evidence to suggest that Borough Watch Committees, established by the 1835 Municipal Corporations Act exercised considerable authority over their chief constables.[26] Thus, the suggestion that the constable is immune from direction runs contrary not only to the history of the office, but also to the realities of police organisation.

It is generally accepted that the case of Fisher v Oldham Corporation, decided in 1930,[27] is the progenitor of the concept of police independence in England and Wales. The issue before the King's Bench Division was whether or not the local authority could be held vicariously liable for false imprisonment committed by one of its constables. The court decided that it could not and in the course of giving judgment, McCardie J. commented:

> If local authorities are to be liable in
> such a case as this...then it would indeed
> be a serious matter and it would entitle
> them to demand that they ought to secure
> a full measure of control over the arrest
> and prosecution of all offenders. To give
> any such control would, in my view, involve
> a grave and most dangerous constitutional
> change.[28]

This conclusion can be criticised on two grounds. First, holding a local authority vicariously liable does not necessarily require extending to the local authority control over the arrest and prosecution of offenders and secondly, even if it does, it could hardly be described as "a grave constitutional change" in view of the history of the office of constable.[29] The case remains the authority for the view that constables are not local authority employees. Neither, however, are they crown

31

THE ACCOUNTABILITY OF THE POLICE

servants. Viscount Simonds, delivering the judgment of the Privy Council in Attorney General for New South Wales v Perpetual Trustee Company,[30] expressed the position thus:

> ...he is a ministerial officer exercising statutory rights independently of contract. The essential difference is recognised in the fact that his relationship to the Government is not in ordinary parlance described as that of servant and master.[31]

In 1968, in the first Blackburn Case,[32] Lord Denning MR was sufficiently emboldened by these dicta to state, obiter, "...every constable in the land...is independent of the executive."[33]

The independence of the constable has thus been established by reference to obiter dicta in a trio of relatively recent cases, but despite its weak legal basis, the constable's independence has come to be regarded as a bulwark of individual freedom. Constables do not act at the behest of politically motivated government agencies: neither the Home Secretary, nor the chairmen of Police Authorities can tell them what to do. Their powers are conferred upon them by the law, not by virtue of contract and they exercise them at their discretion. This legal conception of the constable has been supported, by the propagation both by official bodies and by the police themselves, of one of the great policing myths. It was expressed in these terms by the 1929 Royal Commission on Police Powers:

> The police of this country have never been recognised, either in law or by tradition as a force distinct from the general body of citizens...The principle remains that a policeman in the view of the common law is only 'a person paid to perform as a matter of duty acts which if he were so minded, he might have done voluntarily.'[34]

The cosy image presented therefore, is that of the public spirited citizen in uniform, exercising circumscribed powers free from executive influence, for the benefit of the community as a whole. It is not surprising that the police hierarchy should wholeheartedly embrace it:[35] the conflation of the constable's "independence" and the "citizen in uniform" imagery, allows the police to fend off political

32

THE ACCOUNTABILITY OF THE POLICE

interference and helps legitimate the autonomy of chief officers. The problem with this 'Dixon of Dock Green' image, however, is that it entirely ignores the fact that the policeman possesses far greater powers than the ordinary citizen and that these are augmented by the policeman's membership of a technologically advanced and sophisticated service, organised on military lines with an explicit hierarchy and associated chain of command. He is, therefore, no longer merely a citizen in uniform. It also ignores the enormous significance of policing styles. Reactive or "fire-brigade" policing depends for its impact on the assertion of power and the utilisation of modern technology. Police and public meet under conditions of stress and the opportunities for strengthening police/public relations are thereby diminished: an inevitable result of this is the isolation of the police from the community.

Further credibility is given to the cosy imagery by the emphasis upon the patrol officer, the "bobby on the beat" as being in the front-line of policing. According to this thesis, the success of policing will depend upon the efficiency, effectiveness and integrity of the patrol officer in uniform. The autonomy and discretion with which he is endowed derive in part from the legal nature of the office, but are also a consequence of the general nature of the policing function he performs. Such is the variety of the situations that he is likely to encounter from day to day, that he cannot be confined by hard and fast rules and regulations. It is upon his initiative and common sense, rather than upon general policing styles and policies or the use of wide powers, that his success in performing his duties depends.

All of this may reflect the beat constable's traditional role, but there is no doubt that this description needs to be re-appraised in the light of policing developments over the last twenty years. When in the sixties, beat constables were equipped with personal radios, they became easier to supervise and direct. It became possible to deploy and re-deploy them at a moments notice and the discretion which was a consequence of long hours spent unobserved by their superiors and largely isolated on the beat was consequently subject to severe limitations. More effective communications also made it possible to instruct the officer, through, for example, Force standing orders, in the way in which he should carry out his duties.[36] Individual

THE ACCOUNTABILITY OF THE POLICE

initiative was no longer as important as constables faced with a difficult or unexpected situation could now contact the police station for advice and help. Increasingly, also, in the sixties and seventies, constables were taken off the beat and put into cars in which they would be directed from one incident to another. Reactive policing may have been an empirical response to the collapse of the unit beat system and the advent of more sophisticated technological aids,[37] but that it has now become formalised as a policing policy is evidenced by the number of forces moving to computerised "command and control" systems.[38] It is a style of policing characterised by clear lines of control and a lack of individual discretion. The ability of senior officers to control the men on the ground has increased enormously and this incidentally, demonstrates another flaw in the legal theory relating to the office of constable. The legal "independence" of the constable does not extend to independence from command by his senior officers. A police force, according to one view, is simply an organised body of individual constables all claiming the independence traditionally associated with the office. The rigid police hierarchy and the Police Discipline Code, however, make it clear that the constable is a member of a disciplined body subject to the orders of superior officers. There is thus a conflict between legal theory and organisational practice, a conflict which was recognised by the Royal Commission on the Police in 1962, but left unresolved.[39]

The work of the beat constable has thus become more structured and, with the movement towards greater and greater specialisation in police work which again, has accelerated over the last twenty years, more mundane. The preoccupation of the police with crime control and law enforcement and the creation of specialist squads and groups to deal with it, has led to a relative neglect and lowering in status of the patrol officer. The uniformed patrol branch, in manpower terms, is a weak section of the police organisation. A very high proportion of patrol officers will be constables in "initial training or in the early stages of their career and gathering experience."[40] They will also usually be young.[41] To this we might add that their ambition will almost invariably be to move out of patrol work and into a more specialised form of police work. Those who are recognised by their superiors as being good policemen will probably achieve this; those who are thought of as less than adequate for more

34

THE ACCOUNTABILITY OF THE POLICE

specialist work, will remain on the beat.[42]

In what senses then, is the modern police constable accountable for his actions? First, there is a process of internal accountability and control. The Police Act, 1964, placed disciplinary control of the police firmly in the hands of chief constables[43] and this disciplinary function is buttressed by the Police Discipline Regulations[44] which apply nationally, and cover a multiplicity of disciplinary offences. In addition, the chief officer's responsibility to direct and control his force, means that he controls all promotions and transfers[45] within it. There is also a degree of accountability through the complaints system, though how effectively the police investigate complaints against themselves has long been a matter of controversy.[46] Insofar, however, as the Police Complaints Board was able to scrutinise, _ex post facto_, the results of an investigation into a police officers conduct and the Police Complaints Authority is now able to supervise such investigations, and, in exceptional cases, direct that disciplinary charges be brought against an officer,[47] there is a process of accountability, albeit, one that is mainly internal.

Despite the theory of the police officer's _individual_ responsibility to the law for the exercise of his powers, the courts do not play a major part in the control of police activity. It is true that police officers are required to act lawfully in the exercise of their powers, but the strength of this requirement is diminished by the imprecision and vagueness of much of the law relating to police powers.[48] Courts are reluctant to hold that a police officer has acted unlawfully, particularly where the action, though unlawful, appears reasonable in the circumstances. Even where a finding of illegality is arrived at, evidence obtained thereby will normally remain admissible, though the officer will not be in the execution of his duty for the purposes of, for instance, the offence of obstructing an officer in the execution of his duty.[49] In R v _Sang_,[50] the House of Lords ruled that a trial judge has no discretion to refuse to admit relevant admissible evidence merely because it has been obtained by improper or unfair means.[51] Lord Diplock stated the position in forthright terms:

> It is no part of a judge's function to exercise disciplinary powers over the police or prosecution as respects the way in which evidence to be used at the

35

THE ACCOUNTABILITY OF THE POLICE

> trial is obtained by them. If it was
> obtained illegally there will be a
> remedy in civil law; if it was obtained
> legally but in breach of the rules of
> conduct for the police, this is a matter
> for the appropriate disciplinary authority
> to deal with. What the judge at the trial
> is concerned with is not how the evidence
> sought to be adduced by the prosecution
> has been obtained but with how it is used
> by the prosecution at the trial.[52]

This "robust"[53] approach to the issue of admissibility may well have the effect of encouraging the
police to bend the rules in order to short-cut what
might otherwise be a lengthy and complex procedure.
    Finally, it must be said that the continued
emphasis on the individual nature of the constable's
responsibility to the law, allows the police to
evade collective responsibility for policing
policies. The blame for an improper use of, for
example, stop and search powers, can be laid at the
door of the individual who misused them and senior
officers can, if they wish, duck the underlying
question of whether a policing policy which encour-
ages the use of such powers is appropriate.

(ii) Police Authorities

    The tension which developed between police
authorities and their chief constables in the 1970s
and early 1980s has already been referred to in
Chapter One. The problem really derives from the
Police Act, 1964. The 1962 Royal Commission, upon
whose recommendations the Act was based, had
acknowledged the uniquely powerful position of chief
constables but instead of taking the opportunity to
limit it, effectively endorsed it by not recommending
increased powers for police authorities.
    Each of the forty three police forces in England
and Wales is subject to the general oversight of a
police authority. The Metropolitan and City of
London forces are the subject of special arrangements, but outside London, the police authority is
either a committee of the local authority or, in the
case of combined police forces, is a separate body
consisting of representatives of a number of
authorities. In either case, in addition to local
authority members, one third of police authority
members are drawn from the ranks of the local
magistracy. While being committees of local

THE ACCOUNTABILITY OF THE POLICE

authorities, police authorities do not exercise delegated powers: they are statutory bodies exercising powers conferred on them directly by the Police Act, 1964. Nevertheless, it is the general practice that police authorities report regularly to the county council although there is considerable variety in the method of reporting.[54]

The main duty of a police authority is to maintain an adequate and efficient force for its area.[55] In addition, it is responsible for the provision of buildings, vehicles and equipment,[56] determining the establishment of the force[57] and subject to the approval of the Home Secretary, it appoints and if it proves necessary in the interests of efficiency, dismisses the chief constable, deputy chief constables and assistant chief constables.[58] It also controls the expenditure of the force,[59] fifty per cent of which is met from local authority funds and fifty per cent from central government.[60] The chief constable is obliged to make an annual report to his police authority[61] and it may also call for a report from him on any matter connected with the policing of the area.[62] Finally, the police authority is under a statutory duty to keep itself informed about the handling of complaints against the police in its area.[63]

At first glance, this appears an impressive list of powers but a number of important limiting factors must be remembered. The Police Act, 1964, firmly placed operational control of a police force in the hands of the chief constable[64] and in the exercise of this operational power, the chief constable is independent of central and local government and, to a large degree, of the courts.[65] The freedom of action of a police authority to maintain an adequate and efficient force, ensuring that it is properly trained and equipped is also confined by the strongly unifying effect of the Secretary of State's regulations, which ensure uniformity in those areas in which police authorities are most likely to wish to impose their control - uniforms, equipment, training etc. Finally, the police authority's control over the expenditure of its police force, although it can undoubtedly be used as a lever to exert pressure on a "difficult" chief constable, has probably been only rarely so used in the past. Indeed, it has been suggested that police authorities have traditionally been in the position of paymasters with little or no control over the use of the resources made available to chief constables.[66] Where police authorities wish to assert their role,

THE ACCOUNTABILITY OF THE POLICE

however, the financial lever may be their most potent weapon.

The combination of these factors makes it inevitable, therefore, that police authorities operate within confined limits. An authority has no power to give instructions to the chief officer regarding the use of the police, though it does have the right to call for a report from him on any matter connected with the policing of the area. However, when this right to call for reports is examined, it is found that the information which a chief constable is required to provide is confined to that which the police authority needs to enable it to discharge its functions.[67] As a result, although police authorities are entitled to ask questions about any matter connected with the policing of the area, some matters related to the policing of the area are considered to be no business of the authority and that decision is in the hands of the chief constable. The result of this, is that the chief constable is empowered to decide what the powers of the police authority are. In March 1982, for example, Mr. Anderton, chief constable of Greater Manchester, refused to answer questions addressed to him by his police authority on the attendance of the police at a factory engaged in an industrial dispute with its employees. Mr. Anderton was reported as saying that he would not answer questions about the disposition of his force as under the 1964 Act, the information was not needed to discharge the functions of the police authority. He complained about the "political overtones" to the questions which he regarded as "irregular" and "thoroughly unreasonable".[68] The resolution of such disputes is in part provided for by the 1964 Act, because under section 11, the Home Secretary can give a ruling on the admissibility of the question. Not surprisingly, this procedure is rarely resorted to. In this case it was not and the questions remained unanswered.

The ability to ask questions, therefore, does little to diminish the operational autonomy of chief constables and in practice, the respective roles of police authority and chief constable will depend upon the relationships forged between individual authorities and their chief officers. In this connection it is useful to refer to a survey of the forty one police authorities outside London conducted jointly in 1976 by the Association of Metropolitan Authorities and the Association of County Councils. It revealed that in a significant number of cases, the

THE ACCOUNTABILITY OF THE POLICE

chief constable did not report regularly to his police authority on the policing of the area[69] and that in the majority of cases, police authorities only infrequently used their ability to call for reports on specific policing issues.[70]

All of this does tend to bear out the criticism that traditionally police authorities have concerned themselves with the provision of resources to the exclusion of nearly everything else. In other words, they have been unable or unwilling in the past to use their statutory powers, limited though they are, to the full.[71] Even the presentation by the chief constable of his annual report to the authority is not always seen as an opportunity to make him account for the way in which the area is policed. Although he is obliged by statute to present an annual report to his authority, he is not required to consult with the authority over its contents, or refer it to the members in draft. The style of presentation and more importantly, the contents of the report are entirely matters for the chief constable. The result is that some reports are much more informative than others and it is not unknown for annual reports to omit to mention important developments in policing in the area or important statistics.

What then of the community role in securing greater accountability? Local police forces are supposed to facilitate locally responsive policing, but, as has been argued earlier, the amalgamation of forces to create larger (but more remote) units in the name of efficiency and the predominance of a reactive style of policing together ensured that not only was community support more difficult to harness and quantify, it was no longer particularly important. "Community liaison" has thus been a peripheral process in many Forces, conducted through the medium of schools visits and meetings with local authority social services, probation and education departments. Some Forces have adopted more sophisticated arrangements through, for example, participation in crime prevention panels and victim support schemes or by the creation of police liaison officers or Area Beat Officers. Occasionally, arrangements have been made for police officers to attend parish or district council meetings or the meetings of residents' associations, community action groups and the like.

Such arrangements can clearly serve useful purposes, though their voluntary and ad hoc nature has tended to emphasise their essentially peripheral role. In the aftermath of the Scarman Report, considerable attention has been focused on the

THE ACCOUNTABILITY OF THE POLICE

machinery now thought necessary for giving community involvement in policing a higher profile. The difficulty with voluntary consultative arrangements, in the view of Lord Scarman, "...is that they depend too much on the willingness of the parties to participate: if, for any reason, a local difficulty prompts one of the parties to withdraw, the arrangements collapse and discussion stops."[72] These remarks, of course, were particularly directed at the situation in the Metropolitan Police District, where, at the time of the Report, there was no local accountability.[73] The police authority for the Metropolitan Police is the Home Secretary and a major consequence of this was that there was no formal machinery at the London Borough level, for example, through which local communities could make their views known. "The opportunity to ignore local... opinion exists for the Metropolitan Police."[74] Accordingly, Lord Scarman recommended the development of a statutory framework to facilitate consultation between the Metropolitan Police and the community at Borough or Police District level.[75] He also suggested that similar arrangements should obtain in the provinces with a statutory duty being imposed upon police authorities and chief constables to co-operate in the establishment and supervision of community liaison committees.[76]

The governmental response to these proposals was rapid. In June, 1982, the Home Office issued a circular to police authorities and chief constables exhorting the establishment in their areas of formal community liaison procedures.[77] It did not purport to impose a set formula upon police authorities, but suggested means by which liaison machinery might be established, possible membership, matters which might be included in the terms of reference of liaison committees and so on. According to the circular, it was for every authority to discuss whether liaison committees would be desirable in the light of local circumstances and conditions and if it was decided that they would be, to initiate the necessary procedures for their establishment.

By the autumn of 1983, all provincial police authorities had consulted with their chief constables about the desirability of introducing formal consultative arrangements with the community.[78] Indeed, in the majority of police authority areas, such committees had either already been established or were in the throes of establishment. The publicity given to the establishment of the committees varied enormously from area to area. Some police

40

THE ACCOUNTABILITY OF THE POLICE

authorities set up Working Groups to examine the implications of the Scarman Report and the Home Office circular and the consultation process was comprised largely of a dialogue between police authority and senior police officers with comparatively little public involvement. The most adventurous authorities arranged a series of public meetings at which those attending were invited to express their opinions on the form which any formal consultative machinery should take.[79] Not surprisingly, the novelty of the community liaison scheme envisaged by the circular encouraged some authorities to exercise caution by, for example, establishing a limited number of committees on an experimental basis with provision for review after a year or so, or in some cases, by taking a decision not to establish formal machinery but to improve the existing informal police/community contacts.[80]

As has been already stated, the circular did not lay down any uniform system of consultation nor indeed, did it specify an optimum or desirable size for a consultative area, though it did suggest that committees might be based on local authority administrative areas or police administrative boundaries. In practice, most police authorities have based their consultative committees either on police divisional or sub-divisional boundaries or on local authority district boundaries.[81] A similar variety is seen in committee size, with numbers of members ranging from twelve to (exceptionally) fifty though the norm is for a committee of between twenty and thirty members.[82] Such a committee would normally have a "core" membership drawn from the police, the police authority, district and county councils and the statutory agencies, added to which would be nominated members from a wide range of community interests and groups[83] and meet quarterly.

It is entirely consistent with the policy underlying the Home Office circular that the consultative committees should respond to changing local circumstances. Some police authorities have underlined the experimental nature of the arrangements adopted and even where this has not been made explicit, it is clear that the performance and contribution made to policing by the new committees will be closely monitored by both the authorities themselves and the Home Office. The kind of structure described above, therefore, should not be regarded as immutable. Insofar, however, as a pattern has emerged, it does not seem inappropriate to offer some comment on it. Committee size, for example, will to

41

THE ACCOUNTABILITY OF THE POLICE

some degree determine effectiveness: too big and the committee will become unwieldy; too small, and it will not be sufficiently representative. Not only, however, must the committees achieve a balance between these extremes, they must also seek to achieve a proper balance between "official" representatives and "ordinary" representatives. Domination of the committees by the former is to be avoided if the consultative process is really to reach into local communities and reflect local views. It is also undesirable in principle that the police should be seen to control the proceedings of the committees and there is a danger of public cynicism if the secretariat is provided from within the police service and meetings are habitually held on police premises.[84]

Above all, the effectiveness of the new committees will depend upon the limits, self-imposed or otherwise, within which policing is discussed. Lord Scarman thought that wide-ranging discussion was not only permissable, but also necessary:

> Community involvement in the policy and operations of policing is perfectly feasible without undermining the independence of the police or destroying the secrecy of those operations against crime which have to be kept secret...If a rift is not to develop between the police and the public as a whole...it is in my view essential that a means be devised of enabling the community to be heard not only in the development of policing policy but in the planning of many, though not all, operations against crime.[85]

The June 1982 circular suggests some matters which may be usefully discussed by the new committees: issues of local concern which it is desired to bring to the attention of the police; the development of community awareness regarding the police role; ways in which young people can contribute to crime prevention; ways in which police procedures in relation to law enforcement operate and discussion of police responses to crime; and the implications of any general complaints about police response to the public. Certain matters may not be discussed at all, for example, the enforcement of the criminal law in individual cases and allegations against police officers, and others may only be discussed with the approval of the police,

42

THE ACCOUNTABILITY OF THE POLICE

for example, the deployment of officers and the method and timing of police operations. In view of the background to the circular, it is clearly important that chief constables should not indiscriminately assert that operational matters are entirely within their competence and therefore, not suitable for discussion with the local community. Traditionally in their dealings with police authorities, chief constables have been reluctant to initiate or participate in discussion of operational matters. If the new committees are not to be seen as "window dressing" it is crucial that chief constables encourage senior officers to discuss policing policy openly with the committees.

The new system has not been without its critics. Geoffrey Marshall, for example, has criticised the "foggy" image of the consultative process which emerges from the Home Office guidelines and has further suggested that if the committees follow the pattern of consultative devices in other walks of life, they will become "a prey to apathy" or "lend themselves to the objectives of predictable ranters or the spokesmen of special...interest groups."[86] The vast majority of committee members will, of course, be representatives of special interest groups - the police, local authorities and so on. They may well approach the problems of policing from very different perspectives but it should be possible to avoid manipulation or domination of the committees by one group or another where the membership is balanced and wide-ranging. Apathy, however, is quite a different matter. If the committees' role is confined to detailed discussion of policing trivia, they may well become "a prey to apathy." The importance of the police attitude to these committees cannot therefore, be overstated. If they see the system as an irritating adjunct to the main thrust of policing or as an exercise in public relations and no more, the new system will fall lamentably short of its objectives.

Police authorities, by their attitudes, are also in a position to influence the liaison committees' discussions. Most such committees will have police authority members one of whom, often, will be the chairman. A dialogue between committee and police authority is thus facilitated and the more confident the police authority is in its dealings with the chief constable, the more effective are the liaison committees likely to be as they will take their example from their parent authority. In this connection, it is worth noting that police

THE ACCOUNTABILITY OF THE POLICE

authorities did not escape criticism in the Scarman Report, which referred to the fact that "many police authorities are somewhat uncertain of themselves and do not always exercise the firmness which the statute envisages as necessary to the discharge of their awesome responsibility..."[87] It has been argued earlier that the circumscribed nature of their statutory powers is in part, at least, responsible for their failure to involve themselves to any significant degree in the formulation of policing policy. It is a matter for considerable regret, therefore, that when considering community involvement in policing, neither Lord Scarman nor the Home Office, envisaged a broadening of police authorities' power. The new consultative committees together with the initiatives taken voluntarily by some police and local authorities prior to the June 1982 circular,[88] can play a useful function in bringing the police and community closer together but their effectiveness is inevitably limited by the relatively weak position of police authorities. One way forward, which would not involve radical change, would be to place police authorities and chief constables on a more equal footing. This need not necessarily require diminishing the operational powers of chief constables. For example, police authorities could be given enhanced powers to seek reports from their chief constables across the whole range of operational matters and a statutory right to be consulted on general policing policy for their areas. Although apparently modest, these changes in practice would significantly strengthen the position of police authorities and give them the confidence to assert themselves more vigorously on behalf of their local communities.

(iii) Chief Constables

Chief constables occupy positions of immense power and influence. Some of the factors which have contributed to the development of their unique autonomy have already been discussed and will not be rehearsed here in detail but among them are: the decline of magisterial control; the rise of police professionalism; the amalgamation of forces; and the growth of centralisation at the expense of local control. A further factor, their ambiguous legal status, will be examined later in this section as will the implications of the police role in the prosecution process. Although it is undoubtedly true that the power of chief officers has increased

THE ACCOUNTABILITY OF THE POLICE

over the last twenty years, the 1962 Royal Commission's Report identified correctly the fundamental nature of that power in the following terms:

> Thus [the chief constable] is accountable to no-one and subject to no-one's orders for the way in which, for example, he settles his general policies in regard to law enforcement over the area covered by his force, the concentration of his resources on any particular type of crime or area, the manner in which he handles political demonstrations or processions and allocates and instructs his men when preventing breaches of the peace arising from industrial disputes, the methods he employs in dealing with an outbreak of violence or of passive resistence to authority, his policy in enforcing the traffic laws...and so on.[89]

The Commission accepted that "it is in the public interest" that in dealing with "quasi-judicial" matters - for example, the enforcement of the law in individual cases - chief constables should be free from "the conventional process of democratic control and influence"[90] but that the same considerations do not apply in the case of duties of the kind described above.[91] Nevertheless, the rhetoric of the Commission was not translated into effective action to subject chief constables to "democratic control and influence" even with regard to their wider powers, as is apparent from a consideration of the Police Act, 1964.

Under it, while police authorities have the duty to maintain an adequate and efficient force for their areas, operational control of the force is firmly placed in the hands of chief constables.[92] It is true that the Home Secretary, H.M. Inspectors of Constabulary and the police authorities all exercise responsibilities for the maintenance of efficient police forces and have the ability to influence the general manner in which they operate, but none of these bodies possess the authority to direct the chief constable to a particular course of action or to follow particular operational policies and he is under no obligation to justify his decisions to them. The completeness of his operational control is underlined by the fact that he alone is responsible for all appointments and promotions below assistant chief constable and is

45

THE ACCOUNTABILITY OF THE POLICE

the disciplinary authority for these ranks.[93] He is, of course subject to certain constraining influences. The Secretary of State has wide-ranging power to make general regulations concerning the administration of police forces, to authorise expenditure on common services and, through the Inspectorate, to ensure that the conditions for the award of grant are complied with,[94] though these powers give formal expression to the central government relationship with the police authority, as much as with the chief constable. The police authority itself has the power to appoint, discipline and dismiss, (subject to the Secretary of State's concurrence),[95] its chief constable and local control over police expenditure. The framework is, however, one of checks and counter-checks rather than one of direction and command.

To what extent are the courts in a position to exert control over chief constables? In a number of cases they have asserted in wide terms the independence of chief constables from judicial and political control. The best known of these is the first Blackburn case.[96] In it, Lord Denning M.R. said:

> I hold it to be the duty of the Commissioner of Police, as it is of every chief constable, to enforce the law of the land. He must take steps so as to post his men that crimes may be detected; and that honest citizens may go about their affairs in peace. He must decide whether or not suspected persons are to be prosecuted; and, if need be, bring the prosecution or see that it is brought; but in all of these things he is not the servant of anyone, save of the law itself. No Minister of the Crown can tell him that he must, or must not, keep observation on this place or that; or that he must, or must not, prosecute this man or that one. Nor can any police authority tell him so. The responsibility for law enforcement lies on him. He is answerable to the law and to the law alone. That appears sufficiently from Fisher v Oldham Corp., and the Privy Council case of A-G for New South Wales v Perpetual Trustee Co Ltd.
> Although chief officers of police are answerable to the law, there are many fields in which they have a discretion with which the law will not interfere. For instance, it is for the Commissioner of Police, or the chief constable,...to decide in any

46

THE ACCOUNTABILITY OF THE POLICE

particular case whether enquiries should be pursued or whether an arrest should be made, or a prosecution brought. It must be for him to decide on the disposition of his force and the concentration of his resources on any particular crime or area. No court can or should give him direction on such a matter. He can also make policy decisions and give effect to them...[97]

The broad sweep of these remarks has had an enormous impact, not least, upon chief constables who clearly have a vested interest in their acceptance, notwithstanding the fact that they are obiter. They assert a concept of independence which, as has already been argued is unsupportable on historical grounds[98] and is predicated on obiter dicta in the Fisher case and the New South Wales case. They also completely ignore the fact that it is possible to argue that the Metropolitan Police Commissioner is, in law, the chief officer most susceptible to ministerial control as under section 1 of the Metropolitan Police Act, 1829, the Commissioner will perform "...such duties as shall from time to time be directed by one of His Majesty's principal Secretarys of State..." This can clearly be interpreted as giving to the Home Secretary powers of direction over the Commissioner. More generally, however, Lord Denning's observations leave considerable room for doubt as to the extent to which chief officers are subject to ministerial or police authority control. All the examples given by Lord Denning of a chief officers' immunity to direction relate to decisions in particular cases and it has consequently been argued that it may be that he did not intend to indicate that directions as to general policy would be similarly improper.[99]

In the first Blackburn case, the Metropolican Police Commissioner was allegedly failing to enforce the gaming laws. In 1973, Mr. Blackburn once again attempted to subject the Commissioner to an order of mandamus, this time, for failing to enforce the obscene publications laws. The Master of the Rolls reiterated his earlier reasoning to conclude that "...in the carrying out of their duty of enforcing the law, the police have a discretion with which the courts will not interfere."[100] Roskill L.J. added: "It is no part of the duty of this court to presume to tell the [Metropolitan Police Commissioner] how to conduct the affairs of the Metropolitan Police,

THE ACCOUNTABILITY OF THE POLICE

nor how to deploy his...resources,"[101] a view echoed by Phillimore L.J.[102] And, in R v Chief Constable of Devon and Cornwall ex p. CEGB,[103] the Court of Appeal once again turned down a request to issue mandamus, this time, against a provincial chief constable, to compel him to assist the CEGB in dealing with demonstrators preventing survey work on a potential nuclear power station site. Lord Denning stated: "The decision of the chief constable not to intervene was a policy decision with which...the courts should not interfere."[104]

The consistency with which the courts have adhered to the views set out above makes it extremely difficult to gainsay that as a matter of law and in the absence of express statutory authority, chief officers are immune from ministerial, police authority or judicial direction, both with regard to general operational policy and the application of the law in individual cases. An understanding of the constitutional position of the chief constable, therefore, is crucial to an understanding of the accountability debate. His statutory duty to direct and control his force means that he alone is responsible for the orders and policies which result from that duty and the performance of the policing function will depend largely on his views and attitudes. In the words of one commentator: "By decisions over deployment...over training, over resource allocation and within the organisational reward structure, [chief constables] determine the form of police work within local society."[105] The effect of the Force amalgamation process which has taken place over the last twenty years has, there-fore, been to diminish the number of chief officers at the same time as increasing their powers. A relatively small number of individuals now determine policing policy over the whole country and the concept of police independence adumbrated above necessarily means that chief officers can pay lip-service to the ideology of 'policing by consent' while taking decisions for which there is no formal process of accountability.

In England and Wales, this extensive autonomy of chief police officers is especially important because most prosecuting decisions are made by the police. The discretion to prosecute is, of course, only one aspect of the enormous discretionary power vested in the police. The significance of prosec-ution discretion is, however, two-fold. First, selective law enforcement inevitably shades into law-making as by their prosecution policies, the

THE ACCOUNTABILITY OF THE POLICE

police, and in particular, chief constables, decide which laws to enforce and on what occasions. Secondly, prosecution discretion is largely un-challengeable. The courts have made it clear that the power to review prosecution decisions is likely to be reserved for exceptional cases.[106] It is no part of the police authorities' duty to oversee prosecution policies and the impact of central bodies on chief constables' discretion is apparently limited.[107] There is, at the moment, therefore, no effective institutional apparatus to secure account-ability or even uniformity in prosecution decisions.

To summarise then, a chief constable's general decisions regarding the deployment of his force are entirely a matter for him. He is not accountable for those decisions in any meaningful way. Decisions about deployment, however, will have a crucial effect upon what offences are prosecuted and for their prosecution policies, the police are equally unaccountable. Perhaps the most obvious method of reconciling the competing demands of independence and control in this area, would be the establishment of an independent prosecuting service. Removal from the police of their prosecution discretion would diminish their power and have other consequential benefits, for instance, achieving a degree of uniformity in prosecution decisions. Indeed, England and Wales are very unusual in not providing for institutional control over prosecution decisions. The American District Attorney is well-known to film fans. He is an official who not only decides whether or not to prosecute, but also plays a substantial role in the investigative process.[108] Less well-known but closer to home is the Scottish Procurator Fiscal. Although he has investigative powers - for instance, when a serious crime has been committed he may give instructions to the police about the collection of evidence, interview and take statements from witnesses - in the large majority of cases, the Fiscal plays no part at all in the investigation. He merely approves the case for proceeding on the basis of the paper evidence put before him.[109]

In 1981, the Royal Commission on Criminal Procedure recommended that a statutorily based prosecution service should be set up to cover all police areas in England and Wales and that it should have the following general functions:

(a)   the conduct of all criminal cases in which the initial decision to proceed has been taken by the police;

49

THE ACCOUNTABILITY OF THE POLICE

(b) the provision of legal advice to the police on matters relating to the prosecution of offences; and

(c) the provision of advocates in magistrates' courts in all cases prosecuted by the police and the briefing of counsel in all such cases tried on indictment.[110]

The Commission characterised the most obvious method of organising such a service - a centrally directed national prosecution system - as "neither desirable or necessary"[111] recommending instead the establishment of local, independent Crown Prosecutors and the modification of police authorities' powers to enable them additionally to exercise general supervision over them.[112]

These proposals were referred in July 1982 to an interdepartmental Working Party which, while accepting the Royal Commission's formulation of the general functions of an independent prosecuting service, rejected the organisational structure proposed by the Commission. Instead, it recommended the establishment of a national prosecution service headed by the Director of Public Prosecutions and under the superintendence of the Attorney General. This is the model now favoured by the government[113] and legislation to give effect to it is in the course of preparation. When it reaches the statute book it will have a profound effect not only on the prosecution of offences, but also upon the role of the police. Henceforth, they will be confined to the investigation of offences and the disproportionate influence which they have traditionally exercised over the enforcement of the criminal law through their ability to control the prosecution process will be greatly reduced.

(iv) Central Government

The Home Secretary occupies the central position in the constitutional structure of policing, but a recital of his formal statutory powers provides only an incomplete picture of central government influence. It is important also to examine his permissive and persuasory powers, the use of which have contributed significantly to the centralising process. In addition, the decrease in the number of police forces has facilitated centralisation as, clearly, the fewer the number of forces and chief constables, the more easily achievable is national uniformity of practice. We do not have a national police force; but the processes of

50

THE ACCOUNTABILITY OF THE POLICE

regionalisation and centralisation have ensured the development of a common policing pattern and a network of integrated homogeneous forces.

The degree of integration which now exists is, in part, attributable to legislation designed to ensure that the Home Secretary bears ultimate responsibility for efficient policing. As has already been noted, he possesses wide-ranging powers to make regulations for the government, administration and conditions of service of police forces, particularly with respect to qualifications for appointment and promotion, probationary service, discipline, duties, pay, allowances and equipment.[114] It is for him to approve the appointment of chief constables and ultimately to dismiss them or require them to resign in the interests of efficiency.[115] Candidates for appointment as chief constable have to be chosen from a short-list approved by the Home Secretary; he can thus influence the kind of appointment made by approving only the candidacy of men who possess the qualities and qualifications acceptable to him. He, of course, sees the annual reports made by chief constables to their police authorities and may require a chief constable to submit a report to him on any specific matter connected with the policing of an area.[116] He is also empowered to set up a local enquiry into any matter connected with the policing of an area.[117] It is the supervision of police expenditure, the power of the purse, however, which ultimately underpins the Secretary of State's position, as the payment of the central government grant is conditional upon the Home Secretary's certificate that a police force is efficient, co-operates adequately with other police forces, and is properly equipped and administered,[118] though in practice, the threat of grant withdrawal is rarely used in modern times; where it is used, by its very nature, it bears upon the police authority rather than upon the chief constable.

The major link between the provincial forces and the Home Office is the Inspectorate of Constabulary. The establishment of the Inspectorate was designed to ensure more effective central control over the policing standards in the various forces and as such, the Inspectors are an integral part of the Home Secretary's regulatory powers. They inspect and advise police forces but have no power to direct police authorities or chief constables to any particular course of action, reporting instead to the Home Secretary.[119] In recent times, though

51

THE ACCOUNTABILITY OF THE POLICE

their regulatory role cannot be overlooked, they have been heavily involved in policy formulation and strategic planning for the police service as a whole.[120] A final sanction potentially available against a force which departs from the usual standards of efficiency is the power to bring about an amalgamation with a neighbouring force.[121] Whether a force is efficient is entirely a matter for the Home Secretary[122] though the Inspectorate's views will be extremely important.

The Inspectors have been influential in the adoption of uniform standards, the encouragement of inter-force co-operation and the provision of national and regional facilities and it is through these strategems, as much as through the exercise of formal, statutory powers, that the Secretary of State's influence has grown. The Home Office finances and administers a whole range of services which it is either too expensive or impractical for individual forces to set up. Many of these are organised on a regional basis and shared by a number of forces: forensic science laboratories; police training centres; technical support services; major crime operations. Others are organised nationally: command training at the Police Staff College; the Police National Computer at Hendon (criminal records); scientific research; immigration intelligence. It is the Home Office too, which has encouraged the holding of regular conferences between chief constables and Home Office officials on important policing issues, such as the control of pickets and protestors, the utilisation of computer technology to serve policing purposes or the appropriate policies to be adopted with regard to motoring offences. The one hundred or so ministerial circulars issued to the police forces annually also secure uniformity on rates of pay and rest day allowances, the interpretation and implementation of new legislation or law enforcement procedures, such as the use of handcuffs.

What is the role of Parliament in all of this? Traditional constitutional theory has ministerial responsibility to Parliament as the pre-eminent form of political accountability, but the role of Parliament in securing the accountability of the Home Secretary for his policing function is not pronounced. If he is questioned about the policing policies adopted by any particular force, his reply will usually be that operational matters are within the province of the chief constable; similarly, questions about the facilities and resources of

52

THE ACCOUNTABILITY OF THE POLICE

individual forces will receive the reply that these are matters for the appropriate police authority. It is true that regulations made under the police legislation will require the approval of Parliament, but ministerial circulars do not (indeed, they are rarely seen by either House of Parliament before publication), and the latter far exceed the former in number in any given year. Fortunately, Parliament is not entirely dependent upon the Home Secretary for its policing information; it can take its own initiatives, a process much aided by the re-organisation of the parliamentary select committee system in 1979. Each government department is now monitored by a select committee and the Home Affairs Committee has shown a considerable interest in policing as is evidenced by its influential reports on police complaints procedures and the 'sus' laws.

In addition to his general policing responsibilities, the Home Secretary is the Police Authority for the Metropolitan Police. Unlike the provincial forces, therefore, and the City of London Police, the Metropolitan Police Force is not subject to the oversight of a police authority representing the local community it serves and, as might be expected, its unique constitutional position has been the subject of vigorous criticism over the years. It is traditional to justify it by reference to the special nature of the policing tasks performed by the Metropolitan Police. It is, of course, by far the largest police force in the country and the demands made upon it in the course of policing the nation's capital are both qualitatively and quantitatively different from those facing other police forces. London is the focus of political protest and the policing of the hundreds of demonstrations and processions which take place there in any given year make enormous demands upon the Metropolitan Police. Serious crime is also more of a problem - drug-trafficking, racketeering, large-scale fraud, vice, armed robbery - and serves to make the traditional policing tasks of peace-keeping and law enforcement particularly difficult to perform. Finally, it is the Metropolitan Police Force which has primary responsibility for the guarding of diplomatic premises - the Embassies and High Commissions of foreign states - and of Parliament itself. In the light of all this, it is argued, it is right that there should be a form of national accountability for the Metropolitan Police, through the Home Secretary to Parliament. One difficulty with this

THE ACCOUNTABILITY OF THE POLICE

approach is that Home Secretaries, as has already been mentioned, are adept at side-stepping questions from MPs raising operational matters. Another, is that such national accountability as is provided, is at the expense of local accountability. The Metropolitan Police Force does have especially arduous policing responsibilities but these must not be allowed to obscure the fact that the Force also polices communities and relies on public support to the same extent as any other police force. In the aftermath of the Scarman Report, 'community policing' has been given a higher priority in the Metropolitan Police District. The formal consultative committees recommended by Scarman and now required by the Police and Criminal Evidence Act, 1984, have been set up in the London Boroughs based on the Home Office guidelines and, in the City of London, improvements have been made to the liaison arrangements, though the absence of any significant residential community in the generally accepted sense of the word renders the adoption of consultative committees as such, inappropriate.[126]

In the light of governmental proposals for the abolition of the Metropolitan Authorities, it is clear that the Greater London Council's long and vigorous campaign to assume the Home Secretary's mantle as police authority for London is unlikely to be successful. The GLC effectively highlighted the anomalous position of the City of London Police, however, and the relative powerlessness of the London Boroughs to contribute any kind of policy input into the policing of London. The demands for change have, for the time being, been resisted: the government does not intend to alter significantly the London arrangements. But the pressure for reform is likely to be maintained because it is the Boroughs who at the end of the day, contribute a substantial proportion of the cost of policing the capital city.

Notes

1. See particularly, T.A. Critchley, A History of Police in England and Wales, (Constable, London, 2nd ed., 1979), and Reith, A History of Police, (OUP, London, 1948), upon whose accounts this section draws heavily.

2. Contrary to popular belief, therefore, the "posse" of the American Mid-West, was not an

THE ACCOUNTABILITY OF THE POLICE

American invention!

3. Although the system probably pre-dated the statute of Winchester, enacted in 1285, it is with that legislation that "watch and ward" is most closely associated.

4. See Critchley, op. cit., at p.6.

5. The Common Council of the City of London is still the police authority for the City of London police force.

6. See the Report of the Royal Commission for the purpose of inquiring as to the best means of establishing an efficient constabulary force in the counties of England and Wales, (hereafter, the Chadwick Report), B.P.P. 1839 (XC), paras. 172-197.

7. See the Report of the Royal Commission on the Police, Cmnd. 1728 (May 1962), para. 36.

8. Report of the Select Committee on the Police of the Metropolis, 17th June, 1822.

9. By the Metropolitan Police Act 1829, the justice who occupied the "new police office" was styled the Commissioner and all succeeding Metropolitan Police Commissioners, upon appointment, have been created magistrates.

10. The City of London Police Act, 1839, provided for a force along the lines of the Metropolitan Police with a Commissioner. It remained responsible, however, to the Common Council of the City of London.

11. London Review 1, 1829.

12. Ibid., p.67.

13. See the Chadwick Report, op. cit.

14. County Councils were established by the Local Government Act, 1888.

15. Committee on the Police Service, Cmnd. 874, (1920).

16. Police Act, 1946.

17. Police Pensions Act, 1948.

18. All figures have been taken from Appendix 3 of the Report of the Royal Commission on the Police, (1962), op. cit.

19. It was the manner of his dismissal which led, of course, to the famous case of Ridge v Baldwin, (1964) AC 40, which is still the leading authority on "natural justice".

20. The background to the institution of the Royal Commission is set out in Chapter 1 of the Report. See Report of the Royal Commission on the Police, 1962, op. cit., paras. 1.1 - 1.5.

21. Ibid., para. 150.

22. Ibid., para. 18.

23. Ibid., para. 147.

THE ACCOUNTABILITY OF THE POLICE

24. Ibid., para. 149.
25. Ibid., para. 102.
26. See T.A. Critchley, A History of Police in England and Wales, op. cit., p.131-133.
27. (1930) 2 KB 364.
28. Ibid., pp. 377-378.
29. See particularly G. Marshall, Police and Government, (Methuen,: London 1965), Chap. 3.
30. (1955) A.C,.457.
31. Ibid., p. 490. In Lewis v Cattle (1938) 2 KB 454, it was held that a policeman is a person who holds office under His Majesty for the purposes of s.2 of the Official Secrets Act 1911. The view that he is not a crown servant, however, found support in Conway v Rimmer, (1968) AC 910.
32. R. v Metropolitan Police Commissioner, ex p. Blackburn, (1968) 1 All ER 763.
33. Ibid., p. 769.
34. See the Report of the Royal Commission on Police Powers, Cmnd. 3297, (1929), para. 15.
35. See e.g. Sir Robert Mark, Policing a Perplexed Society, (Allen & Unwin, London, 1977), at p.56: "He is only an ordinary member of the community who has undertaken certain duties on behalf of his 'fellow citizens'".
36. Baldwin & Kinsey, Police Powers and Politics, (Quartet Books, London 1984), reproduced in an Appendix a detailed job specification for the duties of an Area Constable.
37. For a fuller discussion of "reactive" policing, see Chapter 1.
38. See Baldwin & Kinsey, Police Powers and Politics, op. cit., pp. 52-57.
39. Report of the Royal Commission on the Police, 1962, op. cit., para. 66.
40. J. Mervyn Jones, Organisational Aspects of Police Behaviour, (Gower, Farnborough, 1980), p.52.
41. J. Mervyn Jones, Ibid., pp. 53-56. In the Force researched by Jones, 40.8 per cent patrol constables were 23 years old or under; 78.1 per cent of the patrol strength were 29 years old or less.
42. Ibid., Chap. 6.
43. See s. 7(2).
44. See Schedule 2 of the Police (Discipline) Regulations, 1977.
45. Police Act, 1964, s. 7(2).
46. See Chapter 3.
47. Police Act, 1976, s. 3(2).
48. See the discussion in Chapters 4, 5, 6 and 7.

THE ACCOUNTABILITY OF THE POLICE

49. The offence derives from the Police Act, 1964, s. 51(3).

50. (1979), 2 All E.R. 1222.

51. An exception to this relates to confessions, admissions and evidence obtained from the accused after the commission of the offence. Breach of the Judges' Rules, for instance, has on occasion been used by trial judges as a reason for excluding evidence of admissions. See the discussion in Chapter 6.

52. R v Sang, op. cit., at p. 1230.

53. See Kuruma v R, (1955), AC 197.

54. See the survey of all police authorities outside London on matters of practice carried out by the Joint Working Party of the Association of County Councils and the Association of Metropolitan Authorities in 1976. Full minutes of police authority meetings were seen by the county council in a minority of cases. It was more usual for selected extracts to be forwarded.

55. Police Act, 1964, s. 4(1).

56. Police Act, Ibid., ss. 4(3), 4(4).

57. Ibid., s. 4(2).

58. Ibid., s. 5(4), 6(5).

59. Ibid., s. 8.

60. The "local" fifty per cent attracts an element of rate-support grant.

61. Ibid., s. 12.

62. Ibid.

63. Ibid., s. 50.

64. Ibid., ss. 51(1), 6(1).

65. See the discussion post at pp. 44-50.

66. See Brogden, op. cit., at pp. 90-91.

67. Police Act, 1964, s. 12.

68. See The Times, 13.3.82.

69. The Chief Constable did not report regularly on the policing of the area in 10/41 cases.

70. It did not happen at all in 7/41 cases and was a frequent occurrence in only 10/41 cases.

71. For instance, the Police Act, 1964, imposes a duty on police authorities to keep themselves informed about the handling of complaints in their areas. That power could be used to ask for details about the pattern of police complaints, the nature of the complaints and whether particular police stations are more involved than others. For most police authorities however, their only exposure to this part of their role is where the statistics on police complaints are presented to them by the chief constable in his Annual Report and the method and form of presentation is entirely a matter for him.

THE ACCOUNTABILITY OF THE POLICE

72. Scarman Report, op. cit., para. 5.69.

73, In Brixton, the ad hoc community/police consultative committee had collapsed under the particular policing strains in that area, prior to the riots of April 1981.

74. Scarman Report, op. cit., para. 5.67.

75. Ibid., para. 5.69. Lord Scarman also suggested the creation of a Police Advisory Board at Force level to ensure consultation between the Home Office, the Commissioner, and the London Boroughs. See para. 5.70.

76. Ibid., paras. 5.65, 5.66.

77. "Local Consultative Arrangements Between the Community and the Police", Home Office circular, 54/1982. See now Police and Criminal Evidence Act, 1984, s. 106.

78. Most of what follows is based on research conducted by the author in August/September 1983, when a letter was sent to all forty one provincial police authorities in England and Wales requesting details of the measures they had taken in the light of H.O. circular 54/1982. A similar letter was sent to the police authority for the City of London Police and to the Metropolitan Police. A more detailed analysis of the response to the letters is given in an Appendix.

79. This was the case, for example, in Hampshire and North Wales. A detailed account of the Hampshire meetings and their response can be found in Atkins and Rutherford, "The Police and the Public : In Search of New Styles of Accountability", (1983) Public Law, 241.

80. See Appendix, Table 1.

81. A detailed breakdown is given in the Appendix, Table 2.

82. Ibid.

83. See the Appendix for a typical membership of a committee of this size.

84. Most Committees will be serviced by the local authority, but a number will be serviced by the police.

85. Scarman Report, op. cit., para. 5.56.

86. See G. Marshall, "Police Complaints and Consultation", (1982), Public Law, 337, 342.

87. Scarman Report, op. cit., para. 5.62.

88. For example, Greater Manchester County Council has appointed a Community Liaison Officer at a senior level, reporting to the Authority, and the Policy Committee of the county council. Northumbria Police Authority has made efforts to set up a Sub-committee to work with the police to improve the

58

THE ACCOUNTABILITY OF THE POLICE

supervision of police stations by senior officers (The Times, 21.6.81). Merseyside Police Authority has appointed a Sub-committee to monitor complaints against the police (The Times, 14.9.81).

89. Report of the Royal Commission on the Police, 1962, op. cit., para. 89.

90. Ibid., para. 87.

91. Ibid., para. 91.

92. See Police Act, 1964, s. 5(1).

93. Ibid., s. 7(2).

94. See the discussion post at pp. 50-54.

95. Police Act, 1964, ss. 4(2) and 5(4).

96. R. v Metropolitan Police Commissioner ex. p. Blackburn, (1968), 1 All ER 763.

97. Ibid., p. 767.

98. See the discussion at pp. 30-36 ante.

99. See G. Marshall, Police Accountability Revisited, in D. Butler and A. Halsey (eds.,) Policy and Politics, pp. 51-65, (London, MacMillan Press, 1978).

100. R v Metropolitan Police Commissioner ex p. Blackburn (No. 3), (1973), 1 All E.R. 324, 331. Lord Denning added: "there might however be extreme cases in which he was not carrying out his duty. And then he would".

101. Ibid., p. 338.

102. Ibid., p. 335.

103. (1981), 3 All E.R. 826.

104. Ibid., p. 833.

105. Brogden, The Police : Autonomy and Consent, op. cit., p. 30.

106. It can be argued that as the result of the prosecutor's decision to proceed comes before the courts, prosecutorial discretion is daily subject to judicial scrutiny. A bad individual decision may be called in question, but general policies are less readily subject to scrutiny.

107. This was a finding in the Report of the Royal Commission on Criminal Procedure, Cmnd. 8072, (January 1981). See particularly discussion at paras. 6.42-6.47.

108. Ibid., paras. 6.32-6.34.

109. Ibid., paras. 6.35, 6.36.

110. Ibid., paras. 7.4, 7.5.

111. Ibid., para. 7.24.

112. Ibid., paras. 7.25-7.32.

113. See An Independent Prosecution Service for England and Wales, Cmnd. 9074, (September 1983). The Report of the interdepartmental Working Party is reproduced as an Appendix.

114. See The Police Act, 1964, s. 33. Many of

THE ACCOUNTABILITY OF THE POLICE

these regulations can be brought into force only after a draft has been submitted to the Police Advisory Board for England and Wales (s. 46). Regulations relating to pay, hours of duty and leave must be shown in draft to the Police Council (Police Act, 1969, s. 4).

115. See Police Act, 1964, s. 29.
116. Ibid., s. 30.
117. Ibid., s. 32.
118. Ibid., s. 28.
119. Ibid., s. 38(2).
120. See T.A. Critchley, A History of Police in England and Wales, op. cit., p. 187.
121. Police Act, 1964, s. 21.
122. Ibid.

Chapter 3

THE POLICE COMPLAINTS PROCEDURE

Introduction

The procedures for investigating complaints made against the police by the public have loomed large in the wide-ranging debate about policing which has taken place in recent years. It is only the intensity of the debate, however, which is new. In 1929, the Royal Commission on Police Powers[1] considered a suggestion that the Director of Public Prosecutions should be furnished with a special staff, independent of the police, to enable him to investigate allegations of criminal conduct committed by police officers. The Commission rejected the suggestion, commenting: "We prefer to continue to trust the police, in the belief that, having the responsibility for their own discipline, they will discharge it more faithfully in the absence of interference from some outside authority."[2] Thus, the responsibility for investigating complaints made against police officers remained with individual chief constables within the framework of police discipline regulations. Even when the complaint alleged criminal conduct on the part of the police, there was no obligation on the chief constable to submit to any outside scrutiny of his decision - some chief constables sought the advice of the Director of Public Prosecutions, but this was by no means the universal procedure and it occurred entirely at the discretion of individual chief officers.

In the 1950's a series of incidents engendered misgivings about the state of the police and led to the institution of the Royal Commission on the Police in 1960, whose terms of reference directed specific attention to "the means of ensuring that complaints by the public against the police are

61

THE POLICE COMPLAINTS PROCEDURE

effectively dealt with."[3] The majority of the Commission rejected a suggestion of independent investigation[4] and concluded that the existing arrangements were fair and effective, but recommended certain improvements to them. Three Commissioners, however, were of the opinion that the measures proposed were inadequate to reassure the public that complaints were properly dealt with and in the interests of justice and good relations with the public, thought that some form of external check should be imposed. They accordingly recommended that a Commissioner of Rights should be appointed to investigate complaints made to him about the way in which a complaint against the police had been dealt with by a chief constable.[5] The majority recommendations were embodied in the Police Act, 1964, and the discipline regulations made under it. Section 49 of that Act required a chief officer of police who received a complaint about a member of his force to record it and cause it to be investigated. Under the police discipline regulations, a complaint which suggested that an offence against the regulations may have been committed had to be investigated by an officer of the rank of superintendent (or above) and from a different division of the force.[6] When the investigation was completed, a report of it was submitted to the deputy chief constable[7] who was required to send it to the Director of Public Prosecutions unless he was satisfied that the officer concerned had not committed a criminal offence. The Director decided whether or not the officer should be charged with a criminal offence and in the light of his decision, the deputy chief constable decided whether to charge the officer with an offence against the Police Discipline Code. The Act further provided that the local police authority was under a duty to keep itself informed about the handling of complaints against the police[8] and Her Majesty's Inspectors of Constabulary were under a similar obligation.[9]

These procedures, however, were not successful in stemming the tide of criticism of the police complaints procedure, and a number of proposals for the introduction of an independent element into the complaints procedure were put forward during the late sixties and early seventies. In 1973, a Private Member's Bill was introduced into the House of Commons which was designed to establish local tribunals to review the handling of complaints and such was the support that it received that the government of the day agreed to begin the process of

THE POLICE COMPLAINTS PROCEDURE

consultation with a view to reform, if the Bill was dropped. The general election of 1974 returned a Labour government to power and the new Home Secretary, Roy Jenkins, forged ahead with the reform of the police complaints procedure, a process which was undoubtedly aided by the revelations of wholesale corruption in the Metropolitan Police Force, which had, by this time, begun to emerge. The government's Police Bill was introduced into the House at the end of 1975 and, by August 1976, had received the Royal Assent.[10] What the Act did, was to institute the Police Complaints Board[11] and thereby, to introduce a modest independent element into the procedures for investigating complaints against the police. Chief constables were opposed to the new procedures because they were fearful that civilian interference in the investigation of complaints would undermine their authority over their men. And the Police Federation, representing rank and file policemen, was only won over to it by a Home office promise that the so-called 'double-jeopardy' rule would be interpreted in a novel way and by the concession that Federation members would be able to sue malicious complainants in defamation.

The Police Act, 1976

Under the Act, the Board's role was grafted on to the section 49 procedure. After any reference to the Director of Public Prosecutions, the 1976 Act required the deputy chief constable to send a copy of the investigating officer's report to the Police Complaints Board, together with a memorandum stating whether he had decided to bring disciplinary charges against the officer concerned and, if he had not, his reasons for not doing so.[12] The Board could request additional information from the deputy chief constable,[13] and, where it disagreed with his decision not to bring disciplinary charges, was empowered to recommend[14] and ultimately to direct,[15] that disciplinary charges be brought. Where the deputy chief constable preferred a disciplinary charge and this was denied by the officer concerned, the Board was required to consider whether exceptional circumstances made it desirable that the charges should be heard by a disciplinary tribunal consisting of the appropriate chief officer and two Board members,[16] rather than by the chief officer sitting alone, which was the normal procedure.

The Board began its operations against a general background of hostility from within the

THE POLICE COMPLAINTS PROCEDURE

police service and very soon it, and the procedures it represented, became the subject of criticism and controversy. In order, partly, to deflect some of the criticisms, the Board consistently emphasised in its Annual Reports to Parliament the statutory limitations imposed upon it and these were indeed considerable. The scheme was entirely geared to complaints made against individual police officers and did not cater for a complainant who was more concerned to raise the issue of, for example, the policy incorporated into a Force's standing orders or the levels of patrols in a particular area. In consequence, the Board's role was restricted to disciplinary matters and thus, it had little chance of acting positively to satisfy complainants or reassure the public generally. Related to this was the fact that the decision to record a complaint as a section 49 complaint was entirely a matter for the appropriate deputy chief constable. To some degree, therefore, the role of the Board and the fate of a complaint were dependent on decisions made by the police themselves. In some cases, for example, it may be possible to view a complaint - say, about routine stop checks on motorists - either as a complaint about an individual officer or as a complaint about general Force policy. If, in the police view, it fell into the latter category, there was, for the purposes of the Act, no complaint. The reverse was equally true. Where a complaint was recorded as a section 49 complaint, the Board had no option but to deal with it on that basis, even if it disagreed with the deputy chief constable's decision that the criticism amounted to a complaint. There was some Home Office guidance issued to deputy chief constables on the requirements of section 49,[17] but it remained extremely odd that the police were not required to have regard to the views of the Board itself on these matters.

The police may also be able to persuade a complainant not to pursue his complaint. The Police Complaints Board estimated that a very substantial number of complaints, (perhaps as many as forty to fifty per cent of the total number of complaints recorded), were never in fact recorded as section 49 complaints.[18] This was because, in practice, most police forces operated some form of preliminary sifting by, for example, arranging for a complainant to be seen by a senior officer to see whether his grievance really was a complaint, even though section 49 specifically required that all complaints should be recorded. The Board expressed its concern

THE POLICE COMPLAINTS PROCEDURE

about this practice on a number of occasions because, of course, this preliminary sifting lent itself to the suggestion that the police brought pressure to bear on complainants not to proceed with their complaint. In 1981, the Board commented: "We have no evidence that this happens but by dealing with complaints outside the system, the safeguard of independent adjudication is lost."[19]

Once a complaint was recorded as such, it was investigated by the police and referred if necessary, to the Director of Public Prosecutions. Whatever his decision on criminal proceedings, it could not be questioned by the Board. Similarly, where a deputy chief constable after reference to the Director of Public Prosecutions, if necessary, and before reference to the Police Complaints Board, decided to prefer disciplinary charges against an officer, the Board had no power to vary those charges and, as has been noted, its sole function in these cases was, where the charges were denied, to decide whether they should be heard before a disciplinary tribunal.

These then, were some of the more technical criticisms of the police complaints procedure. It was the wider aspects of the system, however, that caused greatest concern in recent years. Pre-eminent amongst these, was the fact that the police continued to investigate themselves and that this either actually worked against the complainant, in that the complaint was not adequately investigated, or, even though the complaint was properly invest-igated, there was little public confidence in the nature of the investigation. In other words, justice was not being seen to be done. The feeling that the 1976 Act did not contain a sufficiently convincing independent element was widespread by the beginning of the 1980s and the Police Complaints Board was forced more and more onto the defensive. Even the most cursory examination of the Board's Reports reveals that the percentage of cases in which disciplinary action was taken against an officer was tiny. In 1981, for example, the Board considered 15,198 complaints. Disciplinary charges were brought by deputy chief constables in 138 cases prior to reference to the Board. Of the 15,080 cases in which charges were not brought by deputy chief constables, the Board recommended charges in 26 of these cases and directed charges, (the first time the power to direct the bringing of charges had been used), in one.[20] Statistics like these, provided ample ammunition for those who wanted to

THE POLICE COMPLAINTS PROCEDURE

argue that the main function of the Board was to legitimate inadequate or biased police investigations and forced the Board to explain why complaints led to disciplinary action in so few cases. It advanced three main reasons.[21] First, the evidence very often simply did not support the complaint. Secondly, the evidence more often than not was inconclusive and this problem of conflicting evidence will remain at the root of any system that attempts to attribute blame. Thirdly, the Board cited the operation of the 'double-jeopardy' rule.

It will be recalled that double-jeopardy was a particular concern of the Police Federation during the period prior to the enactment of the 1976 Police Act and the double-jeopardy rule, as operated since the establishment of the Police Complaints Board, proved to be one of the most unsatisfactory aspects of the treatment of complaints alleging the commission of criminal offences by police officers. Section 11 of the 1976 Act provided that where a member of a police force was acquitted or convicted of a criminal charge, he was not liable to be charged with an offence against discipline which was in substance the same offence of which he had been acquitted or convicted. That is a concept of double-jeopardy which is perfectly clear and entirely reasonable. However, soon after the Act came into force, the Home Secretary issued a circular to the effect that where it had been decided, after reference to the Director of Public Prosecutions, that criminal proceedings should not be instituted against an officer, there should normally be no disciplinary charge either, if the evidence required to substantiate the disciplinary charge was the same as that required to substantiate the criminal charge.[22] In practice, therefore, double-jeopardy very often meant no jeopardy because the Police Complaints Board, albeit with some reluctance,[23] regarded itself as bound by the Home office guidance. Opposition to this rule came from the Association of Chief Police Officers, the Director of Public prosecutions, the National Council for Civil Liberties and the Home Affairs Committee of the House of Commons.[24] In 1983, the necessary corrective was supplied, not, as one might expect, by the Home Office reacting to this weighty criticism,[25] but by the Divisional Court on an application for judicial review against the Police Complaints Board.[26] The applicants each made a complaint about the conduct of certain officers. The complaints were regarded as alleging criminal

THE POLICE COMPLAINTS PROCEDURE

offences against the officers and were referred to the Director of Public Prosecutions who decided that there was insufficient evidence to justify criminal proceedings. In the light of this, the police decided not to prefer disciplinary charges and the Police Complaints Board decided, in accordance with its usual practice, that it was not open to it, in view of the Home Office guidance, to question the police decision not to prefer disciplinary charges. The applicants, accordingly, sought an order of certiorari to quash the Board's decision on the grounds that the Board had abdicated its statutory function to consider the complaint and that, alternatively, the Board had unlawfully fettered its discretion. The Divisional Court ruled in favour of the applicants on both grounds, stating the position unambiguously:[27]

> Since the object for which [the Board] was created was the consideration of complaints and the receipt of reports of investigations into those complaints, I cannot see that that object is pursued if, in relation to certain complaints, it accepts as binding on it the decision of another body, even so distinguished a person as the Director of Public Prosecutions...The Board, as an independent body, should be asserting its independence.

The Police Complaints Board was thus freed from the admittedly self-imposed shackles, of the Home Secretary's guidance. The Director of Public Prosecutions decision in any given case not to recommend criminal charges and the Home Office advice, were simply factors to which the Board should have regard in arriving at its independent decision whether to recommend the bringing of disciplinary charges. In practice, this may not have made a significant difference; the adoption of the principle by the Board, however, could have helped to restore some of its credibility.

Finally, it was argued that the system was excessively formal and rigid. Once a complaint had been recorded as a section 49 complaint and, assuming it was not subsequently withdrawn, it was subjected to a protracted investigation by a senior officer followed by reference to the Police Complaints Board. This very formality may itself have acted as a deterrent to complainants and when the complaint was a minor one, it was arguably

THE POLICE COMPLAINTS PROCEDURE

unnecessary to subject it to such a cumbersome procedure.

The Movement for Reform

In 1980, the Board recognised the mounting criticism of the complaints procedure, in its first Triennial Review Report.[28] It firmly rejected independent investigation of complaints on the ground that, "it is neither practicable nor desirable" to establish an independent investigative body.[29] It supported this conclusion by arguing that the number of complaints would necessitate the establishment of a very large investigative body, that the members of the body would need to be invested with all the powers of a constable and that the information enabling the investigation to proceed would largely be in the possession of the police. Further, it suggested that there is no readily available source of recruitment for such a body and even if it could be recruited, training would present formidable problems. However, the Board did suggest that additional safe-guards should be incorporated into the system where the complaint involves an allegation of serious injury caused by a police officer to a member of the public. The area of assault was singled out because "unexplained injury sustained during the course of arrest or while in subsequent police custody represents the focus of present discontent and...violence is the factor which causes the greatest damage to good relations between the police and the public."[30] Of the 31,252 complaints dealt with by the Board in the period under review, allegations of assault comprised by far the biggest category amounting to some twenty per cent of the total. Accordingly, the Board recommended that a specialist body of investigating officers be recruited by secondment from all police forces and that this body should be responsible for investigating allegations of serious injury inflicted by the police upon the public. The Board further recommended that this force should be responsible to a lawyer of experience and repute, preferably one who had exercised judicial office.

Although this was undoubtedly an important recommendation from a body well placed to judge the efficacy of the system, the reasoning underlying it was curious. If, as the Board asserted, "in the vast majority of cases" which came before them "a thorough and fair investigation has been made,"[31] the setting up of a specialist investigative team

68

THE POLICE COMPLAINTS PROCEDURE

would seem to be superfluous. If, on the other hand, there was a clearly identifiable class of cases where the investigation was less than thorough, this was bound to throw doubts on the general standard of investigation of complaints against the police. Also, it was difficult to see how a recommendation which contemplated the introduction of a sort of two-tier system of investigation and which, by its very nature, seemed to admit that the standard of investigation in at least some classes of cases was not all that it should be, was capable of instilling greater public confidence in the effectiveness and fairness of the system. Further, in so far as there was perceived by the Board to be a need to create a specialist squad of experienced and able police officers responsible to an independent figure, it was not easy to see at first glance why its terms of reference should not cover all classes of complaints.

Following the publication of the Triennial Review Report, the Home Secretary, with commendable promptness, set up a departmental Working Party, under the chairmanship of Lord Plowden, (at that time, chairman of the Police Complaints Board), to consider the various recommendations made by the Police Complaints Board.[32] Membership of the Working Party was weighted in favour of the police organisations[33] and their influence on its conclusions was most marked. The Association of Chief Police Officers, for instance, argued that changes on the lines suggested by the Board would significantly interfere with the responsibility of the chief officer for the investigation of all alleged offences within his area and would affect the constitutional relationship between the chief officer and the Director of Public Prosecutions.[34] On this latter point, the Association was supported by the DPP, who suggested that his involvement in the investigation process already constituted an independent element in the section 49 procedure.[35] The Association went on to argue that it was not convinced that a significant body of opinion was dissatisfied with the existing arrangements, that the proposed scheme would be likely to lead to delay, expense and confusion of responsibilities and that within the police service, it would lead to a closing of ranks against the special investigating squad and a corresponding shortage of officers willing to serve in it. The Superintendents' Association and the Police Federation expressed similar views.[36] Apart from these expressions of

69

THE POLICE COMPLAINTS PROCEDURE

general opposition, however, the police also argued that the establishment of a special team of investigators would face strong practical difficulties: for instance, the problems of finding suitable office accommodation, financing the operation, meeting the need for a proper command structure and securing the co-operation of the force whose members are under investigation.[37] These factors together, led the Working Party to reject the proposal. Instead, it recommended that "the possible use of an officer from another force is specifically and independently considered in every case where the complaint is of the prescribed types."[38] The Police Complaints Board's proposal for an independent assessor was similarly watered down by the Plowden Working Party. A non-police supervisor could be involved in deciding which cases were to be investigated under the new arrangements suggested by the Working Party, but it was not necessary that he should be a lawyer. Indeed, the Working Party suggested that the chairman or deputy chairman of the Police Complaints Board should fulfil this role.[39]

It appeared in March 1981, then, that the debate about who polices the police, officially at least, was closed. The modest initiative taken by the Police Complaints Board in its Triennial Review Report had been resoundingly rejected by the Plowden Working Party. The section 49 procedure would continue virtually unaltered. It is true that in cases of serious assault or injury the Working Party had recommended that the use of an officer from another force should be specifically considered, but the section 49 procedure already allowed a chief officer, at his discretion, to use an investigating officer from another force. Most disturbing of all, however, was the united opposition of the police to any further significant changes in the police complaints procedures. The Association of Chief Police officers and the Police Federation differed in their reasons for opposition, not surprisingly, as they represent different and often conflicting vested interests, but together they constituted powerful pressure on the Home Office to preserve the status quo.

It was only the cataclysmic events which took place in Brixton in April 1981 and shortly afterwards, in Toxteth and Moss-side, that made policing an acute and difficult political issue and thrust the police complaints procedure into renewed prominence. Lord Scarman, in his Report on the Brixton

70

THE POLICE COMPLAINTS PROCEDURE

riots,[40] suggested that on the basis of the evidence advanced before him, "there is a widespread and dangerous lack of public confidence in the existing system for handling complaints against the police"[41] and added that if public confidence in the complaints system was to be secured, "the early introduction of an independent element in the investigation of complaints and the establishment of a conciliation process are vital."[42] Lord Scarman's own view was that "any solution falling short of a system of independent investigation for all complaints"[43] was unlikely to be successful in achieving public confidence. Mindful of the resource implications, however, he suggested that the decision to go for independent investigation must rest on a judgment whether the gain in public confidence which would result outweighed the financial costs involved[44] and as an alternative to his radical solution, proposed a series of more limited measures, including some form of independent supervision of investigations and some form of local conciliation procedure for less serious complaints.[45]

Prior to the publication of the Scarman Report, the Home Secretary had appointed a Working Group to report to the Police Advisory Board for England and Wales on complaints and discipline matters and this body reported early in 1982.[46] Once again, the composition of the Group, under the chairmanship of Lord Belstead,[47] was weighted in favour of the police organisations,[48] and while in general terms it thought that the Plowden proposals would be workable, the considerable disagreement amongst the members of the Group was evident from the following comment: "Some of us think the proposals worthwhile, some remain unconvinced as to their value and others believe that more radical change is necessary."[49] Indeed, the opposition to independent investigation of complaints voiced by the police to the Plowden Working Party, had by this time begun to crumble. In October 1981, Albert Laugharne, chief constable of Lancashire, was reported as commenting that the only way to allay public disquiet about the police complaints procedure is to have independent investigation,[50] a view shortly after supported by James Anderton, chief constable of Greater Manchester and Peter Imbert, chief constable of Thames Valley.[51] At the very end of 1981, the Police Federation released a statement in favour of independent investigation[52] and expanded this in its evidence to the Belstead Working Group. In view of the Federation's long history of opposition to

THE POLICE COMPLAINTS PROCEDURE

independent investigation, this was indeed a dramatic volte face, but it was hedged around with a number of important and, to the Home Office, unacceptable qualifications.[53] Cynical observers of this debate also viewed the Federation's change of heart as a crude attempt to play the political game of "I told you so." In this view, independent investigation by lay investigators would soon prove to be less efficient than the existing procedures, ultimately collapse, and the Police Federation could jubilantly claim, "I told you so!"[54]

Despite these developments, it is clear that by early 1982, Home Office policy was based on a combination of Plowden/Belstead/Scarman and had three main characteristics:

1. a new informal procedure, including conciliation, for less serious complaints;
2. examination of more substantial complaints in accordance with the section 49 procedure as amended by the Police act 1976; and
3. investigation of serious complaints, for example, infliction of serious injury by the police and possibly corruption, in accordance with the Plowden recommendations, namely, investigation by a senior officer from an outside force under the supervision of an independent assessor (probably the Police Complaints Board itself).

In the meantime, yet another official investigation of the police complaints procedure was embarked upon, this time by the influential Home Affairs Committee of the House of Commons. It reported in May, 1982.[55] In the long term, it felt that the best solution to the problem was represented by the Royal Commission on Criminal Procedure's recommendation that a system of regional Crown prosecutors should be set up in England and Wales.[56] According to the Home Affairs Committee, the prosecutors should be given responsibility for the investigation of complaints against the police.[57] This new twist to the debate, however, was not without its difficulties. Nowhere in the Royal Commission's report is it suggested that the Crown prosecutors might have a role to play in the police complaints procedure. What the Home Affairs Committee did, therefore, was to graft onto a recommendation solely concerned with the arrangements for the prosecution of offences, a further role for the Crown prosecutors not adverted to by the Royal Commission itself, whose view on the

THE POLICE COMPLAINTS PROCEDURE

nature and functions of the institution it recommended would almost certainly have been different if it had considered the Crown prosecutors having this expanded role. For instance, the Royal Commission did not envisage the prosecutors having investigative powers, such as the power to interview witnesses. Under its proposals, the conduct of all investigations would remain in the hands of the police.[58] The Home Affairs Committee recommended that the prosecutor should be able to interview witnesses in connection with the complaints against the police.[59] A further point was that the Home Affairs Committee did not, in its report, delineate sufficiently clearly the function of the prosecutor in the complaints procedure. It stated that "there is no inherent reason why...local Crown prosecutors ...should not also be given responsibility for the investigation of complaints against the police"[60] but it did not further explain what it meant by "responsibility for the investigation of complaints" and as the proposal stood, it conflicted with the Royal Commission's view that Crown prosecutors should not have investigative powers as such. It may be that the decision to charge a police officer with a criminal offence could be taken by the new prosecutors instead of by the Director of Public Prosecutions as at present, but again, if this is what the Home Affairs Committee had in mind, it does not accord with the view of the Royal Commission which recommended that the Crown prosecutor should take over the conduct of a prosecution only after the decision to prosecute has been taken by the police.[61] In addition, the Home Affairs Committee did not consider specifically what the function of the prosecutor should be where a complaint against a police officer does not allege the commission of a criminal offence. The approach of the Home Affairs Committee to this matter was far too generalised and this interesting and useful recommendation required far closer consideration before it could be implemented. And we might add, before leaving this matter, that the recommendation might not have had the effect of allaying public disquiet about the police complaints system. To a public used to police control over prosecutions, the Crown prosecutor may not have seemed sufficiently distant from the police to amount to a convincing independent element in the police complaints procedure.

In the short term, however, and until such a system was established, the Committee recommended immediate changes, among which were:

THE POLICE COMPLAINTS PROCEDURE

1. a re-wording of the double-jeopardy rule to restore the position to that set out in the Police Act 1976;[62]
2. the establishment of regional complaints offices headed by independent assessors who would assume overall responsibility for the investigation of complaints alleging serious criminal offences;
3. the introduction of a conciliation process for complaints not involving criminal offences.[63]

The Committee did not recommend independent investigation because it was not convinced that an independent organisation would do a better job than the police in investigating complaints.[64]

While the Committee was deliberating, the Home Secretary announced that he was prepared to be guided by it. By the autumn of 1982, therefore, there were no less than five sets of official proposals on the table and it is significant that four of the five completely rejected independent investigation. When the Police and Criminal Evidence Bill was published shortly afterwards, it confirmed that the Home Office intended to settle for modest changes in the procedures based largely on the Plowden/Belstead/Scarman recommendations, namely, greater use of officers from outside forces, the appointment of an independent assessor to supervise the investigation of serious complaints (who, under the Bill, would have been the chairman or deputy chairman of the Police Complaints Board) and informal resolution of minor complaints.[65]

In April 1983, the Police Complaints Board published its second Triennial Review Report.[66] It did not take the opportunity to reiterate those proposals for reform so resoundingly rejected by Plowden and Belstead, not surprisingly, because by this time, as we have seen, the government's legislative proposals were before Parliament. Instead, it expressed its continued concern at the high proportion of withdrawn complaints and recommended that some form of scrutiny of cases in this category should be undertaken.[67] It also expressed the view again that its effectiveness as an institution should not be judged solely on the relatively small number of times its views, especially on the preferment of disciplinary charges, diverged from those of chief officers. "It is our impression" it reported, "that the role of the Board has become more widely acceptable to the police service as a part of the procedure for dealing with

74

THE POLICE COMPLAINTS PROCEDURE

complaints. In an area where the potential for disagreement with chief officers is considerable, the fact that we differ from them so infrequently is not an indication of the Board's ineffectiveness, but rather, that in our approaches to the question whether disciplinary charges should be brought in consequence of a complaint, our standpoint and responsibilities are understood and respected."[68] In other words, the Board was asserting that chief officers deal with complaints in a manner which they know the Board will approve. This, of course, did not deal with the main point of those who used statistics to query the effectiveness of the Board, namely, that it was inconceivable that only approximately one per cent of those officers against whom complaints are made and which were then reported to the Board, deserved to be charged with disciplinary offences.

The second Triennial Review Report in the event, turned out to be the last to be made by the Police Complaints Board. The General Election announced for June 1983 and consequent dissolution of Parliament ensured that the Police and Criminal Evidence Bill could not complete its parliamentary stages and was therefore lost. A Conservative government was returned to power and a new Home Secretary appointed.[69] When Parliament reassembled in October, the Police and Criminal Evidence Bill was reintroduced, but in the meantime, it had undergone considerable reformulation in the Home Office. Nowhere were the changes more marked than in the area of complaints against the police. The government's new policy was explained in a White Paper.[70] Under it, a new Police Complaints Authority was to replace the Police Complaints Board and exercise substantially widened powers to supervise the investigation of complaints in certain classes of cases and it is to the details of this scheme, enacted by the Police and Criminal Evidence Act, 1984, that we must now turn.

The Police Complaints Authority

> The changes are designed to ensure that the procedure to be adopted in any case reflects the seriousness of the allegation. A new Police Complaints Authority will be created which will be required to supervise the investigation of the most serious cases and will be empowered to 'call in' any other complaint where it believes that independent

THE POLICE COMPLAINTS PROCEDURE

supervision of the investigation is appropriate.71

Under the Act, the new Authority has two quite distinct functions, the supervisory function; and the disciplinary function. In its latter role, it operates very much as its predecessor the Police Complaints Board; it is the totally new supervisory role which is the government's main response to all the criticisms of the old scheme.

It is important to stress at the outset that the new procedures still depend on the police investigating complaints from the public. The rethinking of the procedures which occurred between the demise of the first Police and Criminal Evidence Bill and the introduction of the second into Parliament did not result in any change in the Home Office's attitude that independent investigation would be impracticable and undesirable. Neither do the 1984 Act procedures place an investigatory corps of police officers under the control of the new Authority as recommended by the Police Complaints Board in its first Triennial Review Report. It is not apt therefore, to refer to the Authority's investigatory functions, as the 1983 White Paper consistently does; the Authority's role is to supervise investigations carried out by the police service.

In what circumstances then, do the new procedures operate? Sections 84 and 85 of the Act require a chief police officer who receives a complaint against a member of his force from or on behalf of a member of the public to record it and to take any steps that appear to him to be desirable for the purpose of obtaining or preserving evidence relating to the matter complained.72 As soon as a complaint is received, the chief officer will make such preliminary inquiries as are necessary to decide whether the matter necessitates formal investigation or is suitable for informal resolution,73 and may appoint an officer of at least chief inspector rank to assist him.74 Where the case is one which the Police Complaints Authority will supervise, the choice of investigating officer must be approved by the Authority.75 Such cases fall into a number of different categories:

(a) Mandatory Reference and Mandatory Supervision

Under the Act, a chief officer is required to refer to the Authority76 any complaint which alleges that the conduct of a member of his force resulted

THE POLICE COMPLAINTS PROCEDURE

in the death of or serious injury[77] to some other person[78] and the Authority is required to supervise it.[79]

(b) <u>Discretionary reference and discretionary supervision</u>

Chief officers are empowered to refer to the Authority any other section 84 complaint which they consider should be brought to its attention.[80] In such a case, the Authority will supervise its investigation if it considers that to do so "is desirable in the public interest."[81] The legislation also entitles chief officers to notify the Authority of cases which are not strictly speaking complaints, but which nonetheless involve allegations of serious misconduct against individual officers or are in some other way exceptional.[82] Again, the Police Complaints Authority may supervise the investigation of such an allegation if it is desirable in the public interest.[83] In either case, the Authority is under a duty to inform the chief officer of its decision regarding supervision.[84]

(c) <u>Reserve Powers</u>

The Act provides a safeguard against improper use of the discretionary power to refer complaints to the Authority vested in the chief officer. By s. 87(2) of the Act, the Authority is empowered to require a chief officer of police to submit to it any s. 84 complaint which has not already been referred and the Authority may at its discretion supervise the investigation of such a complaint.

In practice, the Police Complaints Authority operates through a supervisory division and a discipline division, each presided over by a full-time deputy chairman. The chairman of the Authority is Sir Cecil Clothier QC, formerly Parliamentary Commissioner for Administration and his high public standing and experience as ombudsman are a clear indication of governmental commitment to restoring credibility to the procedures for investigating complaints against the police. Although members of the Authority are not appointed to one or other of its divisions as such, as a matter of practice they do specialise in one or other side of the Authority's work and the task of supervising an investigation is allocated to a specific member of the supervisory division.[85]

77

THE POLICE COMPLAINTS PROCEDURE

As has already been mentioned, the first task of the Authority in performing its supervisory function is to approve the appointment of an investigating officer and this power can be used to require the appointment of a particular individual or to veto an appointment.[86] The extent to which the Authority can exercise a controlling function over the investigation is governed by statutory regulations.[87] Under them, the Authority can require that an investigative team be augmented in respect of manpower or other resources and has the power to give investigating officers such reasonable directions as it considers necessary for the proper conduct of the investigation:

> The powers...enable it to require
> investigating officers to account for
> their actions; to explain the strategy
> and tactics of their investigation; and
> to justify particular lines and depth of
> questioning and any apparent delay in the
> investigation as a whole or particular
> parts of it.[88]

Before giving directions on evidential matters to the investigating officer, the Authority is required to consult the Director of Public Prosecutions and obtain his consent to them.[89]

Where a complaint is made against a senior police officer - an officer holding a rank above that of chief superintendent[90] - the chief officer is required under the Act to pass it to the disciplinary authority for officers above that rank. This will normally be the appropriate police authority.[91] Where a police authority receives such a complaint against a senior officer it is required to record it and cause it to be investigated. The supervisory role of the Police Complaints Authority operates in exactly the same way as for junior officers and the relationship between the Police Complaints Authority and the police authority is identical to that between the Authority and chief police officers.[92]

At the end of any investigation supervised by the Authority, the investigating officer submits his report on the investigation to it and sends a copy to the chief officer to whom the complaint was made.[93] After considering this report, the Authority finally issues its own report on the investigation, copies of which are sent to the appropriate chief officer and to the person who made the complaint or allegation[94] stating whether or not the investigation was conducted to its satisfaction and specifying

78

THE POLICE COMPLAINTS PROCEDURE

any respect in which it was not so conducted.[95] Where the investigation has been conducted satisfactorily, a statement to that effect is issued and no decision on disciplinary or criminal action can be taken until such a statement has been issued. The Authority's supervisory role ends with the issue of its certificate.

Complaints, the investigation of which are not supervised by the Authority and which are not dealt with by the informal procedures sanctioned by the Act, continue to be dealt with in much the same manner as heretofore. An investigating officer, who may be from another force, is appointed and his investigation culminates in a report to the chief officer.[96]

The duties of the chief officer are the same irrespective of whether or not the investigation has been supervised by the Police Complaints Authority. His first task is to decide whether the investigating officer's report indicates that a criminal offence may have been committed by the officer concerned.[97] If the report does so indicate, the chief officer must then decide whether the offence indicated can be dealt with by preferring disciplinary charges instead.[98] If he decides that it can be, he must send to the Authority a signed memorandum to that effect, stating whether he proposes to prefer disciplinary charges and if not, his reasons for not so doing.[99] If on the other hand, he concludes that the criminal offence indicated by the report is too serious for him to deal with by the preferment of disciplinary charges, he must send a copy of the report to the Director of Public Prosecutions for his decision whether criminal charges are appropriate in the circumstances.[100] If the Director decides that criminal charges are not appropriate, the chief officer must send to the Authority a memorandum indicating whether he intends preferring disciplinary charges and if he does not, his reasons for not doing so.[101]

On receipt of the investigating officer's report, a chief officer may decide of course, that it does not indicate that criminal offences may have been committed. In such a case, he is under a duty to send to the Authority a signed memorandum to that effect. The memorandum must give particulars of any disciplinary charges which the chief officer has preferred or proposes to prefer and if he has decided not to prefer discplinary charges his reasons for not doing so. It must also state the chief officers opinion of the merits of the complaint

79

THE POLICE COMPLAINTS PROCEDURE

and set out any exceptional circumstances affecting the case which indicate that the charge should be heard by a disciplinary tribunal, rather than by the chief officer sitting alone.[102]
As can be seen, a chief officer of police is given wide and important powers to make the initial decisions about how complaints should be dealt with. Safeguards against bad decision making by chief officers are, however, provided by the Act. Where the Police Complaints Authority receives a memorandum from a chief officer indicating either, that he has decided that although a criminal offence may have been committed he intends to deal with it by the preferment of disciplinary charges, or, that no criminal offence appears to have been committed, it is entitled to take a different view and if necessary, to direct the chief officer concerned to refer the investigating officer's report to the Director of Public Prosecutions.[103] Alternatively, it may recommend the chief officer to prefer disciplinary charges where he has indicated that he does not propose to do so and if the recommendation is not complied with, the Authority is ultimately entitled to direct him to prefer such disciplinary charges as are indicated by it.[104]
Many complaints against police officers are of a relatively trivial nature and one important criticism of the pre-existing procedures was that they did not differentiate between the trivial and the more serious complaints: once a complaint was recorded as such, it had to be subjected to formal investigation followed by reference to the Police Complaints Board. The need for a more informal procedure for dealing with certain classes of complaint was pressing and the 1984 Act now provides for informal resolution. An officer appointed to investigate a s. 84 complaint will advise the chief officer whether the matter can be handled by informal means. However, informal resolution is only possible in certain confined circumstances: first, the chief officer must be satisfied that the conduct complained would not in practice justify a criminal or disciplinary charge; and secondly, the complainant must consent to the use of informal procedures.[105] The Act, therefore, gives recognition to the fact that the use within the police service of informal warnings and advice means in practice that disciplinary charges do not generally follow trivial breaches of the Police Discipline Code.
No fixed procedures are imposed on officers

80

THE POLICE COMPLAINTS PROCEDURE

administering informal resolution although detailed guidance on the subject has been issued to all police forces by the Home Secretary. The Police Complaints Authority has no formal role to play in respect of informal resolution, but the use of the technique is subject to the general oversight of police authorities and HM Inspectors of Constabulary.[106]

Conclusions

Changes in the way in which complaints against the police are investigated, monitored and supervised cannot in themselves create or maintain public confidence that the police are using their powers properly or pursuing policies which accord with community expectations and desires. The formulation of police powers, the way the police are recruited, trained and supervised, the policies which determine how they are deployed and the extent to which they are seen to be responsive to community needs and aspirations are all factors which will have a determining effect upon public confidence in and respect for, its police forces. Indeed, it can be argued that concentration upon the complaints procedures deflects attention from the more important need to avoid or reduce the kind of behaviour which gives rise to justified complaints in the first place. Police complaints procedures are important however, for a number of reasons; first, there is a clear link between police effectiveness and public confidence that complaints will be fully and properly dealt with; secondly, a police complaints procedure acceptable to the public is an essential part of the process of keeping the police in touch with the community they serve; thirdly, the principle of policing by consent depends upon good police/community relations and an effective police complaints procedure can help to cement these; fourthly, because the ability of the police to control individual freedom is so wide-ranging they themselves must not just act within the law, but be seen to be acting within the law. Few things are more calculated to produce distrust and suspicion of the police than a public perception that the police themselves are able to act improperly or above the law with impunity.

In this area, however, as in all aspects of policing, difficult issues of balance arise. What is the primary purpose of the police complaints procedures? Is it to ensure that complaints against

81

THE POLICE COMPLAINTS PROCEDURE

the police are effectively and properly investigated and disposed of? Or is it to reassure the public that improper police behaviour will not escape undetected? The Police Complaints Board, for instance, consistently argued that the vast majority of investigations into complaints against police officers were conducted thoroughly and impartially, though it must be said that this view was undermined by its own proposals for reform. Yet there can be little doubt that the procedures over which the Board presided did not command public confidence. Is it possible for a police complaints procedure to fulfil both of these objectives adequately? The changes introduced by the 1984 legislation are designed to do precisely that but it must be queried whether they go far enough. The government has chosen to build upon existing procedures rather than looking for more radical solutions. The powers of the Police Complaints Authority to supervise investigations are confined to the most serious classes of complaints. The investigation of the bulk of the complaints is not therefore subject to supervision and for these, the role of the Authority is as restricted as that of its predecessor. By concentrating on the disciplinary aspects of complaints, the statutory framework once again denies to the Authority the opportunity to play a more positive part in reassuring the public generally that complaints are properly investigated.

The Home Office has thus settled for the soft option of introducing changes, the effect of which will be mainly cosmetic because they do not tackle the fundamental issue - that the police investigate themselves. No system, however elaborate, which concentrates on supervision and ex post facto review of police investigations will satisfy the demand that justice will only be seen to be done when the investigation of complaints against the police is taken out of the hands of the police themselves. Governmental rejection of independent investigation has been based not so much on the principle, but on the practical difficulties of implementing such a procedure. According to the Home Office,[107] there are three main ones. The first is the difficulty which an independent system would create for chief officers who are accountable for their forces and responsible for discipline. This assertion does not withstand close scrutiny, however, but simply illustrates the strength of the Association of Chief Police Officers which fears that its members' power and influence would be undermined or diminished by

THE POLICE COMPLAINTS PROCEDURE

independent investigation. The second, and this is far more substantial, is the difficulty of staffing an independent investigatory force. We will return to this after considering the final main reason for opposition by the Home Office to independent investigation - cost.

A number of estimates of the cost of an independent investigatory force have been ventured though they have to be treated with caution as it is impossible to tell which elements of expenditure have been costed into the calculation and which have not. Sir Cyril Phillips, former chairman of the Police Complaints Board, has suggested that the additional cost of a special force recruited by secondment from within the police service to investigate complaints of assault, could be as high as £10 million per annum.[108] In contrast, the Home Office has suggested that an independent investigatory force to investigate all complaints would require 800 investigators and cost, again, £10 million per annum.[109] Compared with the direct costs of the Police Complaints Board in its last year of operation of around £500,000, these estimates appear astronomical, but it must be remembered that under the present system the police themselves bear the costs of investigating complaints and these run into many millions of pounds. The Metropolitan Police, for instance, has estimated that the cost of investigating complaints against its officers is nearly £6 million per annum.[110] It must also be borne in mind that independent investigation would allow those officers currently involved in investigating complaints to return to normal police duties. The crucial question, therefore, remains that suggested by Lord Scarman - whether the benefits of independent investigation outweigh the costs involved, which incidentally, in the context of departmental and policing budgets of hundreds of millions of pounds, are hardly substantial.

One model for radical reform would be the establishment on a regional basis of a system of police ombudsmen.[111] The ombudsman device, since its adoption into our constitutional structure in 1967 has worked reasonably well and could usefully form the basis of a new independent investigatory system, as some people have recognised.[112] The police ombudsmen should have their own staff consisting of lawyers, investigators and conciliation officers and be responsible for deciding the appropriate manner for dealing with complaints and

THE POLICE COMPLAINTS PROCEDURE

carrying out the necessary investigations. After the investigation of complaints alleging criminal offences, a report of the investigation should be sent to the Director of Public Prosecutions, unless the ombudsman is satisfied on the advice of his legal staff, that no question arises of a criminal offence having been committed. Where the complaint alleges a disciplinary matter, after the investigation the report should be sent to the relevant chief officer with an appropriate direction. A conciliation process should be available for minor complaints which do not indicate the commission of a criminal or disciplinary offence.

The crux of this model is that investigation should be taken out of the hands of the police and this is where formidable problems arise. From where could lay investigators be recruited and, more importantly, could they do the job effectively? Many government departments employ investigative staff, sometimes in considerable numbers and frequently the main concern of such investigators is the investigation of criminal offences. Bodies such as the Customs and Excise, the Inland Revenue and the Department of Trade and Industry readily come to mind but there are others such as the Department of Health and Social Security, the Post Office and the local authority ombudsmen. The experience of these bodies is that efficient investigation of unlawful behaviour is not the sole prerogative of police officers. Initially, therefore, it would be necessary to second or transfer some of these investigators to the staff of the police ombudsmen to assist in the recruitment of staff, to devise training programmes and so on. A common criticism of this idea is that while lay investigators might be able adequately to deal with members of the public, they would not be able to cope with the investigation of experienced police officers. How would it be possible, for instance, for a lay investigator to subject to interrogation a detective fully versed in all the stratagems and nuances of the questioning process? While we must not underplay this difficulty neither must we elevate it to the realms of an insuperable problem. Interrogation techniques can be taught. And more importantly, although interrogation of suspects can be of central significance in the construction of a case against them, crimes and offenders are most usually discovered and prosecuted by the painstaking process of accumulating and sifting[113] evidence - interviewing the victim, compiling lists of suspects and so

84

THE POLICE COMPLAINTS PROCEDURE

on. Experienced lay investigators with the necessary local knowledge might therefore be capable of investigating complaints against the police.

But what of their investigative powers? They clearly will need to be able to demand access to any relevant information in the hands of the police and, on occasion, may need to arrest people and search them and their premises. Because of this, it has been suggested that the investigators will need to be endowed with all the powers of a constable and thus, to all intents and purposes, will be police officers. It would have to be emphasised, therefore, that the lay investigators would belong to the civilian staff of the police ombudsmen and would not be attached to any recognised police force. In any event, it would be preferable to confer the necessary powers directly on the investigators in the statute instigating the scheme (by analogy, Inland Revenue investigators possess special powers conferred directly by statute), thus making it clear that they exercise their powers _qua_ civilian investigators.

Whether such a scheme would actually work is a matter for conjecture. It would not be popular with the police service itself which might well close ranks against lay investigation. Without co-operation from the police, the lay investigators might find their task increasingly difficult and, if ultimately the scheme should collapse, public confidence would be dealt a severe blow. The merit of such a scheme, however, is that it goes to the heart of the problem of policing the police and given commitment by government and police service alike, could resolve it.

Notes

1. _Report of the Royal Commission on Police Powers_, Cmnd. 3297, (1929).
2. _Ibid._, para. 283.
3. _Report of the Royal Commission on the Police_, Cmnd. 1728 (1962). The background to the setting up of the Commission is outlined in paras. 10-12.
4. _Ibid._, para. 478.
5. _Ibid._, Appendix V. This proposal was closely modelled on the ombudsman recommendations of the Whyatt Report, _The Citizen and the Administrat-_

THE POLICE COMPLAINTS PROCEDURE

ion : the Redress of Grievances, published by Justice, Nov. 1961.

6. In the Metropolitan Police, the requirement was for an officer of the rank of chief inspector or above and from a different division of the force.

7. To whom the duties of the chief officer in this respect are normally delegated.

8. Police Act, 1964, s. 50.

9. Ibid.

10. For an excellent account of the background to the Police Act, 1976, see D. Humphrey, The Complaints System, in Hain (ed.,) Policing the Police, (John Calder, London, 1980), Vol. 1, pp. 41-103.

11. The Board was composed of not less than nine members appointed by the Prime Minister. No person who had been a constable in any part of the U.K. was eligible for membership. Police Act, 1976, s. 1(2). See now Police and Criminal Evidence Act, 1984, Schedule 4.

12. Police Act, 1976, s. 2(1).

13. Ibid., s. 3(1).

14. Ibid., s. 3(2).

15. Ibid.

16. Ibid., s. 3(5).

17. See Home Office Circular, No 63/1977.

18. See the Report of the Police Complaints Board for 1981, H.C. 275, para. 24.

19. Ibid.

20. Ibid.

21. See para. 14 of the Memorandum submitted by the Police Complaints Board to the House of Commons Home Affairs Committee, (reprinted as Appendix D to the Report of the Police Complaints Board for 1981, ibid.).

22. The circular was originally issued in 1977 (Home Office Circular No 63/1977). See also Home Office Circular 32/1980 (as amended by Home Office Circular 15/1982).

23. See, for example, the comments made in the Report of the Police Complaints Board for 1981, op. cit., at para. 31.

24. See the Fourth Report of the Home Affairs Committee of the House of Commons, Session 1981-1982, Police Complaints Procedures, HC 98-1, Vol. 1 paras. 13-15.

25. Indeed, the Home Office, in its evidence to the Home Affairs Committee of the House of Commons, stated that Home Office guidance on double-jeopardy "struck an acceptable balance". See the

THE POLICE COMPLAINTS PROCEDURE

Fourth Report of the Home Affairs Committee of the House of Commons, Session 1981-1982, Minutes of Evidence, HC 98-2.

26. See R v Police Complaints Board ex parte Madden, (1983) 2 All E.R. 353.

27. Ibid., at p. 373.

28. Police Complaints Board, Triennial Review Report, Cmnd. 7966 (1980).

29. Ibid., at para. 67.

30. Ibid., at para. 69.

31. Ibid., at para. 62.

32. Report of a Working Party on the establishment of an independent element in the investigation of complaints against the police, (hereafter, the Plowden Report), Cmnd. 8193 (March 1981).

33. In addition to the chairman, the Working Party comprised three representatives of the Association of Chief Police Officers, two representatives of the Superintendents' Association, two representatives of the Police Federation, one HM Inspector of Constabulary, the Director of Public Prosecutions, a representative of the Police Complaints Board and a representative of the Home Office.

34. Plowden Report, op. cit., para. 8.

35. Ibid., para. 11.

36. Ibid., paras. 9, 10.

37. Ibid., para. 18.

38. Ibid., para. 20.

39. See the discussion at paras. 21-28, ibid.

40. Lord Scarman was appointed on 14th April 1981, to hold a local inquiry under s. 32 of the Police Act, 1964, by the Home Secretary. The terms of reference were "to inquire urgently into the serious disorder in Brixton on 10-12 April 1981 and to report, with the power to make recommendations." The Report was published in November 1981, Cmnd. 8427.

41. Scarman Report, ibid., para. 5.43.

42. Ibid., para. 7.28.

43. Ibid., para. 7.21 (emphasis added).

44. Ibid.

45. Ibid., paras. 7.24-7.26.

46. The Report of the Working Group was not published separately, but is reproduced in the Fourth Report of the Home Affairs Committee of the House of Commons, op. cit., Minutes of Evidence.

47. At that time, Under-Secretary of State at the Home Office.

48. Apart from Lord Belstead, the Working Group comprised one representative from the

THE POLICE COMPLAINTS PROCEDURE

Association of Chief Police Officers, one from the Metropolitan Police, one from the Police Superintendents' Association, one from the Police Federation, one from the Association of County Councils, one from the Association of Metropolitan Authorities, one from the Home Office and one HM Inspector of Constabulary.

49. Report of the Belstead Working Group, op. cit., para. 29.

50. The Times, 12.10.81.

51. The Times, 9.11.81.

52. The Times, 9.11.81.

53. The Police Federation demanded that a Bill of Civil Rights be written into any new legislation which would give a police officer against whom a complaint was made the protection of the Judges' Rules, the right to appear before an independent tribunal with full legal representation and the right of appeal to a Crown Court. However, independent investigation should only apply to complaints of a disciplinary nature. Complaints alleging criminal offences should continue to be investigated by the police. See The Times, 10.12.81.

54. See, for example, the memorandum submitted by K.W. Lidstone of Sheffield University to the Belstead Working Group, op. cit.

55. Fourth Report of the Home Affairs Committee of the House of Commons, op. cit.

56. Report of the Royal Commission on Criminal Procedure, Cmnd. 8092, (Jan. 1981), para. 7.3.

57. Fourth Report of the Home Affairs Committee of the House of Commons, op. cit.

58. Report of the Royal Commission on Criminal Procedure, op. cit., para. 7.7.

59. Fourth Report of the Home Affairs Committee, op. cit., para. 42.

60. Ibid., para. 40.

61. Report of the Royal Commission on Criminal Procedure, op. cit., para. 7.7.

62. See now R v Police Complaints Board ex parte Madden, supra.

63. Fourth Report of the Home Affairs Committee, op. cit., paras. 15, 57-58, 63-64.

64. Ibid., para. 55.

65. The Bill had completed all its House of Commons stages when the General Election was called in June 1983.

66. Police Complaints Board, Triennial Review Report, Cmnd. 8853, (April 1983).

67. Ibid., paras. 3.3, 3.5.

68. Ibid., para. 3.1.

THE POLICE COMPLAINTS PROCEDURE

69. Mr. Leon Brittan QC succeeded William Whitelaw, who was made a peer.

70. Police Complaints and Discipline Procedures, Cmnd. 9072, (October 1983).

71. Ibid., para. 10.

72. It will continue to be the norm for these duties to be delegated to deputy chief constables, See Police and Criminal Evidence Act, 1984, (hereafter, PCE Act, 1984), s. 99(2)(k).

73. See PCE Act, 1984, s. 85(2).

74. See PCE Act, 1984, s. 85(8)(a). A chief officer may request the chief officer of police for any other police area to provide an officer to carry out the investigation. Such a request must be complied with. See s. 85(7).

75. PCE Act, 1984, s. 89(4)(a) and (b).

76. Such reference shall be made not later than the end of a period specified in regulations made by the Secretary of State. See s. 99 generally.

77. Serious injury is defined by the Act as "a fracture, damage to an internal organ, impairment of a bodily function, a deep cut or a deep laceration." See s. 87(4).

78. The duty is imposed on the chief officer by s. 87(1).

79. See s. 89(1)(a). In addition, the Act provides that the Secretary of State may extend by regulation the kinds of complaints which must be referred and supervised. See ss. 87(1)(a)(ii) and 89(1)(b).

80. See s. 89(1)(b).

81. See s. 89(2).

82. See s. 88.

83. See s. 89(2).

84. See s. 89(3).

85. This was how the White Paper, Police Complaints and Discipline Procedures, envisaged the scheme working.

86. Where the Authority is not required to supervise the investigation and does not exercise its discretion so to do, the appointment of the investigating officer would not appear to be subject to the Authority's approval.

87. See s. 89(5) and Police (Complaints) (General) Regulations 1985, (No. 520).

88. Police Complaints and Discipline Procedures, op. cit., para. 22.

89. Police (Complaints) (General) Regulations, op. cit.

90. In provincial forces, these are the ranks of assistant chief constable, deputy chief constable and chief constable. In the Metropolitan Police,

THE POLICE COMPLAINTS PROCEDURE

they are the ranks of commander, assistant commissioner and deputy commissioner. The 1984 Act does not lay down a procedure for dealing with complaints against the Metropolitan Police Commissioner. Were such a complaint to be made, it would be referred to the Home Secretary.

91. The Metropolitan Police Commissioner remains the disciplinary authority for the senior ranks in his force, even though the Home Secretary is the police authority. See s. 84(4).

92. See generally s. 86.

93. See s. 89(6).

94. See s. 89(7), (8), (9).

95. See s. 89(10).

96. See s. 85 generally.

97. See s. 90(3)(b)(i).

98. See s. 90(6).

99. Ibid.

100. See s. 90(4)(b).

101. See s. 90(5).

102. See generally s. 90(8). Disciplinary tribunals are constituted under s. 94.

103. See s. 92(2).

104. See s. 93 generally.

105. See s. 85(10).

106. See s. 95.

107. See the Fourth Report of the Home Affairs Committee, Minutes of Evidence, (Home Office Memorandum), op. cit.

108. See The Times, 27.10.81.

109. See The Times, 11.3.82.

110. Fourth Report of the Home Affairs Committee, op. cit., para. 47.

111. Such a scheme has the qualified support of the Commission for Local Administration and the Association of Metropolitan Authorities. See the Fourth Report of the Home Affairs Committee, ibid., paras. 34, 35.

112. For example, in October 1981, Alf Dubs MP introduced into the House of Commons a Private Member's Bill which was designed to establish regional police ombudsmen.

113. The Royal Commission on Criminal Procedure commissioned research on the interrogation of suspects. While not wishing to draw hard and fast conclusions (see the discussion in Chapter 7), it appears from the research that interrogations are not usually crucial in the detection of crime. See B. Irving, Police Interrogation : A Case Study of Current Practice, Royal Commission on Criminal Procedure, Research Study No. 2, (1980), HMSO;

THE POLICE COMPLAINTS PROCEDURE

P. Softley, Police Interrogations : An Observational Study in Four Police Stations, Royal Commission on Criminal Procedure Research Study No. 4 (1980), HMSO; J. Baldwin and M. McConville, Confessions in Crown Court Trials, Royal Commission on Criminal Procedure Research Study No. 5 (1980) HMSO. See also, B. Mitchell, Confessions and Police Interrogations of Suspects, (1983) Crim. LR 596.

Chapter 4

ARREST AND DETENTION

Introduction

It is axiomatic that police forces need powers of
coercion in order to function efficiently and that
powers to detain suspects against their will on the
street or in police stations are essential elements
of the investigative process. The degree to which
it is necessary to use these powers will vary
enormously from case to case. Much crime is detected as a result of information received from the
public enabling an offender to be identified. In
other cases, suspects will voluntarily co-operate in
the investigative process. There will always be
circumstances, however, in which if the police are
to do their job successfully, they will need to stop
and question people, search them and their premises
or vehicle and take them to the police station in
order to proceed with the investigation, if need be,
by force. The exercise of such powers will inevitably infringe individual freedom and it is a primary
duty of the law, therefore, to grant such powers
sparingly and control their exercise rigorously.
Thus, one major problem permeates the whole field of
police powers: how to frame the law to give the
police adequate powers to perform their law enforcement duties, while at the same time ensuring that
such powers do not allow arbitrary and unreasonable
interference by the police with the freedom of the
individual.

That the law has not satisfactorily resolved
this problem is attributable, in part at least, to
the way in which police powers have evolved in
England and Wales. Traditionally, legislation has
built upon common law foundations in a sporadic and
piece-meal fashion. Until the passing of the Police
and Criminal Evidence Act, 1984, there was nothing

ARREST AND DETENTION

resembling a code of police powers. The law could only be discovered by searching through the cases and statutory provisions. The result was confusion and complexity. The public was consequently largely ignorant of the extent and nature of police powers and the police themselves were compelled to operate within a framework which was uncertain and ambiguous. To a degree, such a situation suited the police; public ignorance could be utilised to their own advantage. But it also gave rise to difficulties. Many of the cases of alleged and substantiated misuse of power involved officers acting in a manner which they thought was lawful.

The need for clarity in this area of the law has often been recognised, though not always in the right quarters. In 1962, for instance, the Report of the Royal Commission on the Police stated blandly:

> British liberty does not depend and never has depended upon the dispersal of police power...It depends on the supremacy of Parliament and on the Rule of Law.[1]

As a statement of classic constitutional theory that view cannot be faulted; but it is cold comfort to the man who has been unlawfully detained or whose person or property has been unlawfully searched. A more realistic view was taken by the Criminal Law Revision Committee, when in its Seventh Report it said:

> Ideally, the law should define clearly the rights of the police and private persons in all the situations that might confront them.[2]

More recently, the Royal Commission on Criminal Procedure recognised that "there is a critically important relationship between the police and the public in the detection and investigation of crime"[3] and suggested that public confidence in police powers required that these conform to three principal standards: fairness, openness and workability.[4] The Royal Commission recommended far reaching changes to the law and central to its proposals was the notion that the major and most frequently used powers should be collected together in one statute or code. Powers to arrest and detain suspects lie at the heart of the law enforcement process. Their content and, as importantly, the way they are used, are crucial to the relationship between police and public.

93

ARREST AND DETENTION

Arrest

The purpose of arrest is to render a person who has committed an offence or is reasonably suspected of so doing amenable to the criminal process. In many cases, of course, it is not necessary to arrest a person in order to ensure his presence before a court: the summons procedure is a very extensively used alternative. Around a quarter of those proceeded against for summary offences will have been brought to court by summons. Because arrest deprives a person of his liberty, its use traditionally has been restricted to offences which carry the penalty of imprisonment. Arrest can be made with or without warrant, though arrest on the authority of a warrant is relatively unusual.[5] The law contains very extensive powers of arrest without warrant.

By arrest an individual is deprived of his liberty. It was laid down in _Bird_ v _Jones_[6] that there is no arrest unless the restraint is total and it was this requirement that led to the view put forward in some of the older authorities that an arrest is not complete unless there is an actual seizing or touching of the arrested person. The court in _Bird_ v _Jones_ itself recognised, however, that the pronouncing of words of arrest followed by acquiescence in the arrest by the suspect would constitute a valid arrest.[7] The modern view is best seen in the case of _Alderson_ v _Booth_, where the Divisional Court stated the rule as follows:

> An arrest is constituted where any form of
> words is used which in the circumstances
> of the case were calculated to bring to the
> accused's notice and did bring to the
> accused's notice that he was under compulsion
> and thereafter, he submitted to the
> compulsion.[8]

Both Lord Parker and Donaldson J. remarked in this case upon the necessity of using very clear words to bring home to a person that he is under compulsion, particularly in circumstances in which a person's understanding may be dulled.[9]

Problems can arise where the words used do not make it clear to the suspect that he is under arrest. _Alderson_ v _Booth_ itself provides a good example of this, as does the case of _Inwood_.[10] Inwood went voluntarily to a police station in order to assist inquiries into certain thefts. After some questioning, he was told that the police proposed to charge

ARREST AND DETENTION

him with the thefts. Shortly afterwards, Inwood decided to leave the police station, was prevented from doing so, and in the ensuing struggle injured two police officers. He was charged with and convicted of assaulting a police officer in the execution of his duty. On appeal, the Court of Appeal held that the issue of whether it had been made clear to Inwood that he had been arrested was a matter of fact for the jury. The trial judge had withdrawn the issue from the jury and therefore the conviction was quashed. In the course of delivering the judgment of the court, Stephenson L.J. made the following comments:

> It all depends on the circumstances of any particular case whether in fact it has been shown that a man has been arrested and the court considers it unwise to say that there should be any particular formula followed...There is no magic formula; only the obligation to make it plain by what is said and done that he is no longer a free man.[11]

The Police and Criminal Evidence Act, 1984, now provides by s. 29 that where a person voluntarily attends at a police station to assist with an investigation, he shall be entitled to leave at will unless he is placed under arrest. If the police wish to prevent him from leaving "he shall be informed at once that he is under arrest." The regrettable ambiguity in Stephenson L.J.'s dictum has thus been clearly resolved in the legislation which reasserts the principle that voluntary attendance at a police station means precisely that and that if a suspect is to be prevented from leaving the police station, this is only permissible in law where his attendance is no longer voluntary; he is consequently under restraint and the only restraint recognised by the law in this context is by arrest. The suspect must be informed that he is under arrest and the legality of the arrest in the circumstances will be adjudged in any later proceedings.

(a) <u>Arrest without warrant for breach of the peace</u>

Historically, the major common law powers of arrest without warrant developed at a time prior to the establishment of professional police forces. Consequently, the duty of keeping the peace and apprehending offenders lay on each individual and

ARREST AND DETENTION

this explains the right of individuals to effect arrests which still persists today in certain circumstances. Traditionally at common law therefore, any person was entitled to arrest anyone who committed a breach of the peace in the presence of the arrestor or who was suspected of being a felon. In 1967, after a Report by the Criminal Law Revision Committee,[12] the distinction between felonies and misdemeanours was abolished by the Criminal Law Act and the common law power to arrest without warrant for a felony was replaced by new statutory powers to arrest without warrant for arrestable offences, which have since been extended by the 1984 Act. The only common law power of arrest which survives today, therefore, is the power to arrest without warrant for a breach of the peace.

In the absence of specific statutory authority, a police officer can arrest without warrant for nonarrestable offences only if a breach of the peace has taken place in his presence or if he reasonably apprehends that a breach of the peace may occur.[13] What constitutes a breach of the peace has never been authoritatively defined, though the Court of Appeal has suggested that "there is a breach of the peace whenever harm is actually done or is likely to be done to a person or in his presence to his property or a person is in fear of being so harmed through an assault, an affray, a riot, unlawful assembly or other disturbance."[14] Because the power extends to situations where a police officer has reasonable grounds of suspecting that a breach of the peace may occur, it has been established that there must exist proved facts from which a police officer could reasonably have anticipated such a breach and there must be a real and not merely a remote possibility of a breach.[15] Despite this ruling, the turning back of pickets' cars, when they were still a substantial distance away from the picket lines, as happened during the recent Miners' strike, on the basis that there was a reasonable apprehension that the occupants of the cars would commit breaches of the peace when they got to the picket lines, was upheld by magistrates as lawful.

The law requires that the breach of the peace should take place in the presence of an arresting officer. This is established by a clear line of authority which has never seriously been challenged.[16] In most American jurisdictions it is settled that an officer need not actually see the breach of the peace being committed: it is sufficient if the breach is "perceived through the senses."[17]

ARREST AND DETENTION

Professor Glanville Williams has suggested that
English courts would adopt a similar test.[18]
 The power to arrest without warrant for a
breach of the peace is limited to situations which
require immediate action by the police officer:
when the emergency is over, the power ceases.[19]
 It must be remembered, however, that in this
area of arrest, in common with all others, there is
no legal obligation on a constable to make an arrest.
The police officer has a discretion to choose what
appears to him to be the best course of action in
the circumstances. Should he make the arrest that
can properly be made, attempt to mediate, give a
warning and so on? The discretion vested in the
policeman on the beat is just one aspect of the
enormous discretionary power exercised by the police
at varying levels of decision-making. This ability
to make choices has been particularly recognised
where a breach of the peace is reasonably apprehended. The leading case is Humphries v Connor.[20] The
plaintiff, walked through the streets of Swalinbar
wearing an orange lily. A hostile and threatening
crowd gathered. The defendant, a police inspector,
removed the emblem after the plaintiff refused his
request that she should remove it herself. In the
subsequent action for assault, the plaintiff claimed
that the wearing of the lily, even if it was a
recognised party emblem, was a lawful act and in
removing it, the inspector had committed a trespass
to the person. Hayes, J., who delivered the leading
judgment in the Irish Court of Queen's Bench, said:

> A constable, by his very appointment, is
> by law charged with the solemn duty of
> seeing that peace is preserved. The law
> has not ventured to lay down what precise
> measures shall be adopted by him in every
> state of facts which call for his inter-
> ference. But it has done far better; it
> has announced to him and to the public over
> whom he is placed, that he is not only at
> liberty, but he is bound, to see that the
> peace be preserved and that he is to do
> everything that is necessary for that
> purpose...When a constable is called upon
> to preserve that peace, I know of no better
> mode of doing so than that of removing what
> he sees to be the provocation to the breach
> of the peace.[21]

There have been many cases since Humphries v

ARREST AND DETENTION

Connor in which the right of a police officer to take preventive action falling short of arrest where he suspects that a breach of the peace might occur, has been upheld.[22] Despite the unease which has been on occasion expressed about the implications of the ruling,[23] its effect is to give to a police officer a very wide measure of discretion to adopt appropriate actions to prevent a breach of the peace and provided that there exists evidence upon which he could have reasonably concluded that a breach was likely and that the steps he takes to prevent it were strictly necessary, he will be completely protected by the law against civil actions in trespass.

Finally, it should be mentioned that while there is no general legal duty on individuals to assist the police, an officer who sees a breach of the peace committed is entitled to call on any bystander for assistance if this is reasonably necessary and the person called is bound in law to assist him.[24]

(b) Arrest without warrant for Arrestable offences

The most important and widely used powers of arrest are those which relate to arrestable offences. The concept of the arrestable offence was originally introduced into the law by the Criminal Law Act, 1967 which defined it as an offence "for which the sentence is fixed by law or for which a person (not previously convicted) may under or by virtue of any enactment be sentenced to imprisonment for a term of five years and to attempts to commit any such offence." The wording of the section made it clear that the definition applied to offences normally regarded as serious, such as the major offences against the person, robbery, theft, criminal damage, arson and so on, but also gave rise to some anomalies. The offence of indecent assault upon a woman, for example, was not under this definition an arrestable offence, as it does not carry a penalty of five years imprisonment.

The Royal Commission on Criminal Procedure looked at a number of possible solutions to this "awkward dilemma".[25] One would have been to abandon the five year criterion altogether in favour of a different criterion of seriousness which did not rely upon the penalty available. Another was to leave the statutory provisions as they were. The solution ultimately favoured by the Royal Commission, however, was that an arrestable offence should be defined as any offence punishable with imprisonment[26]

98

ARREST AND DETENTION

but that the exercise of the arrest power should be subject to certain restrictions.[27] This recommendation, which if adopted would have had the effect of introducing a coherent basis for distinguishing between arrestable and non-arrestable offences only at the expense of significantly extending powers of arrest, was rejected by the government. Instead, the Police and Criminal Evidence Act, 1984 retains the five year criterion as the basis of the concept of arrestable offence but in addition, expressly brings within the concept certain other offences, which do not satisfy the five year criterion.[28] The result is a rather untidy provision, but the ambit of the arrestable offence is thereby drawn more narrowly than had been recommended.

The powers of arrest without warrant attached to arrestable offences are the same as those provided originally by the Criminal Law Act, 1967. Under the 1984 Act, any person may arrest anyone who is in the act of committing an arrestable offence or whom he has reasonable grounds for suspecting to be committing such an offence.[29] Additionally, any person may arrest another who is, or whom he with reasonable cause suspects to be guilty of an arrestable offence, which he knows to have been committed.[30] Where, however, there is reasonable cause to suspect that another is about to commit an arrestable offence, or where there is merely reasonable suspicion that an arrestable offence has been committed, the power to arrest without warrant is conferred upon constables only.[31] A clear distinction is, therefore, drawn between the powers of arrest possessed by a constable, and those possessed by the private individual, which are appreciably more limited.

It has already been pointed out that the ability of private citizens to make valid arrests is a legacy from the time before the establishment of professional police forces. The continued existence of these powers is, however, of considerable importance to those relatively small classes of private individuals, such as store detectives, engaged in duties which may involve the apprehension of suspected offenders. There are also occasions on which even the ordinary citizen might be envisaged exercising a power of arrest, for example, the householder who has the misfortune to interrupt a burglar on his property. By conferring these powers on the ordinary citizen, therefore, the law is sanctioning interference with another's personal liberty, which would otherwise amount to trespass to the person. However,

ARREST AND DETENTION

whilst a police officer is empowered to arrest without warrant any person whom he reasonably suspects
to have committed an arrestable offence which he
reasonably suspects to have been committed, the
individual may only arrest a person whom he reasonably suspects either to be in the act of committing
an arrestable offence or, to have committed an
arrestable offence which he knows to have been
committed. In 1965, the Criminal Law Revision
Committee gave serious consideration to recommending
the abolition of this distinction, but eventually
concluded that it would not be "desirable or acceptable to public opinion to increase the powers of
arrest enjoyed by the private person."[32] The effect
of the distinction therefore, is to encourage the
private individual to exercise caution before using
his powers of arrest.[33]

(c) General Arrest Powers

The 1984 Act introduces into the law general
powers of arrest without warrant applicable to all
offences, subject to certain conditions. The likelihood is that they will be very commonly used.
The new powers are based on the recommendations
of the Royal Commission on Criminal Procedure.
Prior to the Act, if there was no power to arrest an
offender without warrant by statute or at common
law, the police were compelled to proceed by way of
summons or by applying to a magistrate for an arrest
warrant. If a suspect refused to provide his name
and address however, there being no legal duty upon
him to do this, in the absence of specific statutory
provision,[34] he could prevent the law being enforced
because it was not possible to serve a summons upon
him. The Royal Commission accordingly recommended
that in such circumstances, there should be a power
of arrest without warrant available provided that
the police officer had seen an offence being committed and that any detention consequent upon arrest,
should terminate immediately the required information was forthcoming.[35] Building upon this, the
1984 Act provides that where a constable has reasonable grounds for suspecting that any offence which
is not an arrestable offence has been committed or
attempted, or is being committed or attempted, he
may arrest the person whom he has reasonable grounds
to suspect of having committed it or attempted to
commit it "if it appears to him that service of a
summons is impracticable or inappropriate because
any of the general arrest conditions are

100

ARREST AND DETENTION

satisfied."[36] That this is in wider terms than the power recommended by the Royal Commission is evident. Some of the general arrest conditions relate to uncertainty about or failure to provide name and address. The first four conditions are that the name and address of the suspect is unknown to or cannot be readily ascertained by the constable; that the constable has reasonable grounds for doubting whether the name provided is the suspect's real name; that the suspect has failed to furnish a satisfactory address (i.e. one which is satisfactory for the purposes of service of a summons); or that the constable has reasonable grounds for doubting whether an address provided is satisfactory.[37] The other general arrest conditions are that a constable has reasonable grounds for believing that arrest is necessary to prevent the arrestee causing physical injury to another or causing or suffering physical injury to himself; causing loss or damage to property; committing an offence against public decency; causing unlawful obstruction to the highway; or for the protection of a child or other vulnerable person.[38]

These very wide powers mean that there is now no offence for which an arrest cannot be made without warrant "if it appears" to a constable that service of a summons is impracticable or inappropriate. The broad and subjective nature of the discretion conferred upon a police officer would be extremely difficult to challenge in a court. He may exercise the arrest power where a suspect has not provided a name and address or has provided a name and address believed to be false. There is no substantive offence of refusing to provide name and address in English law. Neither has it been usual to attach an arrest power to the commission of minor summary offences. These new powers do not allow arrest for refusing to provide name and address per se; rather the refusal is a sort of aggravating factor rendering arrest possible where, in the absence of those provisions, it would be impermissible. It should be noted also that the Act does not explicitly enact, as recommended by the Royal Commission, that detention following arrest should only continue until the required information is provided. The legislative solution, therefore, to what must be a relatively minor problem, that is, granting a power to deprive a person of his liberty for an offence which cannot carry a prison sentence, is likely to prove highly controversial and in the long term, do nothing to improve relationships

ARREST AND DETENTION

between the police and the public.

The "general arrest conditions" must relate to the service of a summons. The power is a power to arrest if it appears that service of a summons is "impracticable or inappropriate because any of the general arrest conditions are satisfied." Whatever their merits, the name and address provisions are clearly referable to the impracticability of the service of a summons. The link between some of the other conditions and service of a summons is not quite so obvious, but they are all circumstances which may render the service of a summons inappropriate - for example, the suspect who is obstructing the highway and refuses to desist can only be dealt with by way of arrest. However, other powers of arrest may be perfectly adequate to deal with some of the situations envisaged by the general arrest conditions. Where a constable has reasonable grounds for believing that a suspect may cause physical injury to any other person, the common law power to arrest for an apprehended breach of the peace will be available. Similarly, a suspect who is threatening to damage or destroy property could normally be arrested under the statutory powers to arrest for an arrestable offence.

It is difficult to resist the conclusion, therefore, that these "general powers" are ill-conceived and in terms which are unnecessarily wide. Their open-ended nature and the subjective language in which they are conferred cannot fail but to increase the use of arrest in relation to minor crime. Finally, they increase the prospect of police officers arresting even where the service of a summons would be feasible, simply to give a suspect a difficult time.

(d) Requirements of a Valid Arrest Without Warrant

A society which is mindful of individual free-dom must give careful consideration to the extent to which powers of arrest are necessary in the law enforcement process. An American judge once commented that arrest can involve, "intense humiliation, publicity, disgrace, mental suffering, injury to reputation, pain to family and friends, frequently great physical discomfort."[39] In its first Triennial Review Report, the now defunct Police Complaints Board using more moderate language, expressed the view that the police are so involved with the process of arrest and detention, that they fail at times to understand the sense of alarm and

ARREST AND DETENTION

dismay felt by some of those who suffer such treatment.[40]

Ideally then, arrest powers should be granted sparingly and defined with precision. But even more is required. The law should seek to develop a set of criteria for the exercise of arrest powers. When should they be exercised? Or put another way, on what evidentiary basis should the decision to arrest be justified? How should they be exercised? For example, what information if any, should be given to an arrested person concerning the reason for arrest? When will it be justifiable to use force to effect an arrest? Finally, once an arrest has been made, for how long may a suspect be held in right of the arrest? Some of these issues go to the substance of the arrest decision - for example, how much evidence is required to justify an arrest - and others go to procedure - for example, what should an arrested person be told upon arrest?

The focus of this section, therefore, is upon the criteria for the exercise of arrest powers developed by both courts and parliament: what are they; what interests are they designed to protect, and how effective are they?

In one of the leading police powers cases, Christie v Leachinsky decided in 1947, Lord Simonds said:

> A citizen is free from arrest unless there is in some other citizen, whether constable or not, a right to arrest him.[41]

English law has traditionally taken the view that arrest is prima facie illegal. Those who effect arrests, therefore, must be able to point to some legal authority justifying their action. In the absence of such authority, the individual wrongfully arrested may seek redress through the civil courts by pursuing an action for false imprisonment. In addition, because it is no part of a policeman's duty to infringe individual rights where such infringements are not specifically sanctioned by the law, the policeman who wrongfully arrests will not be "in the execution of his duty" for the purposes of the offences of assaulting or obstructing a police officer in the execution of his duty.

This neat analysis begins to break down, of course, when arrest and detention powers are examined in detail. Arrest powers may derive from common law or statute. They may be exercisable with or without warrant. Some may be exercisable by

103

ARREST AND DETENTION

private citizens, others only by police officers. In some cases, the exercise of the power will only be available for specified offences. In others, the powers will be exercisable over a whole range of offences. At common law, it is often said that there is no halfway house between freedom and arrest. Yet, by statute, the police have considerable power to detain persons against their will without having to justify that detention as a lawful arrest. It is true that many pre-existing statutory powers of arrest without warrant have been repealed by the Police and Criminal Evidence Act 1984, but others have been expressly preserved.[42] We still, therefore, lack a comprehensive powers of arrest statute.

Most arrest powers require the presence of "reasonable suspicion" or "reasonable cause to suspect" or "believe" that an offence has been committed and that an individual has committed it. Indeed, the requirement of reasonable suspicion is a feature of coercive powers possessed by the police generally. Street stops can only be carried out where e.g. a police officer reasonably suspects someone of possessing prohibited articles. Most search powers are only exercisable where there are reasonable grounds to suspect that certain items or evidence will be found on the person or on private premises. By employing this notion of reasonable suspicion as a central criterion of the legality of coercive powers, the law is attempting to balance the interest of effective policing against the interest of individual liberty. Thus, in the context of arrest, the notion of reasonable suspicion is intended to ensure freedom from arbitrary or capricious arrests and to require some objective evidentiary basis justifying the arrest of any particular person. It is as well in this context, to remember the main purpose of arrest, namely, to render a suspected offender amenable to the criminal process. Random arrest is outlawed by the reasonable cause requirement; the suspicion must precede the arrest. It is well-known, however, that the criterion of "reasonableness", in whatever branch of the law it arises, produces difficulties. In the context of arrest, the question of what constitutes reasonable cause or reasonable suspicion has been described as "one of those unclassified problems that is not a question of fact, in the sense that it is not an objectively appreciable proposition and is not a question of law, in the sense that there are no standards or guides for its determination."[43]

104

ARREST AND DETENTION

To say that such standards should exist is to state the obvious and yet judges have found great difficulty in articulating them. This may be because of the inevitable problem of giving specific content to a generalised requirement. A more likely explanation, however, is a judicial desire to retain flexibility in the wide variety of situations faced by the police. Unfortunately, this reticence ensures that the reasonable cause concept remains ambiguous. In Wills v Bowley,[44] the House of Lords was faced with the interpretation of a power, now repealed, to arrest without warrant where any person "commits" one of a range of specific offences.[45] The House, by a majority, rejected the literal interpretation of the power, that is, that the arrest was lawful only if the offence had actually been committed, opting instead for the wider interpretation, that is, that the arrest was justified if at the time of making it, the police officer believed honestly and upon reasonable grounds, that the offence had been committed.[46] In other words, the power required not "reasonable suspicion" but "honest and reasonable belief". The majority disagreed with the view of Lord Denning MR in Wiltshire v Barrett that "the constable is justified if the facts as they appeared to him at the time, were such as to warrant him thinking that the man was probably guilty".[47] This, according to Lord Bridge, "substitutes suspicion for belief".[48] The honest belief formula sometimes finds its way into legislation. For instance, s. 8(1) of the Road Traffic Act, 1972, employs the formula reasonable cause to suspect whereas s. 8(2) refers to reasonable cause to believe.[49] Does anything turn on this distinction? In Baker v Oxford,[50] the Divisional Court thought that the requirements are distinguishable but did not indicate the nature of the distinction. Lord Bridge in Wills v Bowley suggests that the distinction is "fine"[51] but does not further explore it. It thus remains a matter for the greatest regret that the judiciary are unable to articulate meaningful guidelines on the necessary legal conditions which govern the exercise of arrest powers. The expressions "belief" and "suspicion" clearly indicate different states of mind. But when both are qualified by a requirement of reasonableness and applied to arrest powers, the practical distinction becomes less easy to grasp. Perhaps, of course, the courts think the distinction so self-evident as not to require elaboration. The consequence of this, however, is that the police are left to develop

105

ARREST AND DETENTION

their own standards.

R v Tooley[52] is one of the earliest cases to recognise that an arrest must be made on reasonable grounds. The court rejected an argument that the fact that a constable recognised a girl as one he had previously arrested for disorderly conduct gave him sufficient grounds to arrest in the present case, stating: "It is not a constable suspecting that will justify his taking up a person, but it must be just grounds of suspicion."[53] However, nowhere is "just grounds of suspicion" defined. Subsequent decisions have stated that the actions of the police must be "justified by the facts as they appear at the time and not on any ex post facto analysis of the situation,"[54] and that "the police are not called upon before acting to have anything like a prima facie case for conviction."[55] But when does suspicion amount to reasonable cause to effect an arrest? It has been said that whereas prima facie proof consists of admissible evidence, "suspicion can take into account matters that could not be put in evidence at all."[56] The police must not shut their eyes to the obvious; they are required to be "observant, receptive and open-minded and to notice any relevant circumstances which point either way, either to innocence or to guilt."[57] Finally, the police officer is told that "once there is what appears to be reasonable suspicion against a particular individual, he is not required to hold his hand in order to make further inquiries, if all that is involved is to make assurance doubly sure."[58]

A number of awkward questions remain unanswered, however. For instance, the requirement of reasonable cause sets a minimum standard by which arrests must be justified, but is that minimum standard constant - does it always require the same evidentiary quantum? A related question, is whether the test is capable of taking into account variable factors such as the seriousness of the offence involved or the exigency of the situation. There is some authority to the effect that it is,[59] though the question remains largely unresolved. Similar issues are raised by the use of informers. For instance, can an arrest or search be legally justified solely on the basis of information received implicating an individual in particular criminal activities? Does it make any difference if the information is relayed by a respectable citizen doing his public duty or by another criminal in return for payment or some future favour? There is old authority to the effect that an arrest cannot be justified solely on the basis of

ARREST AND DETENTION

information received,[60] but the use of informers has not been fully considered by the courts in modern times except in the context of using informers as agents provocateurs. In this context, it has been ruled that it is wrong for the police to encourage the commission of an offence which otherwise might not be committed.[61] It is one thing for the police to make use of information concerning an offence that is already laid on. But it is quite another thing to use an informer to encourage another to commit an offence. This, of course, is no help in deciding the extent to which information received should contribute to reasonable cause. In practice, informers play an important part in the detection of crime and the police make no secret of this. It must also be recognised, however, that the use of informers can severely compromise individual liberty, particularly where information received is made the sole basis upon which arrests are made or premises searched. There is a clear need for the judges to articulate standards.

In a Report published in 1970, the Advisory Committee on Drug Dependence considered the requirement of reasonable cause in the context of the dangerous drugs legislation.[62] It suggested that among the factors influencing a police officer's decision to detain are the following: demeanour of suspect; gait and manner of suspect; any knowledge of suspect's background and character; whether suspect carrying anything and its nature; mode of dress, bulges in clothing etc.; time of observation; any remarks made to third parties overheard by the officer; the street or area involved; information from a third party; any connection between that person and any other person whose conduct at that time is reasonably suspect; suspect's apparent connection with any overt criminal activity.[63] The conclusion the Committee came to was that there are so many factors influencing a police officer's judgement that "we are unanimously of the opinion that it is impossible to draft any definition in positive terms... the factors influencing a police officer's judgement cannot be reduced to simple formulae."[64]

In the light of this conclusion and of the unsatisfactory case-law on the meaning of reasonable cause, it is a matter for particular regret that the Royal Commission on Criminal Procedure made no attempt to invest that concept with some positive content, even though its importance was recognised. It stated, for example, "...the principal safeguard

ARREST AND DETENTION

must be found in the requirement for and stricter application of the criterion of reasonable suspicion. Some have complained that the police interpret this too loosely at present and that the courts are not as a matter of course required to test it; this increases the risk of random stops."[65] However, having established a case for the application of strict standards and the need for guidance to avoid dilution of the concept, the Commission lamely concluded "that the variety of circumstances that would have to be covered makes this impracticable."[66] There is consequently no attempt to analyse the concept and it is not even clear from the Report that the reasonable cause requirement should be a minimum standard applying to the exercise of all coercive powers.

Challenges to the use of arrest or other detention provisions on the grounds of absence of reasonable cause are rare. Where they do occur, some guidance can be gleaned from the words of Lord Devlin in Shabin bin Hussein v Chong Fook Kam: "The circumstances of the case should be such that a reasonable man acting without passion or prejudice would have fairly suspected the person of having committed the offence."[67] In practice, however, the police are left to develop their own standards and these are likely to be far less stringent.[68]

It is possible for an arrest still to be unlawful even if there is a clear power of arrest and reasonable cause to suspect a particular offender. Certain procedural requirements must be adhered to if an arrest is to be valid. An arresting officer must make it clear to the person arrested that he is under arrest and ensure that he is aware of the reason for the arrest and this common law rule has now been given a statutory basis by section 28 of the 1984 Act. A citizen is thus legally entitled to know on suspicion of what crime he has been arrested, because, as has already been noted, the detention of one person by another is prima facie unlawful. He is only required to submit to restraints upon his freedom if he knows in substance the reason why it is claimed that this restraint should be imposed. The 1984 Act accordingly provides that "where a person is arrested, otherwise than by being informed that he is under arrest, the arrest is not lawful unless the person arrested is informed that he is under arrest as soon as is practicable after his arrest". The Act further provides that "no arrest is lawful unless the person arrested is informed of the ground for the arrest at the time of or as soon as is practicable

108

ARREST AND DETENTION

after, the arrest."[69] It was made clear by the House of Lords in <u>Christie</u> v <u>Leachinsky</u>,[70] that there is no need for the officer to use technical language and that the law does not require a precise charge to be framed at the time of arrest; the arrested person must simply be told for what act he is being arrested. <u>Gelberg</u> v <u>Miller</u>[71] illustrates the point. The appellant parked his car in a street subject to a no-waiting restriction. When requested by a police officer to remove it, he removed the rotor arm instead (thus immobilising it) and refused to give his name and address. He was arrested, the officer explaining that the arrest was for obstructing him in the execution of his duty, for failing to give his name and address and for refusing to remove the car. The Divisional Court upheld the validity of the arrest even though the officer possessed no power to arrest on two of the three gounds advanced. The appellant had been told in sufficient detail the act for which he was being arrested.

Where insufficient or no disclosure is made of the reasons either at the time of the arrest, or, at the earliest time when it is practicable to give such information, and the arrested person is later told why he has been arrested, the law regards the arrest as lawful from the time that full disclosure was made. Consequently, the custody during the time between the purported arrest and later compliance with the legal duty, is unlawful and amounts to false imprisonment.[72] This is so even if the ground of the arrest is obvious.[73] Generally, however, a police officer need only do what is reasonable to inform the person of the reasons for the arrest.[74] In particular, the person arrested cannot complain that he has not been supplied with the required information if he himself produces the situation which makes it impossible to inform him by, for instance, running away.[75]

If a suspect whom an officer is purporting to arrest responds with violence, he need not be informed of the ground of the arrest until it is practicable to do so, that is, when the resistance has been overcome. The more immediate problem for the police officer in such a situation, will be that of dealing with the violence. When making an arrest, an officer is entitled to use force, but no more than is necessary. By section 3(1) of the Criminal Law Act, 1967, "a person may use such force as is reasonable in the circumstances in the prevention of crime or in effecting or assisting in the arrest of offenders or suspected offenders or offenders unlawfully

ARREST AND DETENTION

at large." It will be noted that section 3 draws no distinction between constables and private persons and its effect is to afford a wide measure of protection to any person acting reasonably in the prevention of crime or apprehension of criminals. The wording "such force as is reasonable in the circumstances" deliberately leaves a large measure of discretion to a reviewing Court which will obviously take into account all the relevant circumstances including the nature and degree of force offered by the suspect, the way in which the officer responded to it, the seriousness of the offence committed, the possibility of securing the suspect's compliance by other means and so on. It is not possible, therefore, to formulate rigid rules.[76]

If the arrest is <u>unlawful</u>, the suspect may use such force in self-defence as is reasonable and necessary.[77] It has been pointed out, however, that this so-called "right" to resist an unlawful arrest is more apparent than real, as the individual being arrested will rarely be in a position to know whether the arrest is valid or invalid.[78] Private individuals are unlikely to be conversant with the minutiae of police powers and how, for example, is an individual to know if an officer's suspicions about him are based upon reasonable grounds? Further, it has been ruled that an honest and reasonable belief that the arrest was invalid is no defence to a charge of assaulting a police officer in the execution of his duty, if in fact, the arrest was valid.[79] By utilising his right to resist an unlawful arrest, therefore, the individual is compelled to take the risk that the view he forms as to the illegality of an officer's conduct will not be borne out by subsequent judicial examination. Equally, some who resist police activity, indifferent to its legality or illegality, may find <u>ex post facto</u> that they have committed no offence <u>arising from</u> the resistance if there was some defect in the procedure adopted by the police.

A general duty is imposed upon a police officer to take an arrested suspect to a "designated police station."[80] If an arrest is effected by a private individual, the suspect should be handed over to the police without unreasonable delay.[81] A constable who takes custody of an arrestee from such an individual is under the same general duty.[82] In the majority of cases, an arrestee will be taken to a police station immediately. This will not always be "practicable" however, and delay in some cases will be both inevitable and justifiable. If between

110

ARREST AND DETENTION

arrest and arrival at a police station a constable is satisfied that there are no grounds for keeping the suspect under arrest, he is obliged to release him.[83] Indeed the 1984 Act specifically provides that notwithstanding the general duty imposed upon a police officer to take an arrested suspect to a police station as soon as is practicable, an officer is entitled to delay doing this if the presence of the arrestee elsewhere "is necessary in order to carry out such investigations as it is reasonable to carry out immediately."[84] To the extent that this procedure works to the advantage of a suspect, who may thereby be spared the humiliation of the police station procedures in a case where some simple "checking up" on him may conveniently be done prior to arrival at a police station, it is both useful and sensible. Its use needs to be carefully monitored, however, by courts and the police alike, both to ensure that officers do not go off on "frolics" of their own and to ensure that the provision is not made the excuse for carrying out after arrest those investigations which can and should be carried out prior to arrest.[85]

Detention

Police, public and courts alike are prone to use the terms "detention", "custody", "arrest" and "imprisonment" in senses which are both ambiguous and confusing. A police officer may say "I am taking you into custody", when he means "I am arresting you". The phrase "detention for questioning" may refer to the situation where an arrested suspect is being questioned at a police station or it may mean that a suspect who has not been lawfully arrested is being held in a police station and questioned to see if there are grounds to arrest and charge him. It is important at the outset, therefore, to make it clear that in this section we are using the word "detention" to refer to detention in a designated police station following arrest for the purpose of further investigation.

There has traditionally been much confusion over the circumstances in which the police could hold an arrested suspect in custody without either charging him or bringing him before a court. Although there were undoubtedly many instances of suspects being held incommunicado prior to charge for very lengthy periods (and the much revered but seldom granted remedy of habeas corpus was usually ineffective in these situations), research undertaken for the Royal

111

ARREST AND DETENTION

Commission on Criminal Procedure found that 75 per cent of suspects were charged within six hours of arrest and 95 per cent within twenty four hours.[86] The principal statutory provision required that a person arrested for a "serious" offence be brought before a magistrates' court "as soon as practicable" and for any other offence within twenty four hours if he had not been released on bail or otherwise before then.[87] As the Royal Commission on Criminal Procedure rather blandly commented: "The lack of definition of the terms 'serious' and 'as soon as practicable' gives flexibility but produces uncertainty both for the police and the suspect."[88] In practice, of course, it was the suspect who suffered most from the uncertainty because courts were singularly reluctant to give the phrase "as soon as practicable" a restricted meaning.[89] The Royal Commission proposals for reform[90] formed the basis of the 1984 Act's provisions and it is to these provisions that we must now turn.

(i) Custody Officers and their Duties

The Act requires that at each designated police station, one or more custody officers, who must normally hold at least the rank of sergeant and be detached from the investigation of offences for which suspects are being held in custody, will be available to perform the duties set out in the legislation.[91] Custody officers are under a general duty to ensure that all persons in police detention at a police station are treated in accordance with the Act and Codes of Practice issued under it.[92] In this regard they have significant functions to perform both before and after a suspect is charged. One of the most important of these is the keeping of a custody record for each arrested suspect in detention.

When a suspect arrives at a designated police station having been arrested without warrant (or under a warrant not endorsed for bail) the custody officer "shall determine whether he has sufficient evidence to charge him with the offence for which he was arrested" and may detain him for such period as is necessary to enable him to do so,[93] subject to the requirement that the duty is performed as soon as practicable after the arrest.[94] If the custody officer does not have such evidence, the suspect "shall" be released (with or without bail) unless he has reasonable grounds for believing that the suspect's continued detention without charge is "necessary to secure or preserve evidence relating to an offence for

112

ARREST AND DETENTION

which he is under arrest or to obtain such evidence by questioning him."[95] Where he authorises continued detention on this basis he shall "as soon as practicable" make a written record of the grounds for the detention in the presence of the arrestee who shall be informed by the custody officer of those grounds?[96] With the exception of suspects arrested for "serious arrestable offences",[97] the maximum period of time for which a suspect may be held in police detention without charge is twenty four hours,[98] the time running from the time of arrest or the time at which the suspect arrives at a designated police station, which ever is the earlier.[99]

If there is sufficient evidence to charge the suspect with the offence for which he was arrested, he shall be charged or released without charge either with or without bail.[100] Once a suspect has been charged the custody officer "shall order his release" (with or without bail) unless (a) his name or address is not known or the custody officer has reasonable grounds for doubting whether a name or address provided is his real name or address; or (b) he has reasonable grounds for believing that the suspect's detention is necessary for his own protection or to prevent him causing injury to any other person or damaging property; or (c) he has reasonable grounds for believing that the suspect will fail to answer bail or interfere with the administration of justice or the investigation of offences if released.[101]

If a suspect's continued detention after charge is authorised by the custody officer, he must make a written record of the grounds in the suspect's presence and inform him of the grounds for his detention.[102] A suspect who is detained in this way after charge must be taken before a magistrates' court as soon as is practicable and in any event not later than the first sitting after he is charged with the offence.[103]

(ii) Review of Detention

The Act requires that reviews of the detention of each person in police detention for the investigation of an offence shall be carried out periodically by the custody officer in the case of a person who has been charged and by an officer of at least the rank of inspector who has not been directly involved in the investigation, in the case of a person who has not been charged. The officer to whom it falls to carry out a review is referred to in the Act as the

113

ARREST AND DETENTION

review officer.[104] The first review shall be carried out not later than six hours after the detention was first authorised; the second review shall be not later than nine hours after the first. Subsequent reviews shall be at intervals of not more than nine hours.[105] However, a review may be postponed if it is "not practicable" to carry it out at the relevant time, because, for example, no review officer is available or because at the relevant time the suspect is being questioned and interruption of the interrogation to carry out the review would prejudice the investigation.[106] Where a review is postponed, the reason for postponement should be recorded in the custody record and the review carried out "as soon as practicable".

The purposes of the review procedure are not clearly stated in the Act. The primary purpose would appear to be to see if continued detention of a suspect is justified. This is implicit in the requirement that "before determining whether to authorise a person's continued detention" the review officer shall give the suspect (unless he is asleep) or any solicitor representing him who is available at the time of the review an opportunity to make representations about the detention either orally or in writing, subject to the proviso that a review officer can refuse to hear oral representations from the suspect if he considers that "he is unfit to make such representations by reason of his condition or behaviour."[107] A further purpose of the review procedure is presumably to see that the provisions of the Act and Codes of Practice are being complied with. Again, this is implicit in and consistant with the general duties imposed upon custody officers but is not made explicit in the Act.

(iii) Detention for Serious Arrestable Offences

Among the most controversial provisions of the Act are those which allow the detention of suspects without charge in police stations for periods of up to 96 hours. In order for these procedures to be invoked, the suspect must have been arrested for a "serious arrestable offence". The concept of the serious arrestable offence is new to the law and is important not only in the context of detention but also in the context of search as we will see in Chapter 6. The origins of the concept can be found in the Report of the Royal Commission on Criminal Procedure which recommended that certain coercive powers should be exercised only in relation to

114

ARREST AND DETENTION

"grave" offences.[108] In such cases, according to the Royal Commission, "there are circumstances which prolong an investigation and delay charging... and where the police should not release the suspect because, for example, he is likely to abscond. Such cases are a small minority, but provision must be made for them if the police are to be able to solve grave offences and bring persons accused of them before the courts."[109] Under the Act, certain arrestable offences, for example, serious offences against the person, hijacking, possession of firearms with criminal intent, are always serious.[110] Other arrestable offences will be serious only if their commision has led to any of the following conseconsequences: serious harm to the security of the State or to public order; serious interference with the administration of justice or with the investigation of offences; the death of any person; serious injury to any person; substantial financial gain or loss to any person.[111] Whether any of these exacerbating factors exist will, of course, fall initially to be determined by the police. Continued detention under these provisions may only be authorised by "an officer of the rank of superintendent or above who is responsible for the police station at which a person is detained" who must have reasonable grounds for believing that the detention of the suspect without charge is necessary to secure or preserve evidence relating to an offence for which he is under arrest or to obtain such evidence by questioning him; that the offence for which he is under arrest is a serious arrestable offence; and that the investigation is being conducted diligently and expeditiously.[112] If all of these conditions are believed to be satisfied, the suspect may, on the authorisation of the superintendent, be kept in detention for up to 36 hours after the time he first arrived at the police station or was arrested, whichever is the earlier, ("the relevant time") provided that the authorisation does not take place before the second statutory review has been carried out or after twenty four hours.[113] The same rules regarding the recording of the continued detention and the giving to the suspect or his solicitor an opportunity to make representations concerning it apply as to the statutory reviews.[114] Where continued detention has been authorised in this way, a suspect must be released from detention not later than 36 hours after the expiry of the relevant time unless either he has been charged with an offence or his continued detention has been authorised by a magistrates' court.[115]

115

ARREST AND DETENTION

A magistrates court may issue a warrant of further detention under section 43 of the Act where it is satisfied that there are reasonable grounds for believing that the further detention of a suspect is justified. The procedure must be initiated by an application made on oath by a constable supported by an information. The application must be made inter partes, the suspect appearing in court and given the opportunity of legal representation.[116] A warrant of further detention can only be justified on the same terms as those which relate to police authorisation of continued detention, namely - detention without charge must be necessary to secure or preserve evidence relating to an offence for which he is under arrest or to obtain such evidence by questioning him; the offence must be a serious arrestable offence, and the investigation is being conducted expeditiously.[117] Application may be made at any time before the expiry of 36 hours after "the relevant time". Where it is made after 36 hours and the magistrates take the view that it would have been reasonable for the police to make application before the expiry of that period (this will usually be the case), it must dismiss the application.[118] If, in any event, the court is not satisfied that adequate grounds have been shown to justify further detention, the application must be either dismissed altogether, or adjourned until a time not later than 36 hours after the suspect's arrest or first arrival at the police station.[119] Where an application is refused by a court, no further application may be made in respect of the suspect unless supported by new evidence which has come to light since the refusal[120] and the suspect must either be charged or released "forthwith".[121] A warrant of further detention may authorise continued detention for up to 36 hours.[122] A suspect must be charged or released by the end of this period[123] unless a successful application has been made under s. 44 of the Act for the warrant of further detention to be extended. A magistrates court may authorise such an extension, again following an application made on oath supported by an information, if it is satisfied that there are reasonable grounds for believing that continued detention of the suspect is justified.[124] Any extension authorised must not be longer than 36 hours or end later than 96 hours after the relevant time, though if an extension is authorised for a period shorter than 36 hours, the police may make a further application to hold the suspect in detention for up to 96 hours.[125] Again, where an application for

116

ARREST AND DETENTION

extension is refused, the suspect must be charged or released forthwith.[126]

These rather complex statutory provisions have been set out in some detail. In brief, what they mean is that provided the appropriate statutory conditions are complied with, the police may self authorise the detention of a suspect following arrest, without charge, for up to 36 hours. Thereafter, continued detention without charge may only be authorised by magistrates courts for periods up to 36 hours at a time provided that the total period of detention without charge so authorised does not exceed in any case, 96 hours, i.e. four days. In the normal case, therefore, a suspect who is held in detention without charge for the maximum period permitted under the Act, will have had his detention reviewed by magistrates at least twice. Both the details and the implications of this new procedure will be subjected to scrutiny after certain aspects of the provisions relating to the treatment of persons in detention have been considered.

(iv) Treatment of Detained Suspects

The way in which suspects in police detention are to be treated is governed both by the 1984 Act itself and the various Codes of Practice issued under it.[127] The provisions relating to the conducting of searches of suspect whilst in custody, the taking of intimate and non-intimate samples and the interrogation process are dealt with in Chapters 6 and 7 respectively. In this section, the main focus will be on the right to have someone informed when arrested, the right of access to legal advice and the new provisions relating to the finger-printing (and photographing) of suspects.

Before 1977, there was no legal right in a suspect to have someone informed of the fact that he was under arrest and being held in police detention. The Judges' Rules and Administrative Directions, however, provided that a person should be allowed to speak on the telephone to his solicitor or friends, that he should be provided with writing materials and his letters sent with the least possible delay and that he should be allowed to send telegrams at his own expense.[128] The Judges' Rules did not have the force of law and, in any event, the facilities set out above were subject to the overriding proviso that no hinderance was reasonably likely to be caused to the process of investigation or the administration of justice by a suspect availing himself of them.

117

ARREST AND DETENTION

The proviso was sufficiently vague that its effect was to enable the police to allow the suspect to exercise the "rights" when it suited them. In 1977, the Criminal Law Act, by section 62, granted to suspects under arrest and being held in police custody, the right "to have intimation of his arrest and of the place where he is being held sent to one person reasonably named by him, without delay." In essence, this was a statutory right not to be held incommunicado. Its effect was limited, however, first, because it was subject to the proviso that delay could be authorised where the interests of the investigation or the prevention of crime or the apprehension of offenders made delay necessary, secondly, because it was a right to have someone informed of the fact of the arrest and not the reason for it, thirdly, because the person to be informed had to be "reasonably" named and fourthly, because a suspect frequently only became aware of the right after he had been charged.[129]

By the Police and Criminal Evidence Act, 1984, the Criminal Law Act, 1977, provision is repealed and replaced, in section 56 with a far more comprehensive provision. Under it, an arrested suspect being held in custody is entitled, if he so requests, to have one friend or relative or other person, who is known to him or likely to take an interest in his welfare, told as soon as is practicable that he has been arrested and where he is being detained. Delay is only permitted in the case of suspects arrested for serious arrestable offences and only where an officer of at least the rank of superintendent authorises it. For the vast majority of suspects, therefore, the exercise of the right cannot be delayed by the police and the impact of the provision is underlined by the obligation imposed upon the custody officers to inform a suspect when he is brought to a police station, inter alia, of his right under section 56.[130] Even where delay can be authorised, the justifications for it are more tightly defined in the 1984 Act than was the case under either the Criminal Law Act or the Judges' Rules. The officer authorising delay must have "reasonable grounds for believing" that telling the named person of the arrest (a) will lead to interference with or harm to evidence connected with a serious arrestable offence or interference with or physical injury to other persons; (b) will lead to the alerting of other persons suspected of having committed such an offence but not yet arrested for it; or (c) will hinder the recovery of any property

118

ARREST AND DETENTION

obtained as a result of such an offence.[131] In no case can the exercise of the right be delayed longer than 36 hours.[132]

There is no doubt that for the majority of suspects, this provision is an improvement on the preceding position.[133] It must be emphasised, however, that it cannot really be seen as a *quid pro quo* for the vastly increased powers of detention conferred upon the police by this legislation. Those powers, as we have seen, relate only to suspects arrested for serious arrestable offences and the effect of section 56 is to sanction the holding of such suspects incommunicado for up to 36 hours.

The Royal Commission on Criminal Procedure gave high priority to securing an effective scheme for access to legal advice to arrested suspects in police detention.[134] Prior to the passing of the 1984 Act, English law did not grant such a right to arrested suspects. The general principle that "every person at any stage of an investigation should be able to communicate and to consult privately with a solicitor" was affirmed by the Judges' Rules but the Rules, as we have seen, lacked the force of law and in any event, the "right" conferred by them was subject to an overriding proviso that access to legal advice would be denied by the police where to allow it would cause unreasonable delay or hindrance to the processes of investigation or the administration of justice.[135] It was frequently alleged that the effect of these provisions was to give the police a virtually uncontrollable discretion to deny suspects access to legal advice while in custody and that very often suspects were not informed of the right given to them by the Judges' Rules. That there was a great deal of substance in these allegations is undeniable.[136]

The right of access to a lawyer has now been given a statutory basis by the 1984 Act. By section 58, an arrested suspect in police detention in a police station or other premises "shall be entitled, if he so requests, to consult a solicitor privately at any time,"[137] and the availability of this right must be drawn to a suspect's attention by the custody officer, both orally and by giving him a written notice, when he is brought to the police station.[138] Where a suspect requests legal advice he must be permitted to consult a solicitor "as soon as practicable."[139] The right can only be withheld where a suspect has been arrested for a serious arrestable offence and only then, where delay has been authorised by an officer of at least the rank of

119

ARREST AND DETENTION

superintendent.[140] In no case, however, may access to legal advice be delayed for longer than 36 hours. The grounds for justifying delay are the same as those justifying delay of the right to have someone informed when arrested and set out earlier.[141] The effectiveness of the scheme is enhanced by the provisions in the Act for extending the Duty Solicitor Scheme to cover suspects held in police detention.[142] In the areas of the country where the scheme is operative (and it is envisaged that it will ultimately cover all areas) a suspect will not be disadvantaged by the fact that he does not have a solicitor or does not know the name of a solicitor. The Draft Code of Practice contains a number of supplementary provisions. A person who asks for legal advice must not be interviewed or continue to be interviewed until he has received it unless (a) he has been arrested for a serious arrestable offence and delay has been authorised in accordance with the provisions of the Act, or (b) an officer of at least the rank of superintendent considers on reasonable grounds that awaiting arrival of a solicitor would cause unreasonable delay in the investigation or result in an immediate risk of harm to persons or serious loss or damage to property or (c) the suspect has given his consent, either in writing or on tape, to the interview being commenced.[143]

It should be noted that the Act does not grant expressly to a suspect the right to have a solicitor present while he is being interviewed by the police. The Draft Code of Practice provides, however, that where a suspect is permitted to consult a solicitor and the solicitor is available at the time the interview begins or is in progress, the suspect must be allowed to have his solicitor present while he is being interviewed. The solicitor may be required to leave the interview if an officer of the rank of superintendent or above considers that by his misconduct he has prevented the proper putting of questions to the suspect. This provision may be thought to be dangerously ambiguous but would seem to be deisgned to cover the situation where a solicitor is attempting deliberately to obstruct the course of the investigation rather than advising his client in the normal way.[144]

Again, then, these new procedures, it must be conceded, represent a significant improvement on those which they replace, but they are not free from uncertainty and may still be considered to pay undue deference to the police view of operational needs. Nevertheless, access to legal advice will be more

120

ARREST AND DETENTION

readily available, suspects will be informed of their rights early enough for them to make a reaslitic choice about exercising them, in the majority of cases, the police will not be able to deny access to legal advice at all and the improper withholding of these rights from a suspect will be more easily challengeable. None of this applies to the suspect arrested for a serious arrestable offence, however, who can legitimately be denied access to a lawyer for up to 36 hours, despite the fact that it may strongly be argued that the more serious the offence alleged, the greater the need for legal advice.

A suspect in police detention may be requested or required to undergo a variety of procedures including fingerprinting or photographing. Finger-print evidence can sometimes be extremely signifi-cant, though the value of such forensic evidence generally has apparently been greatly overstated.[145] The Royal Commission on Criminal Procedure concluded, however, that the fingerprinting of suspects in custody had become a routine procedure.[146] Prior to the passing of the 1984 Act, a suspect's prints could be taken in the absence of his consent, only after charge and on the authority of a magistrates' court order.[147] It was a common allegation, however, that a suspect's consent was frequently secured by the police by withholding bail until "consent" was forth-coming. The new procedures in the Police and Criminal Evidence Act are based on the Royal Commissions's Report, which regrettably recommended a relaxation rather than a tightening up of the fingerprinting procedures.

Under the Act, the necessity for a magistrates' court order has been abandoned in favour of police authorisation of the taking of fingerprints after charge in the absence of consent. Such authorisation can be given by an officer of at least the rank of superintendent where a suspect who has not had his fingerprints taken in the course of the investigation of the offence has been charged with a recordable offence[148] or informed that he will be reported for such an offence.[149] Authorisation may only be given where the authorising officer has reasonable grounds for believing that the taking of a suspect's finger-prints will tend to confirm or disprove his involve-ment in the offence.[150] A previously convicted suspect's prints may be taken without his consent and without the need for authorisation.[151] By implication reasonable force may be used to take the prints.

If a suspect consents to the taking of his

121

ARREST AND DETENTION

fingerprints, he must now signify that consent in writing "if it is given at a time when he is at a police station."[152] If this is intended to be a safeguard against the police obtaining consent by the strategy of withholding bail, it appears singularly ineffective.

The photographing of suspects in custody is not on all fours with fingerprinting as the police have not possessed traditionally statutory authority entitling them to photograph in the absence of a suspect's consent. Also, whereas the taking of fingerprints in the absence of consent and without lawful authority, will inevitably amount to an assault, the same is not true of the taking of photographs for which physical contact is unnecessary. The Draft Code of Practice on the Detention Treatment, Questioning and Identification of Persons by the Police does however, make explicit reference to the photographing of suspects. It provides that force may not be used to take a photograph but that a suspect's consent to photography is not necessary, inter alia if he has been charged with or reported for a recordable offence and his photograph is not already on record.[153] It is a provision, therefore, which legitimises the taking of photographs in the absence of consent on a virtually routine basis. It is matter both for surprise and regret that these important provisions were not included in the primary Act, rather than being tucked away in the Code.[154]

(v) Criticism of the Detention Provisions

As has already been pointed out, the detention provisions have proved highly controversial. They can be criticised not only on grounds of principle, but also in terms of detail. In this section, attention will be focused on five main areas of criticism: the concept of the serious arrestable offence; the length of time for which suspects may be held in detention; the wide discretion given to police officers and the use in the Act of imprecise terminology; the review procedures and the consequences of failure to comply with these and the other procedures and duties imposed upon custody and review officers; and the alleged attenuation of the right of silence.

Arrest for a serious arrestable offence or one which is reasonably believed to be a serious arrestable offence is the trigger for the initiation of the extended detention procedures in the Act. But the concept of the serious arrestable offence is lacking

122

ARREST AND DETENTION

in the precision which should be a prerequisite of the application of these particularly intrusive coercive powers. Any arrestable offence can be a serious arrestable offence if in the judgement of a senior police officer it has led or is intended to lead to any of the consequences specified in section 116(6) and discussed earlier. The offence, it should be noted, need not in fact lead or be intended to lead to any of them. It is sufficient if the officer "has reasonable grounds for believing" that the offence is a serious arrestable offence. The characterisation of an arrestable offence as serious will thus initially turn on the exercise of a discretion by the police themselves. The list of specified consequences includes, for example, substantial financial gain to any person and serious financial loss to any person. Loss is serious if having regard to all the circumstances "it is serious for the person who suffers it".[155] At what point does financial gain become "substantial" - £500, £1,000, £5,000? The lack of clarity is obvious. Similar problems occur when serious financial loss is considered. If loss is serious when it is serious for the person who suffers it, the theft of a small or even trivial amount of money from a person ill-placed to sustain the loss could be regarded as elevating an otherwise petty theft into a serious arrestable offence.

Such ambiguity renders the concept highly objectionable. Even if a magistrates' court should disagree with the classification of an offence by a sub-divisional commander as a serious arrestable offence, the earliest time at which it could do this is at the first application for a warrant of further detention, by which time a suspect will have been in custody many hours. It would have been far better to base this part of the legislation on the Royal Commission's recommendation that these extended detention powers should only be available (if at all) in respect of a narrowly drawn range of truly "grave" offences.

The pre-existing legal position on the length of time for which a suspect could lawfully be held in police detention was uncertain. That uncertainty could be and was, exploited by the police and in some classes of cases, it had become police practice to detain suspects for well over the 48 hour period suggested to be the limits of the Magistrates' Court Act provision in Re Sherman and Apps.[156] Instead of clarifying the existing legal position and curbing these abuses, Parliament chose, in the 1984 Act, to

123

ARREST AND DETENTION

legitimate previously unlawful police practices. Detention powers which had before the 1984 Act been lawfully available only in exceptional cases, have now been made generally available to the police. The experience of the operation by the police of the terrorism provisions, however, does not inspire confidence. The Jellicoe Review of the terrorism legislation found that the detention provisions (which are analogous, but not on all fours, with the 1984 Act provisions) have been abused by the police. Invocation of the provisions had become a matter of routine and the overwhelming majority of suspects held under the extended detention provisions were ultimately released without charge.[157]

In the light of this, it is a matter for great concern that a suspect arrested for an arrestable offence should be subjected to a similar regime provided that a senior police officer reasonably believes the offence to be a serious arrestable offence. And it is not only the length of time for which a suspect may be held which is important here (though we may note in passing that in Scotland no suspect may be held in police detention without charge for longer than six hours).[158] It is now perfectly lawful for the police to hold suspects in custody totally incommunicado for up to 36 hours.

The governmental and presumably police response to this criticism would be that although police powers have been extended, significant safeguards have been built into the procedures. Regular reviews of detention must be conducted by review officers detached from the investigation. Review officers are not, of course, independent of the police: the value of such scrutiny of a suspect's detention must, therefore, be called into question. It is likely to reassure neither the suspect nor the public at large. The first review must take place not later than six hours after the detention was first authorised by the custody officer and subsequent reviews at nine-hourly intervals. A review officer who authorises continued detention after six hours is unlikely to change his mind at the next or subsequent reviews if a suspect has not in the meantime made a confession or statement. In any event, any review may be post-poned if "it is not practicable" to carry it out at the relevant time. The Act provides that it will not be practicable to carry out a review if no review officer is readily available at the appropriate time and this is indeed a curious provision. The purpose of requiring police stations to be "designated" under the Act is precisely so that all the necessary

124

ARREST AND DETENTION

personnel and facilities are available for the
proper conduct of the detention. It is thus not
acceptable that the statutory reviews should not be
carried out according to the schedule laid down
because a review officer is not readily available.
If a review is postponed, it must be carried out "as
soon as practicable". This formula, which is liber-
ally sprinkled throughout the detention and review
procedures, can, as we have seen, be a convenient
excuse for procrastination and courts will need to
keep a watchful eye on its operation.

The police may "self-authorise" detention without charge in appropriate cases for up to 36 hours.
Detention in excess of this period may be authorised
only by magistrates' courts. Whether this will be a
significant safeguard will depend on the attitude of
magistrates to it. If they see applications for
further detention orders as an opportunity not only
to examine rigorously the grounds put forward to
justify further detention but also, to satisfy
themselves that all aspects of the detention procedures up until the time when the suspect is brought
to court have been properly carried out before making
the requested order, their role may well provide an
important safeguard for suspects. Indeed, the
legislation in this respect would have been more
convincing if it had made the proper carrying out of
the detention procedures a condition of the granting
of any order of further detention. If, on the other
hand, magistrates' courts are unduly deferential to
police requests for further detention orders, or
regard them as matters of routine, then the value of
magisterial involvement will be seriously undermined.

It is not always clear from the Act what action
if any may be taken against the police where the
detention provisions are not properly complied with.
It is trite law that where a suspect has been
unlawfully arrested, he has been falsely imprisoned
and may bring a civil action. It can be taken as
equally axiomatic that a validly arrested but
improperly detained suspect is also falsely imprisoned from the moment that the improper detention is
authorised. So, for example, where a custody officer
authorises detention because he reasonably believes
that detention without charge is necessary to secure
or preserve evidence or to obtain such evidence by
questioning the suspect, and it is found by a court
ex post facto that his belief was not reasonable, the
detention is clearly unlawful and the suspect may
secure redress through civil action in the courts.
Suppose, however, that the custody officer fails to

125

ARREST AND DETENTION

inform a suspect of his rights, as required by the Code of Practice, when he arrives at the police station. Or the statutory reviews are not carried out. Or a suspect is improperly denied the facility of making representations about his detention at the time of a review. Or he is improperly denied access to a solicitor. What effect will any of these defects in the detention procedures have? It is clear that in such circumstances a complaint could be made under the police complaints procedures.[159] Where a suspect is subsequently prosecuted, these are matters which he will no doubt wish to raise at his trial with a view to having any evidence obtained following the breach excluded at the discretion of the court.[160] It is clear, however, that breach of the statutory or Code provisions will not necessarily result in the exclusion of any evidence obtained thereby.[161] Will such breaches render the detention unlawful? In other words, is compliance with all the detention procedures a condition of the legality of the detention? When we look at the language of both the Act and Code, we find that many of the obligations imposed upon custody and review officers are in mandatory terms. Where a custody officer authorises the keeping of a person in detention he shall, as soon as practicable, make a written record of the grounds of detention. The written record shall be made in the presence of the arrestee who shall be informed of the grounds of the detention. Reviews of detention shall be carried out periodically. The review officer shall record the reasons for the postponement of any review in the custody record.

It is submitted that the effect of a breach of any of the mandatory obligations imposed by the Act upon the police in connection with the detention of suspects, should be to invalidate the detention from the time when the breach is committed. In respect of those duties which must be carried out as soon as practicable, the continued detention should be declared unlawful by a court if, taking into account all the circumstances, the duty is not carried out at the earliest time at which it became practicable to do so.

Finally, we turn to the effect of the detention provisions on the right to silence. The Royal Commission on Criminal Procedure recommended that "the present law on the right of silence in the face of police questioning after cautioning should not be altered"[162] and the Police and Criminal Evidence Act, 1984, does not purport, ostensibly at least, to alter

126

ARREST AND DETENTION

it. It is clear, however, that the main purpose underlying the granting to the police of a right to hold a suspect in detention for up to 96 hours is so that he may be questioned. The Act provides that detention in custody without charge is permissable when the custody officer has reasonable grounds for believing that a suspect's detention without charge is necessary to secure or preserve evidence relating to an offence for which he is under arrest or to obtain such evidence by questioning him. The police have thus been given by statute, for the first time, the general right to detain suspects for questioning. The evidence which the police are most likely to wish to secure by questioning a suspect is a confession. The effect of the extended detention provision, therefore, is to give the police up to 96 hours in which to obtain one and for the first 36 of those hours, legal advice may be legitimately withheld from the suspect. It is against this background that the right of silence must be assessed. It will be a very hard-nosed suspect indeed, who is able to maintain silence in the face of 96 hours of psychological pressure to confess. The extended detention provisions are thus predicated on either, the suspect not exercising the right to silence, or, succumbing to interrogation at some point during the period of detention. It is not surprising in the light of this, that an eminent judge, Lord Salmon, should have commented, while the Police and Criminal Evidence Bill was before Parliament, that its enactment would bring us nearer to becoming a police state.[163]

Notes

1.   Royal Commission on the Police, Cmnd. 1728, (1962) para. 135.
2.   Felonies and Misdemeanours, Cmnd. 2659 (1967), p.7.
3.   Report of the Royal Commission on Criminal Procedure, Cmnd. 8092, (1981) para. 2.18.
4.   Ibid., paras. 2.18-2.24.
5.   Arrest under warrant is essential, however, for failure to answer a summons or fine default and is more commonly used in these contexts.
6.   (1845), 7 QB 742.
7.   Ibid., at p. 745.

127

ARREST AND DETENTION

8. (1969), 2QB 216, 220.

9. Ibid., at p. 218. The point is developed in Wheatley v Lodge, (1971), 1 A11 E.R. 173.

10. (1973), 2 A11 E.R. 645.

11. Ibid., at p. 648.

12. Op cit., Felonies and Misdemeanours.

13. See Hawkins, Pleas of the Crown, Vol. 2, Ch. 13. s.8; Barnard v Gorman, (1941), A.C. 378; R v Howell, (1981), 3 A11 E.R. 383.

14. R v Howell, Ibid.

15. See Piddington v Bates, (1960), 3 A11 E.R. 660.

16. See particularly R v G. Light, (1857), 169 E.R. 1029; Cohen v Huskisson, (1838), 150 E.R. 845; Baynes v Brewster, (1802), 114 E.R. 149; Barnard v Gorman, op. cit. For a discussion of the cases, see G.L. Williams, Arrest for Breach of the Peace, (1954) Crim. L.R. 578.

17. See e.g. McBride v United States, 284, Fed. 416; State v McCloud, 173 S.E. 2d 753.

18. Williams, Arrest for Breach of the Peace, op. cit.

19. The power remains exercisable, however, if the officer is in fresh pursuit of the offender (see R v Walker, (1854), Dears C.C. 358), or if he reasonably apprehends a renewal of the breach, (Baynes v Brewster, op. cit.).

20. (1864), 17 Ir. C.L.R. 1.

21. Ibid., at p. 3.

22. See e.g. Piddington v Bates, op. cit., and King v Hodges, (1974), Crim. L.R. 424.

23. See e.g. Fitzgerald J. in Humphries v Connor, itself and D.G.T. Williams, Keeping the Peace, (Hutchinson, London, 1967), at p. 147.

24. The authority is R v Brown, (1841), Car & M 314.

25. Supra, para. 3.82.

26. Ibid., para. 3.83.

27. The Royal Commission recommended that the use of the power to arrest without warrant for an arrestable offence should be subject to the "necessity principle", that is, that detention upon arrest should continue only on one or more of the following criteria;

(a) the person's unwillingness to identify himself;

(b) the need to prevent a continuation or repetition of that offence;

(c) the need to protect persons or property;

(d) the need to secure or preserve evidence relating to that offence or to obtain such evidence from the suspect by questioning him;

ARREST AND DETENTION

(e) the likelihood of the person failing to appear at a court to answer any charge made against him.
Ibid., para. 3.76.
28. See the Police and Criminal Evidence Act, 1984, (hereafter PCE Act, 1984), s. 24(2). Among the offences now regarded as arrestable offences are: indecent assault on a woman; causing prostitution of women, procuration (offences under ss. 14, 22, 23 respectively, Sexual Offences Act, 1956); taking motor vehicle without authority, going equipped for stealing (offences under ss. 12 and 25 respectively of the Theft Act, 1968); and offences under the Customs and Excise Management Act, 1979.
29. PCE Act, 1984, s. 24(4).
30. Ibid., s. 24(5).
31. Ibid., ss. 24 (6) and (7).
32. Supra, Felonies and Misdemeanours, p. 9.
33. The difficulties to which the use of the powers can give rise are well-exemplified by Walters v W.H. Smith Ltd., (1914), 1 KB 595, and Clubb v Wimpey & Co. Ltd., (1936), 1 A11 E.R. 69.
34. See e.g. Rice v Connelly, (1966), 2 A11 E.R. 649.
35. Royal Commission on Criminal Procedure, op. cit., para. 3.86.
36. PCE Act 1984, ss. 25(1) and (2).
37. Ibid., s. 25(3)(a), (b) and (c).
38. Ibid., s. 25(a) and (e).
39. Per Judge Anderson, Park v United States, 294 Fed. 776.
40. Cmnd. 7966, para. 47.
41. (1947), A.C. 573.
42. See PCE Act 1984, Schedule 2.
43. Waite, Some Inadequacies in the Law of Arrest, 29 Mich. L.R. 448, 453.
44. (1982), 2 A11 E.R. 654.
45. The power in this case derived from s. 28 of the Town Police Clauses Act, 1847. It is one of the statutory arrest powers abolished by the PCE Act, 1984.
46. Considerable confusion surrounded the interpretation of arrest powers formulated in this way. In addition to Wills v Bowley, op. cit., see also Barnard v Gorman, (1941), A.C. 378 and Isaacs v Keech, (1925), 2 KB 354.
47. (1966), 1 QB 312, 322.
48. Op. cit., 681.
49. Both refer to situations in which a uni-formed police officer may require a motorist to undergo a breath test.

129

ARREST AND DETENTION

50. (1980), R.T.R. 315. The case is discussed in Bailey and Birch, Recent Developments in the Law of Police Powers, (1982), Crim. L.R. 475, 547, at 549-550.

51. Op. cit., at 681.

52. (1780), 92 E.R. 349.

53. Ibid., at p. 350.

54. Per Lord Denning MR in Wiltshire v Barrett, (1965), 2 All E.R. 271.

55. Per Scott LJ, in Dumbell v Roberts, (1944), 1 A11 E.R. 326. See also Shaabin Bin Hussein v Chong Fook Kam, (1970), A.C. 492.

56. Per Lord Devlin, in Shaabin Bin Hussein, Ibid.

57. Per Scott LJ in Dumbell v Roberts, op. cit.

58. See McArdle v Egan, (1934), 98 JP 103.

59. See particularly Scott LJ in Dumbell v Roberts, op. cit. "They may have to act on the spur of the moment and have no time to reflect and be bound therefore to prevent escape; but where there is no danger of the person who has ex hypothesi aroused their suspicion attempting to escape, they should make all presently practicable enquiries."

60. See Allen v London & S.W. Ry. Co., (1859), 11 Cox C.C. 621.

61. See generally, R v Birtles, (1969), 53 Cr. App. R. 469.

62. Powers of Arrest and Search in Relation to Drug Offences, (London: H.M.S.O. 1970).

63. Compare the list given in Skolnick, The Detection of Crime, (Wiley, New York, 1975), p. 46. See also Powis, The Signs of Crime, (McGraw Hill, London, 1977).

64. Report of the Advisory Committee on Drug Dependence, op. cit., pp. 42-43.

65. Report of the Royal Commission on Criminal Procedure, op. cit., para. 3.25.

66. Ibid.

67. Supra, at p. 948.

68. The issue of reasonable cause or reasonable suspicion is considered in greater detail in Lambert, Reasonable Cause to Arrest, (1973), Public Law, 285.

69. PCE Act 1984, ss. 28(1) and (3) respectively.

70. Supra.

71. (1961), 1 A11 E.R. 291.

72. For an illustration, R v Kulynycz, (1970), 3 WLR 1029.

73. See PCE Act 1984, s. 28(4). In Christie v Leachinsky, op. cit., the House of Lords suggested that at common law, if the reason for the arrest was

130

ARREST AND DETENTION

obvious, the arresting officer was under no duty to communicate it to the suspect.

74. See Wheatley v Lodge, (1971), 1 WLR 29.

75. See PCE Act 1984, s. 28(5).

76. There should, for instance, be no automatic handcuffing. See e.g. R v Taylor, 59 J.P. 393 where it appeared that the prisoner, when arrested for forging electoral nomination papers, had been taken to a police station in handcuffs. The court observed that handcuffing was only justifiable where reasonable necessity existed for it. In its Consolidated Circular to the Police on Crime and Kindred Matters, 1977 ed., para. 4.65, the Home Office gave the following guidance to chief police officers: "Whether a prisoner should be handcuffed must depend on the particular circumstances, as for instance the nature of the charge and the conduct and temper of the person in custody. Handcuffing should not be resorted to unless there is fair ground for supposing that violence may be used or an escape attempted. Handcuffing cannot be justified unless there are good special reasons for resorting to it."

77. The point is well-illustrated by Kenlin v Gardner, (1966), 3 A11 E.R. 931.

78. See Parkin, Resisting Unlawful Police Action, (1979), NLJ 850.

79. See R v Fennell, (1970), 3 A11 E.R. 215; Albert v Lavin, (1982), A.C. 546.

80. A "designated" police station is one designated by a chief constable to be used for the purpose of detaining arrested persons (PCE Act 1984, op. cit., s. 35(1)). Each chief constable is under a duty to designate stations for this purpose (s. 35 (2)). In certain circumstances, a constable may take an arrestee to a non-designated station (ss. 30 (3),(4),(5), but he must be taken to a designated station not more than six hours after his arrival at the first police station (s. 30(6)).

81. John Lewis & Co v Tims (1952), A.C. 676.

82. PCE Act 1984, Ibid., s. 30(1).

83. PCE Act, s. 30(7).

84. PCE Act, s. 30(10). Where there is delay for this or any other reason, the reasons for the delay must be recorded when the suspect first arrives at a police station. See PCE Act 1984, s. 30(11).

85. The provision is not entirely new. In Dallison v Caffery, (1965), 1 Q.B. 348, the Divisional Court arrived at a very similar view, though the authority of the ruling was subsequently doubted - see L.H. Leigh, Police Powers in England

ARREST AND DETENTION

and Wales, (Butterworths, London, 1974), p. 55.
86. See Softley, Police Interrogation: An Observational Study in Four Police Stations, RCCP Research Study No. 4, (London HMSO 1980), p. 61 and Barnes and Webster, Police Interrogation: Tape Recording, RCCP Research Study No. 8, (London HMSO 1980), p. 62.
87. Magistrates' Courts Act, 1980, s. 43 re-enacting Magistrates' Court Act 1952, s. 38. The major exception to this general rule is found in the Prevention of Terrorism (Temporary Provisions) Act, 1984.
88. Royal Commission on Criminal Procedure, op. cit., para. 3.98.
89. Two notable exceptions to this are the cases of R v Hudson (1980, 72 Cr. App. R. 163, and R v Sherman and Apps, (1980), 72, Cr. App. R. 266. In the latter case Donaldson L.J. (as he then was) described the Magistrates' Courts Act 1952 as "unequivocal" and "imperative" in its terms and formed the view that, in the absence of express statutory authority 48 hours was the maximum period of detention following arrest permissible.
90. Royal Commission on Criminal Procedure, op. cit., paras. 3.101-3.113.
91. See generally PCE Act 1984, op. cit., s. 36. An officer of any rank may perform the functions of a custody officer if a custody officer is not available to perform them. Such an officer must, however, be detached from the investigation of the offence (ss. 36(4) and (5)). At a non-designated police station, the functions shall be performed by an officer not involved in the offence under investigation. If such an officer is not available, any officer may perform the necessary duties (ss. 36(7), (8), (9), (10)).
92. Ibid., s. 39(1).
93. Ibid., s. 37(1).
94. See s. 37 (10).
95. See s. 37 (2).
96. See ss. 37 (4) and (5). This latter duty shall not apply when the person arrested is, at the time the written record is made, incapable of understanding what is said to him, violent or likely to become violent, or in urgent need of medical attention - see s. 37(6).
97. See below, pp. 114-117.
98. PCE Act, 1984, op. cit., ss. 41 and 42.
99. Ibid., s. 41 (2).
100. See s. 37(7). Note that the custody officer's duties with regard to juveniles, the

132

ARREST AND DETENTION

position of whom is not separately discussed in this chapter, are set out in detail in ss. 37 (11)-(15).

101. See s. 38 (1).

102. See ss. 38 (3) and (4).

103. See s. 46 (1). Magistrates' Courts do not usually sit on weekends and a person charged on a Friday evening, for example, could not normally be taken before a court until Monday morning. Accordingly, the Act provides that, if no court is due to sit on the day on which a suspect is charged or the next day, the custody officer must inform the local justices' clerk who will arrange for a court to sit not later than the day after the day the suspect is charged - see ss. 46 (3)-(6). Where the day after the day a suspect is charged is a Sunday, Christmas Day or Good Friday, the justices' clerk must arrange for a court to sit not later than the first day after the day of charge which is not one of those days - see s. 46 (8). A person charged on a Saturday will therefore normally go before a court on the following Monday.

104. See ss. 40 (1) and (2).

105. See s. 40 (3).

106. See s. 40 (4).

107. See ss. 40 (12)-(14).

108. Report of the Royal Commission on Criminal Procedure, op. cit., para. 3.7.

109. Ibid., para. 3.106.

110. See PCE Act 1984, op. cit., Schedule 5. The full list is as follows: Treason, murder, manslaughter, rape, kidnapping, incest with a girl under 13, buggery with a boy under 16 or a person who has not consented, indecent assault which constitutes an act of gross indecency. In addition offences under the Explosive Substances Act, 1883, (s. 2, causing explosion likely to endanger life or property); Sexual Offences Act, 1956, (s. 5, intercourse with a girl under the age of 13); Firearms Act, 1968, (s. 16, possession of firearms with intent to injure, s. 17, use of firearms and imitation firearms to resist arrest, and s. 18, carrying firearms with criminal intent); Road Traffic Act, 1972, (s. 1, causing death by reckless driving); Taking of Hostages Act, 1982 (s. 1, hostage-taking) and the Aviation Security Act 1982, (s. 1, hi-jacking); are always serious arrestable offences.

111. Ibid., s. 116 (6).

112. See s. 42 (1).

113. See ss. 42 (1) and (4).

114. See ss. 42 (5)-(8).

115. See s. 42 (10).

133

ARREST AND DETENTION

116. See ss. 43 (1), (2) and (3). The details required to be contained in the information are specified in s. 43 (14).

117. See s. 43 (4).

118. See generally s. 43 (5).

119. See ss. 43 (7) and (8).

120. See s. 43 (17).

121. See s. 43 (15) - though note that a suspect need not be released under s. 43 (15) before the expiry of twenty four hours after the relevant time - see s. 43 (16).

122. See ss. 43 (10), (11), (12).

123. See s. 43 (18). A suspect released under this provision must not be re-arrested without warrant for the same offence unless new evidence justifying a further arrest has come to light since his release - see s. 43 (19).

124. See s. 44 (1).

125. See ss. 44 (3), (4), (5).

126. See s. 44 (7) - though note that the release need not take place before the period specified in any warrant of further detention already obtained has expired - see s. 44 (8).

127. The Secretary of State is under a general duty imposed upon him by s. 66, to issue Codes of Practice in connection with certain statutory powers of search, the detention, treatment, questioning and identification of persons by police officers, and the seizure of property by the police. The Codes must be published in draft, laid before both Houses of Parliament and brought into effect by statutory instrument. At the time of writing, the Codes are available in draft only.

128. See the Judges' Rules and Administrative Directions to the Police, Home Office Circular No. 89/1978, Appendix B, para. 7.

129. In 1978, a circular was issued to Chief Constables explaining the obligations of the section. See Home Office Circular No. 74/1978.

130. See PCE Act, 1984, op. cit., s. 39 (1), and the Draft Code of Practice on the Detention, Treatment and Questioning of Persons by Police Officers, s. 3.1.

131. PCE Act 1984, Ibid., s. 56 (5).

132. Ibid., s. 56 (3).

133. The Draft Code of Practice on the Detention, Treatment and Questioning of Persons, op. cit., provides that if the person initially named by the suspect cannot be contacted, the suspect may choose up to two alternatives. If they cannot be contacted, further attempts may be made at the custody officer's

ARREST AND DETENTION

discretion (s. 5.1). In addition, a suspect may be supplied, on request, writing materials, but any letters he sends may be read (except those to his solicitor (s. 5.6)). He may also speak on the telephone to one person, but unless the call is to his solicitor, a police officer may listen to what is said (s. 5.7). The suspect must be cautioned that anything he says in a letter or telephone call (except communications with his solicitor) may be given in evidence (s. 5.8). Note the extent to which these provisions differ from those in the Judges' Rules and Administrative Directions, which they replace.

134. Report of the Royal Commission on Criminal Procedure, op. cit., paras. 4.81-4.99.

135. Judges' Rules and Administrative Directions, op. cit., Appendix A.

136. Research studies indicated that denial of access to legal advice was commonplace. See Zander, Access to a Solicitor in the Police Station, (1972), Crim. L.R. 342, Baldwin and McConville, Police Interrogation and the Right to See a Solicitor, (1979), Crim. L.R. 145. See also the Fisher Report into the Confait Case, 1977, 78 H.C. 90 and Softley, Police Interrogation: An Observational Study in Four Police Stations, Royal Commission on Criminal Procedure Research Study No. 4 (HMSO 1980), who found that relatively few suspects asked to consult a solicitor.

137. Emphasis added. A suspect arrested under the Prevention of Terrorism (Temporary Provisions) Act 1984, may not be allowed to consult a solicitor privately, see PCE Act 1984, op. cit., ss. 58(13)-(18).

138. Draft Code on the Detention, Treatment and Questioning of Persons, op. cit., s. 3 (c).

139. PCE Act 1984, op. cit., s. 58 (4).

140. Ibid., ss. 58 (4) and (5).

141. See s. 58 (8).

142. See s. 59, which amends s. 1 of the Legal Aid Act 1982.

143. Draft Code on the Detention, Treatment and Questioning of Persons, op. cit., s. 6 (3).

144. Ibid., s. 6.5.

145. Baldwin and McConville, Confessions in Crown Court Trials, (Royal Commission on Criminal Procedure Research Study No. 5, HMSO 1980) suggest that forensic evidence directly implicated the suspect in only five per cent of the cases they examined (see p. 19). Steer, Uncovering Crime; The Police Role, (Royal Commission on Criminal Procedure

ARREST AND DETENTION

Research Study No. 7 HMSO 1980) found that fingerprints were the main source of information which
first established the suspect in the mind of the
investigating officer in about two per cent of
detected indictable crime (see p. 73).
    146. Royal Commission on Criminal Procedure,
op. cit., para. 3.129.
    147. See Magistrates' Courts Act 1980 s, 49
re-enacting Magistrates' Courts Act, 1952, s. 40.
The provision detailed certain conditions which must
be complied with and in R v Jones, (1978), 3 A11
E.R., it was stated that they must be strictly
observed.
    148. i.e. One which is recordable in National
Police Records.
    149. PCE Act, 1984, op. cit., s. 61 (3).
    150. Ibid., s. 61 (4).
    151. See s. 61 (6).
    152. s. 61 (2).
    153. Draft Code on the Detention, Treatment and
Questioning of Persons, op. cit., s. 4.2.
    154. Both fingerprints (PCE Act, ss 64 (1) and
(2)), and photographs (by s. 4.5 of the Draft Code)
must be destroyed (in the suspect's presence if he
so requires) if he is cleared of the offence in
connection with which they were taken or if he is
not prosecuted.
    155. PCE Act 1984, s. 116 (7).
    156. Op. cit.
    157. Review of the Operation of the Prevention
of Terrorism (Temporary Provisions Act 1976, Cmnd.
8803 (1983).
    158. See the Criminal Justice (Scotland) Act
1980.
    159. By s. 67 (8) of the PCE Act 1984, a
police officer shall be liable to disciplinary proceedings for a failure to comply with any of the
provisions of any of the Codes issued under the Act.
    160. The exclusion of unlawfully obtained
evidence is discussed in more detail in Chapters 6
and 7.
    161. Neither will they necessarily give rise.
to civil or criminal liability. See PCE Act 1984,
s.67 (10).
    162. Report of the Royal Commission on Criminal
Procedure, op. cit., para. 4.53.
    163. Sunday Times, 10.4.83.

136

Chapter 5

STOP AND SEARCH AND RELATED PROVISIONS

It commonly happens that the police wish to interview
a suspect at the police station either to eliminate
him from their enquiries or to confirm their general
suspicions. If they lack "reasonable suspicion" or
if they are not sure what sort of criminal activity
he is involved in, they cannot validly arrest him.
It may also occur that a police officer on the street
becomes suspicious about an individual, but again, is
unable legally to justify an arrest. In both cases,
the police can seek the voluntary co-operation of
the suspect: if it is not forthcoming however, the
question arises whether his "co-operation" can be
required.

1.   The Common Law

The response of the common law is reasonably
clear. In Rice v Connelly, Lord Parker said: "...
the whole basis of the common law is that right of
the individual to refuse to answer questions put to
him by persons in authority and a refusal to accom-
pany those in authority to any particular place,
short, of course, of arrest".[1] More recently, Lawton
L.J. has stated "... it must be clearly understood
that neither customs officers, nor police officers,
have any right to detain somebody for the purposes
of getting them to help with their enquiries."[2]
Indeed, as we have seen, it was established at common
law that where a person attends voluntarily at a
police station to assist with enquiries, then changes
his mind, wishes to leave and is prevented from doing
so, he is to be regarded as under arrest; but if it
was not made clear to him that he is under arrest, he
is entitled to leave using reasonable force to do so[3]
and the Police and Criminal Evidence Act 1984
endorses this general view.[4] Again, in R v Houghton

137

STOP AND SEARCH AND RELATED PROVISIONS

and Franchiosy, the Court of Appeal stated: "...
police officers can only arrest for offences. If
they think that there is any difference between
detaining or arresting, they are mistaken. They have
no power save under the Prevention of Terrorism Act
1976, to arrest anyone so that they may make enquiries about him".[5] The general thrust of this statement remains true today, although as we saw in the
last chapter, the police may arrest and subsequently
detain a suspect in custody for the purpose of
questioning him.[6]

In a number of well-known instances, however,
the courts appeared to countenance as valid, detent-
ions which did not purport to be arrests and which
could not in any circumstances have been regarded as
valid arrests. Two of them involved a prosecution
for assaulting a police officer in the execution of
his duty.[7] In such prosecutions, commission of the
offence turns on whether the officer was in the
execution of his duty at the time that the assault
was committed. In one sense, of course, an officer
who is taking steps he thinks appropriate to deal
with suspicious behaviour can be said to be in the
execution of his duty, as it is part of his duty to
prevent and detect crime and apprehend criminals.
This is not, however, the sense in which the courts
usually interpret the phrase. An officer who acts
unlawfully, albeit reasonably, will not be in the
execution of his duty. On this analysis, therefore,
an officer who detains a suspect against his will in
circumstances where the detention cannot amount to a
valid arrest, or is not otherwise authorised,[8] will
not be in the execution of his duty.

In Donnelly v Jackman,[9] a suspect ignored a
constable's repeated requests to stop and answer
some questions. The constable then tapped the
suspect on his shoulder, whereupon the suspect returned the gesture and tapped the officer. When the
officer again tapped the suspect with the intention
of stopping him, he was assaulted. The justices
found that the officer did not touch the suspect for
the purpose of making a formal arrest, but solely
for the purpose of speaking to him. The defendant
was charged with and convicted of assaulting a police
officer in the execution of his duty. On appeal,
Talbot J., who delivered the judgment of the Divisional Court, referred to the words used by Lord
Parker in Rice v Connelly, to the effect that the
duty of a constable was "to take all steps which
appear to him necessary for keeping the peace, for
preventing crime, or for protecting property from

138

STOP AND SEARCH AND RELATED PROVISIONS

criminal injury."[10]   Talbot J. went on to find that the officer concerned was acting in the execution of his duty because, "...it is not every trivial interference with a citizen's liberty that amounts to a course of conduct sufficient to take the officer out of the course of his duties."[11]

The decision is unsatisfactory for a number of reasons. It is not completely clear from the judgment whether the Divisional Court was of the opinion that there was no detention, or that there was a detention, but it was not unlawful because it was so trivial. The former would only be permissable if the justices found as a matter of fact that there was no detention. The latter view is unacceptable because it appears to suggest that the legality of the detention may turn, in part at least, upon the seriousness of the infringement. A third view is that there was a detention and it was unlawful but that it was so trivial that the constable remained within the bounds of his duty, notwithstanding its illegality. This is the least satisfactory alternative. A more acceptable result was arrived at, again by the Divisional Court, in the case of Ludlow v Burgess,[12] where on facts essentially similar to those of Donnelly v Jackman, the court decided that the constable was not within the scope of his duty as the detention of a man against his will without arresting him was an unlawful act and a serious interference with a citizen's liberty.

Shades of the Divisional Court's Donnelly v Jackman reasoning, however, could again be seen in Squires v Botwright.[13] A plain clothes police officer saw a woman driving her car carelessly. He followed her into the driveway of her house, told her that he was a police officer and that he had seen her committing a moving traffic offence and asked her to wait until a uniformed officer arrived. She refused and tried to push past him. He stood in her way and asked for her name and address and driving licence. She thereupon assaulted him and was charged with assaulting a police officer in the execution of his duty. The main issue again, therefore, was whether the officer was in the execution of his duty at the time and the Divisional Court decided that he was. It must be admitted that Lord Widgery C.J. in his judgment referred to the "special and highly peculiar facts of the case" and also that the court interpreted s. 228 of the Road Traffic Act 1960,[14] which authorises an arrest where there is a refusal to provide a name and address, as implicitly authorising the detention of a person in order to make a

139

STOP AND SEARCH AND RELATED PROVISIONS

request for name, address and licence. Nevertheless, the general tenor of the judgment was that a trivial interference with individual liberty does not take a constable out of the course of his duty.

By far the most controversial decision in recent years, however, is that of the Court of Appeal in R v Brown.[15] The defendant was waved down by two police officers after they had seen him cross traffic lights in a slightly dangerous manner. Brown drove on, abandoned his car and ran away. The officers eventually caught him and placed him in the back of the police van. They then noticed that his breath smelled of alcohol and asked him repeatedly to take a breath test. He refused and was arrested for failing to provide a specimen of breath under s. 8 (5) of the Road Traffic Act 1972. He was eventually convicted of driving with a blood alcohol-level above the prescribed limit.

On appeal against conviction, he argued that the police had no power to arrest him for failing to provide a specimen of breath, because he was already under arrest at the time. The procedure for the provision of a specimen of blood was consequently nugatory and the conviction should be quashed. The issue for the Court of Appeal, therefore, was raised in a very clear form. When had Brown been arrested? When first detained and placed in the back of the van, or when the officers purported to arrest him later? If the former, was it a valid arrest or some other form of valid detention short of arrest? If the latter, again, what was the status of the intervening detention?

Upholding the conviction, the Court of Appeal decided that Brown was not arrested until the officers informed him that he was being placed under arrest for failing to provide a specimen of breath. "Arrest", said Shaw L.J., who delivered the judgment of the court, "can only be effective in the exericse of an asserted authority. If a person is put under restraint arbitrarily or for some expedient motive, he is of course imprisoned. In a wide and inexact sense he may be said to be under arrest if the restraint is exercised by a police officer; but it may be neither a purported arrest nor an actual arrest and the officer may have to answer for his conduct in a court of law."[16]

In this perfectly unexceptional statement, Shaw L.J. is making the simple but important point that not every deprivation of liberty will amount to a lawful arrest. In order for there to be a lawful arrest, there must be "the exercise of an asserted

STOP AND SEARCH AND RELATED PROVISIONS

authority." The circumstances in Brown showed that when he was first restrained by the officers, there was no intention to arrest him. There was neither a purported nor an actual arrest. Strictly speaking, this was enough to deal with the argument. However, in one version of the judgment, Shaw L.J. went on to make these (obiter) comments:

> The officers concerned reacted to what they regarded as suspicious conduct by imprisoning him for so long as might be necessary to confirm their general suspicions or show them to be unfounded. In the first event they could then arrest him on a specific charge; in the second event, they would be bound to release him, having perhaps rendered themselves liable to pay damages for trespass and false imprisonment. 17

The passage clearly suggests that the police are at liberty to detain a suspect with a view to seeing if there are grounds for arresting him and only if no grounds are disclosed might they be liable in damages for the tort of false imprisonment. This idea that detention can be justified on an ex post facto basis was severely criticised. Professor Zander, for example, described this part of the Brown judgment as "inadequately argued, badly reasoned, contrary to the overwhelming weight of authority and contrary to accepted legal principle. In short, wrong."[18] Other commentators were equally critical.[19] However, when the Criminal Appeal Reports version of the judgment appeared, it differed significantly in one important respect. In place of the italicised words in the quotation above, Shaw L.J. is reported as saying:[20]

> In the first event they could then arrest him on a specific charge; in the second event, they would be bound to release him. In either case, they may have rendered themselves liable to pay damages for trespass and false imprisonment...

In this version, therefore, the statement accords with accepted authority. A prima facie unlawful detention cannot be justified ex post facto. Whether the detention discloses grounds of arrest or not, it is equally unlawful.

How could this discrepancy arise and which

STOP AND SEARCH AND RELATED PROVISIONS

version should we accept? The case was not reported
in the official law reports and so there is no
definitive version of the judgment. The most likely
explanation, however, is "that their Lordships had
the ghastly consequence of their words pointed out
to them following judgment and amended the offending
sentence before allowing it to see the light of day
in the Criminal Appeal Reports."[21]

It is this version, then, which is to be
preferred and R v Brown, despite the academic controversy, becomes unexceptional. The balance of
authority, therefore, remains strongly against any
right in the police at common law to detain a suspect
against his will to see if there are grounds to
arrest him. The Royal Commission on Criminal
procedure entirely accepted this view: "We do not
propose that the present position should be over-
turned and that the police be given specific power
to detain for enquiries whether in the street or in
the police station on a criterion other or less than
the present one."[22] In other words, in the absence
of specific statutory authority, only those suspected
on reasonable grounds of committing an offence may be
"detained", i.e. arrested. The Royal Commission
added: "...there must be no halfway house between
liberty and arrest...Where we use the words 'detention' and 'detain' we refer only to action taken
after a lawful arrest."[23]

2. Specific Statutory Authority

A number of statutes give powers to stop and
search in different circumstances. Some of these are
well-known and well-used, such as the power to stop
and search for prohibited drugs;[24] others are
hardly known and (presumably) hardly used such as
those under the Poaching Prevention Act, 1862 or the
Conservation of Seals Act 1970.[25] The powers are
exercisable by the police only, sometimes against
restrictively defined classes of people.[26] Most of
the powers have been granted by Parliament in the
last hundred years or so, on a totally ad hoc basis.
Until the passing of the Police and Criminal Evidence
Act 1984, there was no general power to make investigative stops.

The use of some of these powers has proved
highly controversial. Despite the fact that most of
them are couched in terms of reasonable grounds to
suspect an offence against the Act, it has often
been alleged that they are used randomly, arbitrarily
or discriminately. It is also undoubtedly true that

142

STOP AND SEARCH AND RELATED PROVISIONS

through their use, vast numbers of people are caught up in the law enforcement process.

Apart from those powers which apply nationally, some powers were available by local legislation applying within a particular police area. All such local enactments have been repealed by the Police and Criminal Evidence Act 1984.[27] The best known of them was s. 66 of the Metropolitan Police Act, 1839. Its use was restricted to constables within the Metropolitan Police District[28] and it empowered a constable to detain for the purpose of searching any person who was reasonably suspected of having or conveying in any manner anything stolen or unlawfully obtained. The officer could also search any vessel or vehicle on the same terms. In 1981, in one of the rare cases involving s. 66 to come before the courts, Lord Lane C.J. commented that s. 66 conferred on police constables in the metropolis, "powers which extend, to a not insignificant degree, beyond their common law or other statutory powers. In our view, therefore, that section is to be strictly construed."[29]

Detailed statistics on the exercise of powers to stop and search have not traditionally been collected centrally (except in the case of searches under the Misuse of Drugs Act 1971). However, the Metropolitan Police provided information on the use of s. 66 to the Royal Commission on Criminal Procedure.[30] Figures were supplied, broken down by Metropolitan police area, for the months of July 1978 and January 1979 respectively. In the former month, 40,477 stops were recorded resulting in 5,110 arrests (an arrests from stops rate of thirteen per cent), and in the latter, 35,298 stops were recorded resulting in 4,189 arrests (an arrests from stops rate of twelve per cent). On the assumption that those months were not exceptional, a crude calculation supplies a yearly total of s. 66 stops of around 480,000 and these stops resulted in approximately 50,000 arrests. More recent research suggests that these figures seriously underrepresent the scale of the use of s. 66 and other powers. The decision to record an encounter with a member of the public is a highly discretionary decision on the part of the officer concerned. An Official Report by the Home Office Research Unit in 1983 suggested that recorded statistics under-estimate by about one half the number of street stops actually made by the police.[31] In 1981, 716,673 recorded stops[32] were made in the Metropolitan Police District and these stops produced 67,275 arrests.[33] If the Home Office

143

STOP AND SEARCH AND RELATED PROVISIONS

Report is correct, however, the actual number of
people stopped on the streets of London is closer to
a million and a half.[34] The proportion of suspects
arrested following a stop who are then prosecuted is
not accurately known, but it has been suggested that
only four per cent of stops result in prosecutions
in London and the figure could be as low as one per
cent elsewhere.[35]
The Misuse of Drugs Act 1971, re-enacted in
section 23 a power found originally in section 6 of
the Dangerous Drugs Act, 1967. The police are
authorised under this section to search without
warrant and without first arresting, any person whom
they have reasonable grounds to suspect is in
possession of dangerous drugs. Under this provision, a constable may: detain a person for the
purpose of searching him; require a person in
control of any vehicle in which he suspects the drug
may be found to stop it for the purpose of searching
it; and seize and detain for the purpose of proceedings under the drugs legislation anything found
in the course of the search which appears to be
evidence of an offence against the legislation. It
has been held that the power to detain implies a
power to take a suspect to a place where the search
can properly be carried out.[36] When the search is
over the power to detain lapses, unless of course,
the search provides reasonable grounds for an arrest.
The enforcement of drugs legislation obviously
requires wide-ranging powers in view of the particular operational difficulties which beset the police.
Section 23 attempts to prevent arbitrary searches by
the incorporation of the requirement of reasonable
suspicion. When first granted, however, the use of
the power was subjected to much criticism. For
example, both "Release" and the National Council for
Civil Liberties gave evidence to the Advisory
Committee on Drug Dependence in 1970 to the effect
that searches under s. 6 of the 1967 Act were all too
often based merely on the unconventional or weird
appearance of the suspect. Accordingly, one of the
results of the Report of the Advisory Committee[37] was
a Home Office Circular distributed to Chief
Constables, recommending that they keep detailed
statistics on the use of the stop and search power
for the information of H.M.Inspectors of Constabulary. These figures have been available since 1972.
The national use of section 23 is on a modest scale
compared with the figures set out above. In 1978,
the forty one police forces in England and Wales
outside the Metropolitan area, searched 18,107

144

STOP AND SEARCH AND RELATED PROVISIONS

persons and found 4,051 of them (22.4 per cent) to
be in illegal possession of drugs. In the Metropolitan Police district, 6,412 searches were recorded,
leading to 2,483 arrests. In 1981, twenty seven per
cent of persons stopped and searched under the
Misuse of Drugs Act powers were found to be in
illegal possession but the percentage rate varies
enormously from area to area - eleven per cent in
Northamptonshire rising to sixty one per cent in
Dorset.[38]
     Any controversy surrounding the use of these
provisions paled into insignificance when compared
with the controversy which for many years the
notorious "sus" laws excited. Section 6 of the
Vagrancy Act 1824, did not in fact sanction stop and
search. Rather it gave a power to arrest "every
suspected person or reputed thief...loitering with
intent to commit an arrestable offence." The lack
of specificity in the section was an open invitation
to the police to go on "fishing expeditions." Its
use by some police forces in inner city areas with
high immigrant populations, aroused considerable
hostility and was seen by many as one of the most
significant factors in the apparent breakdown of
relations between the police and ethnic communities
in some parts of the country. In 1980, the Home
Affairs Sub-Committee of the House of Commons on Race
Relations and Immigration examined this whole issue
in considerable detail.[39] Shortly afterwards, the
government announced its intention of repealing the
suspected person offence, a measure which was
achieved in the Criminal Attempts Act, 1981.[40]
     The Royal Commission but briefly adverted to
this background of criticism of stop and search
powers. It accepted the arguments, strongly pressed
by the police, for "the retention and rationalisation
of existing powers" subject to the need to improve
safeguards and recommended the enactment of a single
uniform power to apply throughout England and
Wales.[41] The provisions in the 1984 Act are based
upon the Royal Commission's recommendations. By
Section 1, a constable is given the power to stop,
search and detain for the purpose of searching, any
person or vehicle or anything which is in or on a
vehicle, for stolen or prohibited articles, provided
that he has reasonable grounds for suspecting that
he will find such articles. He is entitled to seize
anything which he has reasonable grounds for suspecting to be a stolen or prohibited article. The power
is exercisable by any constable, whether in uniform
or not, in any public place.[42]

145

STOP AND SEARCH AND RELATED PROVISIONS

The term "stolen articles" is not defined in the 1984 Act, though it may be assumed that the Theft Act, 1968, definition will be applicable.[43] A "prohibited article" is either an offensive weapon[44] or an article made or adapted for use in the course of or in connection with burglary, theft, taking a motor vehicle or conveyance without authority, obtaining property by deception, or intended by the person having it with him for such use by himself or some other person.

In addition to providing this general stop and search power, the Act sets out certain safeguards and procedures applicable to all stop and search powers. A search "shall not commence" before certain matters have been brought to the attention of the person to be searched or the person in charge of the vehicle to be searched. These are: where the constable is not in uniform, documentary evidence (i.e. his warrant card), that he is a constable; his name and the name of the police station to which he is attached; the object of the proposed search; his grounds for proposing to make it; the suspect's entitlement to a copy of the record of the search if a copy is requested within twelve months unless it is not practicable to make such a record.[45] It is clear from this that where these duties are not performed before commencing to search, the search and any subsequent seizure, though presumably not the initial detention, will be unlawful. Having made his search, a constable is required to make a record of it in writing as soon as practicable after the completion of the search. The record shall include the suspect's name, or, if this is not known, a description of him together with a statement of the object of the search, the grounds for making it, the date and time when and place where it was made, whether anything was found and whether any, and if so what, injury to a person or damage to property appears to have resulted from the search. The record shall also identify the constable who conducted the search.[46]

The procedures represent a considerable improvement over the pre-existing regime. They go some way to meeting the criticisms made of stop and search powers and may curb some of the abuses that have in the past taken place. They are predicated on the assumption, however, that stop and search powers are necessary, an assumption which is by no means self-evident. It can be strongly argued that such powers are not "cost effective" - that their contribution to law-enforcement is massively out-weighed by the

146

STOP AND SEARCH AND RELATED PROVISIONS

damage which their use can do to police and public relationships. They are associated with a style of policing which has come in for severe criticism in recent years, which has engendered public antagonism towards the police and which has given the lie to the concept of policing by consent. The statistics cited earlier demonstrate that the vast majority of street-stops are unproductive in law-enforcement terms and the available evidence strongly suggests that they have a negative effect on police public relationships.[47]

The argument that they are unnecessary is not solely based on a consideration of acceptable policing styles. Stop and search powers are exercisable only upon reasonable suspicion. Indeed, the Royal Commission saw stricter application of the criterion of reasonable suspicion as the principal safeguard against abuse,[48] though, rather feebly, it did not attempt to give any guidance on the meaning and application of the concept. Arrest powers, as we have seen, are also exercisable only upon reasonable suspicion. A validly arrested suspect may lawfully be searched for anything which might be evidence relating to an offence.[49] It can be argued, therefore, that if there is reasonable suspicion against a suspect he can be arrested and special stop and search powers are thereby rendered unnecessary. The draft Code of Practice on Stop and Search Powers attempts to give some guidance to police officers on the meaning of reasonable suspicion. They are told that "reasonable suspicion, in contrast to mere suspicion, is an objective basis for action. There must be some concrete basis for the officer's belief, related to the individual person concerned, which can be considered and evaluated by an objective third person. The degree or level of suspicion required to establish the reasonable grounds justifying the exercise of powers of stop and search is no less than the degree or level of suspicion required to effect an arrest without warrant."[50]

In practice, of course, the police perceive arrest and stop and search powers as having entirely distinct objectives. A suspect is arrested either when he has been seen committing an offence, or when the belief that he has committed an offence is a strong one. A suspect is stopped and searched mainly to see if there are grounds to arrest him. This operational distinction between arrest and stop and search powers helps to explain the statistics discussed earlier. The low arrests from stops

147

STOP AND SEARCH AND RELATED PROVISIONS

percentage is explicable on the basis that it is likely that reasonable suspicion, as defined in the Code of Practice, was probably absent in most of them. Recent research supports this conclusion. Police officers, it would appear, find great difficulty in articulating in reports their reasons for stopping particular suspects and more often than not content themselves with the entry, "Stop - Re Movements."[51] The legal requirements are, therefore, at odds with the operational use of stop and search powers and the concept of reasonable suspicion is thereby diluted.

The police lobby in favour of extended stop and search powers was, however, a powerful one. That being so, the case for abolishing local stop and search powers was strong. If these powers must be conceded to the police, it clearly makes sense to remove the anomalies and make a general power nationally available. The very act of doing this, of course, appreciably extends the coercive powers available to the police. The quid pro quo for this extension was the stiffening of safeguards to prevent abuse. The obligations imposed on police officers to give suspects clear information about the purpose and grounds of the search is an important one. No such general obligation was previously imposed upon police officers exercising stop and search powers prior to the 1984 Act. It recognises that street stops are by their nature interferences with personal liberty and must be justified to a suspect in the same way as arrests must be. The duty to record all street stops and in so doing, to comply with the details required by the legislation, is equally significant. The entry "Stop - Re Movements" will no longer be adequate and police officers will be compelled to articulate more clearly the basis of their intervention. This will allow both their superiors and the courts the opportunity to scrutinise more closely whether the necessary conditions for the exercise of the power were present and should go some way to preventing random or discriminatory stops. The system will only work, however, if all constables on the streets are given explicit directions both to record every stop and to comply strictly with the requirements now laid down by Parliament.

The Draft Code of Practice on the exercise of stop and search powers contains the following statement:

Statistics on the use to date of powers

STOP AND SEARCH AND RELATED PROVISIONS

of stop and search indicate that in most cases no such article was found and there is strong evidence that on many occasions these powers have been used where reasonable grounds to suspect the individual concerned of having the article in question on him and did not in fact exist. There is strong evidence that such misuse has played an important part in mistrust of the police among some sections of the community. It is therefore important to ensure that the powers are used responsibly and sparingly. Over use of the powers is as likely to be harmful to police effort in the long-term as misuse.[52]

This is a salutory warning which should be heeded by beat constables and senior officers alike. By Section 5 of the 1984 Act, all chief officers of police are obliged to include in their annual reports statistics on the total numbers of searches carried out in each month to which the report relates broken down into searches for stolen articles, offensive weapons and other prohibited articles. In addition, the total number of persons arrested in each month as a consequence of searches in each of the above categories must be supplied. This important provision will enable far more accurate monitoring of the use of stop and search powers than has previously been possible. The statistics thus provided will deserve and should receive the closest scrutiny to ensure that the powers are indeed being used "responsibly and sparingly".

3. Road-Blocks

Section 159 of the Road Traffic Act, 1972, provides that it is an offence for a person driving a motor vehicle on a road to refuse to stop it on being required to do so by a constable in uniform. This is a general power and the officer is not required to have any suspicion that an offence has been committed, though, of course, the purpose of granting it is to ensure conformity with the legislation. There is no associated power of search, though having made his stop, a constable is empowered to require production of driving licence and insurance and test certificates and to demand the date of birth of the motorist and his name and address. That this power was capable of abuse is

STOP AND SEARCH AND RELATED PROVISIONS

self-evident, though the balance of authority was clearly in favour of the ambit of the power being confined to road traffic purposes.[53] The Royal Commission on Criminal Procedure suggested that there there were two circumstances in which the police stopped vehicles in connection with criminal offences where they had no clear authority to do so. The first was where a person sought in connection with a serious crime was known to be moving in a particular area. The second was where the police check the occupants of vehicles passing in and out of an area in which a spate of crime was regularly committed, for example, over weekends.[54] "If such checks are to be allowed," concluded the Commission, "they should be confined to particular types of serious crime and should be regularised by the introduction of a measure of supervisory control."[55]

Accordingly, Section 4 of the 1984 Act, allows an officer of at least the rank of Superintendent[56] to authorise in writing, the setting up of a road-block (the Act uses the phrase "road-check") for the purpose of ascertaining whether a vehicle is carrying a person whom he has reasonable grounds to believe has committed a serious arrestable offence,[57] or who is a witness to such an offence or who is unlawfully at large. In each case, the authorising officer must have reasonable grounds for suspecting that the person sought is, or is about to be in the locality in which vehicles would be stopped.[58] The authorisation shall specify a period not exceeding seven days during which the road-block may be held continuously or conducted at specific times.[59] Further periods of up to seven days at a time may be authorised where necessary.[60] The power allows the police to stop either all vehicles at the road-block or to stop vehicles selected by any criterion.[61] The authorisation must specify the name of the officer giving it, the purpose of the road-block and the locality in which vehicles are to be stopped.[62] Every chief officer's annual report shall contain information about road-blocks including the reason for and results of each of them.[63] In addition, any person stopped at a road-block is entitled to obtain a written statement of its purpose if he applies for it within twelve months of the day on which his vehicle was stopped.[64]

It is entirely understandable that in legislation designed, inter alia, to rationalise police powers, an explicit power to mount road-blocks for investigative purposes should be granted. Indeed, it is a power which most people would probably have

150

STOP AND SEARCH AND RELATED PROVISIONS

assumed the police to possess prior to the passing of the Act. Because it operates by extending the Road Traffic Act 1972, s. 159 power,[65] it is subject to two limitations. First, it is confined to constables in uniform, and secondly, it is a power only to stop and not a power to search.[66] Accordingly, the vehicle may only be searched if (a) the police have reasonable grounds to suspect that the particular vehicle stopped contains a person whom they reasonably suspect has committed or is intending to commit a serious arrestable offence or a person unlawfully at large, and they arrest him,[67] or (b) they reasonably suspect that the vehicle contains stolen or prohibited articles.[68] Despite these limitations, however, a number of criticisms of the power can be made. Both the Act and the various Codes of Practice are silent as to the manner in which a motorist stopped under s. 4 is to be treated. He apparently need not to be told of the reason why he has been stopped, nor the purpose of the road-block nor of his entitlement to a written statement of its purpose. Related to this is a second criticism. The Act permits the stopping of vehicles according to any criterion and this clearly is capable of abuse. Finally, we have noted elsewhere the substantial discretion accorded to police officers in deciding whether arrestable offences are "serious" for the purposes of the Act.

Notes

    1.   (1966), 2 All E.R. 649 at 652.
    2.   In R v Lemsatef, (1977), 2 All E.R. 835.
    3.   See e.g. R v Inwood, (1973), 2 All E.R. 645.
    4.   See Police and Criminal Evidence Act, 1984, (hereafter PCE Act 1984), s. 29.
    5.   (1978), 66 Cr. App. Rep. 197.
    6.   See the discussion of the detention provisions in Chapter 4. See also Mohammed - Holgate v Duke, (1983), 3 All E.R. 526.
    7.   An offence under the Police Act, 1964, s. 50.
    8.   Under specific statutory authority. See the discussion below.
    9.   (1970), 1 All E.R. 987.
    10. Rice v Connelly, op. cit., at p. 989.

151

STOP AND SEARCH AND RELATED PROVISIONS

11. Op. cit., at p. 989.
12. (1971), Crim. L.R. 238.
13. (1972), R.T.R. 462.
14. Re-enacted by Road Traffic Act 1972, s. 164.
15. (1977), R.T.R. 160; (1976) 64 Cr. App. Rep. 231.
16. (1977), R.T.R. (1976), 64 Cr. App. Rep. 234-235.
17. (1977), R.T.R. 165-166. Emphasis added.
18. Zander (1977), 127 New L.J. 352, 379.
19. See e.g. Telling, Arrest and Detention: The Conceptual Maze, (1978), Crim. L.R. 320; Lidstone, A Maze in Law, (1978), Crim. L.R. 332.
20. (1976), 64 Cr. App. Rep. 231 at 235. Emphasis added.
21. Clarke and Feldman, Arrest by Any Other Name, (1979), Crim. L.R. 705.
22. Report of the Royal Commission on Criminal Procedure, Cmnd. 8092, (1981), para. 3.89.
23. Ibid., para. 3.25.
24. Misuse of Drugs Act 1971, s. 23.
25. In addition to these, there are nationally available powers under the Firearms Act 1968, s. 7; Deer Acts 1963 s. 5 and 1980, s. 4; Badgers Act 1973, s. 10; Wildlife and Countryside Act 1981, s. 19; Prevention of Terrorism (Temporary Provisions) Act, 1984, Schedule 3.
26. See e.g. Airports Authority Act 1975, s. 11.
27. See PCE Act 1984, s. 7.
28. It was available by virtue of local legislation in many other parts of the country.
29. See Pedro v Diss, (1981), 2 A11 E.R. 59, 64.
30. See the Report of the Royal Commission on Criminal Procedure, Law and Procedure, Vol. 1 (Cmnd. 8092-1) Appendix 3.
31. See Willis, The Use, Effectiveness and Impact of Police Stop and Search Powers, Home Office Research and Planning Unit Paper No. 15 (HMSO) 1983, p. 5.
32. Ibid., p. 17.
33. Out of a total number of 113, 144. In the provinces, however, stops are much less important in producing arrests. Willis suggests that about three per cent of arrests are the result of stops.
34. The Policy Studies Institute Report, on the Metropolitan Police (1983), suggested a figure of a million and a half also.
35. Willis, op. cit., at p. 17.

152

STOP AND SEARCH AND RELATED PROVISIONS

36. See Farrow v Tunnicliffe, (1976), Crim.
L.R. 126.
37. Powers of Arrest and Search in Relation to
Drug Offences, HMSO, 1970.
38. See Willis, The Use, Effectiveness and
Impact of Police Stop and Search Powers, op. cit.,
p. 17.
39. Race Relations and the "Sus" Law, Second
Report from the Home Affairs Committee, Session
1979-80, HC 559 (1980).
40. See Criminal Attempts Act, 1981, s. 8.
Note, however, that it was thought necessary in view
of the abolition of "sus" to create a new offence of
interfering with vehicles - see s. 9.
41. Report of the Royal Commission on Criminal
Procedure, op. cit., para. 3. 17.
42. By s. 1 (i) of the PCE Act 1984, a
constable may exercise the stop and search powers
"in any place to which at the time when he proposes
to exercise the power, the public or any section of
the public has access, on payment or otherwise, as
of right or by virtue of express or implied
permission; or in any other place to which people
have ready access at the time when he proposes to
exercise the power but which is not a dwelling." A
trespasser in the garden or yard of private property
can be searched if the constable has reasonable
grounds for believing that he does not reside in the
dwelling and that he is not there on the express or
implied permission of the occupier, s. 1(4). A
vehicle on private property may be searched if the
constable has reasonable grounds for believing that
the person in charge of the vehicle does not reside
in the dwelling and that the vehicle is not there
with the express or implied permission of a person
who resides in the dwelling - s. 1(5).
43. See, Theft Act 1968, s. 24.
44. "Offensive weapon" is defined by PCE Act
1984, s. 1(9) as "any article made or adapted for
use for causing injury to persons or intended by the
person having it with him for such use by him or by
some other person." The definition is virtually
identical to that in the Prevention of Crime Act
1953, s. 1(4).
45. PCE Act 1984, ss. 2(2) and (3).
46. Ibid., ss. 3(3), (4), (6).
47. See particularly Willis, The Use, Effectiveness and Impact of Police Stop and Search Powers,
op. cit., and McConville, Search of Persons and
Premises: New Data from London, (1983), Crim. L.R.
605.

153

STOP AND SEARCH AND RELATED PROVISIONS

48. Royal Commission on Criminal procedure, op. cit., para. 3.25.

49. PCE Act 1984, s. 32.

50. See Draft Code of Practice for the Exercise by Police Officers of Statutory Powers of Stop and Search, Annex B.

51. See Willis, The Use, Effectiveness and Impact of Police Stop and Search Powers, op. cit.

52. See Draft Code of Practice for the Exercise by Police Officers of Statutory Stop and Search Powers, op. cit., Notes for Guidance, para. 1B.

53. See e.g. Hoffman v Thomas, (1974), 1 WLR 374. In Steel v Goacher, (1983), RTR 98, the Divisional Court ruled that stopping a vehicle might be justified at common law if there were reasonable grounds to suspect criminal activity.

54. Royal Commission on Criminal Procedure, op. cit., para. 3.32.

55. Ibid.

56. The PCE Act 1984, provides that an officer below the rank of Superintendent may authorise the setting up of a road-block if it appears to him that it is required "as a matter of urgency" - s. 4(5). In such a case, the authorising officer is required to make a written record of the time when he gives his authorisation and to inform an officer of the rank of Superintendent or above that it has been given - s. 4(6). These duties must be performed "as soon as practicable" - s. 4(7).

57. The concept of the "serious arrestable offence" is discussed in detail in Chapter 4, ante.

58. PCE Act, 1984, s. 4(4).

59. Ibid., s. 4(11).

60. Ibid., s. 4(12).

61. s. 4(2).

62. s. 4(13).

63. s. 5.

64. s. 4(15).

65. See PCE Act 1984, s. 4(2).

66. Indeed, the 1984 Act does not even make it clear that the vehicle, once stopped, may be detained, for so long as is necessary to ascertain whether it contains an appropriate person.

67. Under s. 17 of the PCE Act, 1984, the police will be entitled to enter the vehicle and search it for the purpose of effecting an arrest for an arrestable offence or to arrest an offender unlawfully at large. Under s. 32 of the Act, if an arrest has been made, the vehicle may be searched consequent upon that arrest.

154

STOP AND SEARCH AND RELATED PROVISIONS

68.   In which case, they may search it under
PCE Act 1984, s. 1.

Chapter 6

SEARCH AND SEIZURE

Introduction

In no other area of the law relating to police powers was the need for reform more clearly manifested than in the law of search and seizure. Confusion and uncertainty were rife: almost all questions of importance were capable of a range of answers; underlying legal principles were imprecisely stated, and the judges in their attempts to fill in the gaps left by statute and common law alike, spawned case law which obfuscated rather than clarified the legal issues. In the words of one commentator:

> English law consists of a mass of separate and widely differing statutory provisions punctuated by serious gaps... and supplemented by confusing judicial decisions...which usually raise more problems than they solve.[1]

As in the law of arrest and detention, the sporadic development of the law over some three hundred years had contributed to its lack of coherence. Common law foundations had been overlaid with ad hoc statutory powers, usually tied to the investigation of specific offences and granted on a haphazard basis. The result was an accumulation rather than a development of powers. The lack of a comprehensive statute authorising necessary searches and seizures and hedged around with clear safeguards for individual freedom not only gave rise to anomalies - for example, the lack of a statutory power authorising the issue of a warrant to search for evidence of a murder - but also ensured that individuals who wished to resist searches or seizures of their

156

SEARCH AND SEIZURE

property could not be certain of the circumstances in which the law would give its imprimatur to their actions. The complexity and confusion also affected the police. It aided deliberate bending or flouting of the law as much as it contributed to innocent abuses of power. Where a police officer was found ex post facto to have exceeded his powers he rendered himself liable to civil action and took himself outside the execution of his duties for the purposes of the special protection provided by the law against those who obstructed or assaulted him.[2] And, of course, the absence in English law of an exclusionary rule resulted in evidence being admitted by a court, even where it could be established that it was obtained as result of an illegal search or seizure.

Traditional legal dogma has it that neither a police officer nor any other person[3] may enter private premises without the permission of the occupier unless affirmative justification exists in law. The principle derives most clearly from the famous case of Entick v Carrington,[4] in which the practice of issuing general warrants was declared to be unlawful. In one of the best-known dictums in English law, Lord Camden CJ said:[5]

> The great end for which men entered into
> society, was to secure their property.
> That right is preserved sacred and in-
> communicable in all instances where it
> has not been taken away or abridged by
> some public law for the good of the whole
> ...By the laws of England, every invasion
> of private property, be it ever so minute,
> is a trespass. No man can set foot upon
> my ground without my licence...If he admits
> the fact, he is bound to show by way of
> justification that some positive law has
> empowered or excused him.

Not only is the language picturesque, but the social and economic climate has changed enormously since Lord Camden's time. In particular, the sanctification of private ownership which lies at the core of the dictum is today anachronistic.[6] The central principle of Entick v Carrington is of enduring significance,[7] however, particularly in its declaration that search and seizure laws confer exceptional powers and in its rejection of 'state necessity' or 'executive discretion' as a justification for the exercise of such powers. The limitation of the case

157

SEARCH AND SEIZURE

is that while it asserts that otherwise unlawful intrusions must be justified by the law, it does not indicate criteria by which the grant of such powers should be limited. In other words, it says nothing about the substance of such powers; judges are thus able, on occasion, to genuflect to Entick v Carrington while in the same judgment sanctioning appreciable extensions to police powers of search and seizure.[8]

In this chapter, we will attempt to answer three questions. When are the police entitled to enter private premises? When are they entitled to search persons or premises? When are they entitled to seize and retain items found during a search? The partial codification of search and seizure powers provided by the Police and Criminal Evidence Act, 1984 ensures that the sources to which reference has to be made in order to answer those questions are not as disparate as they were prior to its enactment. The controversial nature of that legislation and its tortuous path through Parliament also serve to remind us that society as a whole has a crucial interest in the nature of search and seizure powers because they conflict with interests rightly regarded as fundamental in liberal democratic societies - the dignity of the person, the security of possessions and the concept of privacy.

Entry on to Private Premises

In the absence of specific legal authority, a police officer may enter private premises only with the consent of the occupier. Where an entry is made without consent, the police officer will be a trespasser. It also follows that where the lawfulness of an officer's presence on private premises is dependent upon the occupier's consent, withdrawal of that consent renders his continued presence unlawful.[9]

Legal authority to enter private premises in the absence of the occupier's consent is not co-terminus with the rights of search and seizure. Over the years, police officers have been granted the right to enter private premises for purposes other than searching them. Broadly speaking, the circumstances in which entry on to private premises, in the absence of consent, is legally permitted, fall into four categories: for the purposes of inspection; to deal with disorder or criminal offences; to arrest offenders or suspected offenders without warrant, and to execute search or arrest warrants. Until recently, the police have lacked any power to enter

SEARCH AND SEIZURE

for the purposes of carrying out general evidentiary searches. At common law, rights of entry were relatively restricted. A police officer was entitled to enter private premises to deal with a breach of the peace actually taking place on the premises or where he anticipated on reasonable grounds that a breach of the peace might take place on the premises.[10] In addition, a constable was entitled to enter private premises in fresh pursuit of a person who had committed a breach of the peace in his view,[11] or who had escaped from lawful custody,[12] or to effect a warrant of arrest,[13] or to save life or limb or prevent serious damage to property. The Royal Commission on Criminal Procedure concluded that the common law powers to enter premises without consent or a warrant are essential to deal with the situations for which they exist and recommended that they should be put on a statutory basis.[14] The Police and Criminal Evidence Act, 1984 by s. 17(1) gives effect to this recommendation with the exception of the powers to enter private premises to deal with or prevent breaches of the peace, which are expressly preserved as common law powers by the Act.[15] The decision to leave these powers outside the ambit of the Act is a curious one in the light of the fact that the statute purports, inter alia, to codify powers of entry, search and seizure and that the limitations of the breach of the peace powers are ambiguous. The general aim of clarity in the law would have been far better served by a statutory restatement of them.

Apart from these common law powers, a wide range of statutory entry powers were (and continue to be) available to the police.[16] The most important of them relate to entry for the purposes of executing a search warrant or effecting a lawful arrest. Some fifty public general statutes give the police the right to enter private premises under the authority of a warrant[17] to search for persons or property or simply for the purposes of inspection. According to the Royal Commission on Criminal Procedure, most searches are carried out in connection with property offences[18] and one of the most frequently used powers is that provided by s. 26 of the Theft Act, 1968, which authorises magistrates, where there is "reasonable cause to believe that any person has in his custody or possession or on his premises any stolen goods," to issue a warrant to search for and seize the same. A constable armed with such a warrant may enter and search the premises and "may seize any goods he believes to be stolen goods," even

159

SEARCH AND SEIZURE

though they are not the goods specified in the warrant.[19]

Not all statutory powers of arrest carry with them the right to enter private premises in order to effect the arrest. A constable is entitled to enter private premises in order to effect an arrest under warrant,[20] but whether he is so entitled when making an arrest without warrant for a non-arrestable offence will depend on the precise wording of the statutory authority. In Morris v Beardmore,[21] the House of Lords made it clear that rights of entry must be given expressly by legislation. In the words of Lord Diplock, "...if Parliament intends to authorise the doing of an act which would constitute a tort actionable at the suit of the person to whom the act is done, this requires express provision in the statute..."[22] Since 1967, the most widely used power to make arrests without warrant has been the power to arrest for an arrestable offence. In the exercise of this power, a constable is expressly given the right to enter private premises by force if necessary, if he has reasonable grounds for believing that the person whom he is seeking is on the premises.[23]

The Police and Criminal Evidence Act, 1984, now sets out the major circumstances in which an officer is entitled to enter private premises with or without a warrant. They may be summarised as follows. A constable may enter private premises without the consent of the occupier: to execute a search or arrest warrant or a warrant of commitment;[24] to arrest a person without warrant for an arrestable offence;[25] to arrest a person without warrant for certain other specified offences;[26] to recapture a person who is unlawfully at large and whom he is pursuing;[27] to save life or limb or prevent serious damage to property;[28] to search for evidence after the arrest of the occupier.[29] In this respect, the Act is largely confined to codifying and clarifying existing powers rather than introducing new ones. It is important to note, however, that it does not provide a comprehensive statement of entry powers and many such powers will continue to derive from specific legislation rather than from the 1984 Act.

Search

(a) On arrest

It is common practice for suspects under arrest to be searched either immediately after arrest or when taken to a police station. Indeed, many

SEARCH AND SEIZURE

suspects will be cursorily searched upon arrest and
then subjected to a more extensive search at the
police station. Force standing orders will often
incorporate guidance on the carrying out of such
searches. In addition to a search of the person,
however, a suspect may find that any premises
occupied or controlled by him may also be subjected
to a search, irrespective of whether he was arrested
at those premises or some other place. A search of
a suspect's premises is usually designed to uncover
evidence of a crime, normally the crime for which
the suspect has been arrested. Search of the person
can also be directed to safeguarding the arresting
officer by discovering weapons secreted on the
person or discovering any other items which a
suspect may use to harm himself or effect an escape;
it may be directed to discovering evidence of
identity or address where none has been furnished by
the suspect; it is commonly used to identify and
list all items in the possession of the suspect at
the time he enters police detention. The nature of
the search may also vary according to the circumstances of the arrest and the offence for which the
suspect has been arrested and range from a pat-down
or 'frisk' of the outer clothing, to a more extensive search through the pockets and clothes of a
suspect, to a strip-search or even an intimate body
search, i.e. a complete search of the naked body and
its orifices. An even more extreme form of search
is the examination of a suspect's body by scanning
devices to detect, for instance, objects swallowed
and their subsequent removal.[30] The extensiveness
of the search will thus vary from case to case; but
a search of some kind will routinely be carried out.
It is perhaps surprising, in the light of this,
that the power of the police to search suspects and
their premises following arrest has, until recently,
been one of the murkiest corners of the common law.
Although the power has been judicially recognised,
the case-law is sporadic and rudimentary. It was
reasonably clear at common law, however, that the
power to search in these circumstances was a
consequence of an actual arrest and could not be
exercised where there was authority to arrest but no
arrest had been made.[31] Despite some dicta to the
contrary,[32] it was also relatively clear that the
common law did not recognise any general right of
search following arrest. The early case-law
suggested that a suspect could be searched upon
arrest only where it was reasonable to do so in the
circumstances[33] and more recent cases have generally

161

SEARCH AND SEIZURE

adhered to this view. In <u>Lindley</u> v <u>Rutter</u>,[34] for example, an arrested woman's brassiere was removed in police custody following her arrest for being drunk and disorderly. The police constable who removed the garment was acting in accordance with Force standing orders which required the searching of every prisoner and the removal of certain garments for the prisoner's own protection. The defendant, who resisted the search, was charged <u>inter alia</u>, with assaulting a police officer in the execution of her duty. On appeal against conviction, Donaldson LJ in the Divisional Court, had this to say:[35]

> It is the duty of any constable who lawfully
> has a prisoner in his charge to take all
> reasonable measures to ensure that the
> prisoner does not escape or assist others to
> do so, does not injure himself or others,
> does not destroy or dispose of evidence and
> does not commit any further crime...What
> measures are reasonable...will depend on
> the likelihood that the prisoner will do
> any of these things unless prevented...
> What can never be justified is the adoption
> of any particular measures without regard
> to all the circumstances of the particular
> case.

Accordingly, because the police officer concerned had not considered whether, <u>in the particular circumstances</u>, removal of the garment was justified, the defendant's conviction was quashed. This line of reasoning was endorsed by the Divisional Court in the later case of <u>Brazil</u> v <u>Chief Constable of Surrey</u>,[36] where again, standing orders indicated the routine search of a suspect 'for her own safety.' A police officer, in the view of the court, could not justify a search simply on the basis of a general rule requiring the searching of all arrested suspects irrespective of whether a search was necessary in the circumstances.[37] The Divisional Court also suggested, by analogy with the rule in <u>Christie</u> v <u>Leachinsky</u>,[38] that because a search involved an affront to the dignity of the person, a police officer was not normally entitled to carry out a search without first explaining to the suspect why it was necessary.

    The authorities appear to establish then, that although the common law recognised the right to search a suspect following arrest, the exercise of the right was limited to those situations where there

162

SEARCH AND SEIZURE

was reasonable cause to believe that a search was necessary to prevent attack, injury or escape or the disposal of evidence. On this basis, even the routine listing and removing of a suspect's possessions by the police, in the absence of consent, would in many cases be unlawful at common law.

As was pointed out at the beginning of this section, searches of the person can be of varying degrees of intrusiveness and the greater the intrusion, the greater the affront to the dignity of the person. English courts have not had the opportunity of considering whether strip searches, or the taking of body samples, or intimate body searches, would be sanctioned by the common law. If the guiding principle, as suggested by the authorities, is that a police officer may do what is reasonable in the precise circumstances to ensure that, for example, the suspect does not have evidence of an offence committed by him hidden on his person, the strip-searching of a suspect arrested for drugs offences to see whether drugs are hidden in his underclothes might have been sanctioned by the common law, provided that there were reasonable grounds to believe that drugs would be found as a result of the search. It is also a matter of conjecture whether, at common law, an intimate body search would in any circumstances have been regarded as valid, given the degree of intrusion and humiliation that such a search necessarily entails.

The extent to which a suspect's premises were susceptible to search following arrest was also unclear at common law. In Ghani v Jones,39 Lord Denning MR said that where police officers arrest a man lawfully with or without a warrant, they may take any goods which they find in his possession or in his house which they reasonably believe to be material evidence in respect of the crime for which the suspect is arrested. The statement is, however, obscure (as is much of the Master of the Rolls' judgment), because it is not clear whether Lord Denning had in mind that the arrest must take place in the house, or whether he meant that a suspect's house could be searched even though the arrest took place elsewhere. In Jeffrey v Black,40 the defendent was arrested for the theft of a sandwich from a public house and then taken some distance to his house which was searched and cannabis discovered. The Divisional Court ruled this search to be illegal on the basis that where a police officer arrested a suspect at one place and then searched his house at another place, the search was unlawful when the

163

SEARCH AND SEIZURE

contents of the house bore no relation to the offence for which he was arrested. In other words, the search would have been lawful had the police expected to find at the suspect's house evidence of sandwich thefts. It must be said, however, that the judgments in the Divisional Court are less than a model of clarity and the correctness of the Jeffrey v Black formulation was doubted as being too wide, i.e. that the right to search following arrest extended only to a search of the person of the arrestee and the premises where the arrest is made.[41]

That the common law governing search following arrest was in need of clarification is self-evident. Sporadic, ad hoc decision making, which turns on the facts of the case before the court is not the ideal way to develop coherent legal principles capable of application on a general basis and which are mindful both of the needs of law enforcement and of the protection of civil liberties. The Royal Commission on Criminal Procedure accepted that the power to search following arrest is necessary and that it should be placed on a statutory footing. With regard to searches of the person, the Commission, in line with the authorities cited earlier, agreed that they should not be applied routinely in every case but doubted "if it is practicable to lay down all encompassing guidelines on the circumstances in which people should or should not be deprived of their property or of articles of clothing which they might use to harm themselves or others or to effect an escape."[42] Strip-searching, described by the Commission as an "extreme and manifestly disagreeable form of search"[43] was accepted as being on occasion necessary, but in need of careful supervision. Where strip searches involved examination of intimate parts of the body, "they should be carried out only by a medical practitioner and only in respect of the most serious offences."[44] With regard to the searching of the premises of an arrested person, the Royal Commission noted the uncertainty of the present law and commented that because of the uncertainty, there is scope for abuse: "the police may be tempted to arrest someone on one charge in order to search his premises for evidence of some completely different offence."[45] Consequently, the Commission recommended that the power to search premises following arrest should be placed on a statutory basis and should be available where there are reasonable grounds to believe that there are on the premises occupied by or under the control of the arrested person, articles material to the offence for which the person has been

SEARCH AND SEIZURE

arrested or a similar offence.[46]

When we turn to the Police and Criminal Evidence Act, 1984, however, we find that there are significant differences between the powers it contains and the common law powers it replaces and between it and the recommendations of the Royal Commission, notwithstanding that in this respect, the Act purports to codify and clarify the law rather than to extend it. Under s. 32, where a person is arrested outside a police station, he may be searched if a police officer has reasonable grounds for believing that he may be a danger to himself or others. In addition, he may be searched for any article which he might use to assist his escape from police detention or for evidence relating to the offence for which he has been arrested, provided that in either case, a police officer has reasonable grounds for believing that the suspect has such an article concealed on his person. The Act expressly provides that a constable conducting a search under section 32 may use reasonable force if it is necessary to do so for the purposes of the search[47] and that relevant articles found during the search may be seized and retained,[48] but does not require that the arrested person be told why he is being searched. As under the pre-existing law, the statutory power to search the person following arrest applies to all arrest powers (and not just to arrestable offences) and its ambit is limited by the purposes for which the power can be properly exercised (purposes which are broadly in line with the common law as set out in Lindley v Rutter),[49] which are declared in the Act and subject to the requirement that reasonable grounds exist for believing that the suspect has relevant items about his person. If no such grounds exist, the carrying out of the search is unnecessary and unlawful. The Act also gives some guidance on the manner in which a search of the person following arrest should be carried out. This is important because the section 32 powers are powers to search outside the police station. They are limited in two ways. First, the Act provides that the power is only a power to search to the extent reasonably required for the purpose of discovering the article suspected to be concealed on the person. Secondly, in any event, in the exercise of the power a constable may require a suspect to remove in public only an outer coat, jacket or gloves.[50] The combination of these limitations makes it clear that s. 32 envisages and authorises only a relatively superficial search immediately following an arrest.

The Act draws a clear distinction beween

SEARCH AND SEIZURE

searches of the person of an arrested suspect in the street and searches of an arrestee after he has arrived at a police station.[51] The former search powers are relatively limited; the latter powers are appreciably more extensive and explicit provision is made for the taking of body samples and intimate body searches. It has already been pointed out that at common law, the <u>routine</u> searching of a suspect following arrest to ascertain the property in his possession almost certainly could not be legally justified. The Police and Criminal Evidence Act, 1984, now gives explicit authority to the custody officer at a police station to ascertain and record a prisoner's possessions.[52] More often than not, of course, a suspect will not be physically searched at this stage; rather, he will be invited to turn out his pockets. Where he refuses to co-operate with this request, the Act allows him to be searched (but only to the extent necessary for ascertaining his property) by a constable of the same sex.[53] Linked to the power of search is the power to seize and retain any property[54] which an arrested person has with him when he arrives at the police station.[55] Clothes and personal effects may be retained only where the custody officer believes, (the Act does not require that the belief must be based on reasonable grounds), that they may be used by the arrestee to injure himself or others, to damage property, interfere with evidence, or assist him in escaping from custody,[56] <u>or</u>, where there are reasonable grounds to believe that they are evidence of an offence committed by the arrestee or any other person.[57] Where property is seized under these provisions, the person from whom it is seized should normally be told the reason for the seizure.[58]

Here again, then, we see that the statutory powers go considerably further than those which pre-existed them. All prisoners can now quite lawfully be searched as a matter of routine. The extent and manner of the search will be governed not by a legal requirement of reasonableness, but by the custody officer's 'belief' that they may be used by the arrested person for one of the purposes specified in the Act. The seizure of evidentiary material must be justified upon reasonable grounds, but the right of seizure is not limited to evidence of the offence or offences for which the suspect has been arrested. <u>Any</u> evidentiary material may be seized. It need not implicate the suspect in any crime at all; it is sufficient if it implicates <u>somebody</u> in <u>some</u> crime. To some, such a power smacks of the <u>general</u> search

166

SEARCH AND SEIZURE

power outlawed in Entick v Carrington and is an inducement to 'fishing expeditions'.[59]   A contrary view is that if in the course of a search the police find evidence of a crime, it is an affront to justice and common sense to forbid them to seize it because society has an overriding interest in the detection of crime. It is this view which the statute endorses. Section 54 effectively provides that all arrested persons in custody in police stations will be searched and any evidentiary material found in the course of the search can lawfully be seized, whether it relates to the suspect or the offence for which he is arrested or not. It is submitted that the common law, quite properly, would not have sanctioned such an enormous extension of search powers consequent upon arrest.

The searching of the body's intimate cavities is not, it must be emphasised, a routine police procedure. However, for some objects, a body cavity can be a suitable place of concealment - the obvious examples are illicit drugs, stolen jewels, small weapons.[60] If it is conceded that for certain types of offences, an intimate body search might sometimes be necessary, the degree of intrusion and danger inherent in such searches, together with the humiliation and degradation which a suspect subjected to might suffer, indicate that intimate body searches should be rigorously regulated and controlled. The issue has been considered by law reform bodies in Australia and Canada. The Australian Law Reform Commission recommended that intrusive searches of the surface of the body or its cavities should be carried out only by a medical practitioner under the specific authority of a judicial order.[61] The Law Reform Commission of Canada similarly recommended that such searches should be subject to stringent controls: the power should be confined to specific serious offences; and the search should be authorised by a warrant naming the person to be searched and conducted only by a qualified medical practitioner in circumstances respectful of the privacy of the suspect.[62] The Royal Commission on Criminal Procedure, as we have seen, also recommended that limitations should be imposed by the law on intimate body searches, though they are not as stringent as those set out above. It proposed that they should be confined to 'grave' offences[63] and carried out by a medical practitioner, although it must be said that the Royal Commission's consideration of this aspect of search in its Report is scant.

The provisions governing intimate body searches

SEARCH AND SEIZURE

in the Act are loosely based on the recommendations of the Royal Commission, although they underwent considerable modification during the progress of the Bill through Parliament. By section 55, it is provided that an intimate search may only be conducted at a police station (unless it is a drugs search), a hospital, a medical practitioner's surgery or other place used for medical purposes. The purpose for which such a search may be conducted is more limited than the Royal Commission suggested though the power is not confined to serious or "grave" offences. An intimate search may be conducted only where a superintendent has reasonable grounds for believing either that the person to be searched may have concealed on him an article which could be used to cause injury to himself or others and which might be so used while he is in police detention or the custody of a court and that it cannot be found without an intimate search, or that such a person may have a Class A controlled drug concealed on him which he was in possession of with intent to supply to another or export with intent to evade a prohibition before his arrest.[64] It can immediately be seen, then, that the Act does not authorise intimate searches for general evidentiary purposes though such material may be seized and retained if the custody officer has reasonable grounds to believe that it may be evidence of an offence committed by any person.[65] Police practices prior to the Act by which intimate body searches would usually have been general evidentiary searches are now clearly unlawful. Drugs searches must be carried out by a suitably qualified person (i.e. a registered medical practitioner or a registered nurse) but regrettably, the Act does not require all intimate searches to be conducted by medically qualified persons, adopting instead a formula which allows a police officer of the same sex as the suspect[66] to carry out the search where a superintendent considers that examination by a medical practitioner "is not practicable".[67] By the nature of things, a suspect who has a weapon, (or anything else), concealed in a body orifice is unlikely to be able to extricate it without this being obvious to someone keeping observation. In these circumstances, therefore, the Act should have made it clear that intimate body searches should always be conducted by a medically qualified person.[68] Even with this safeguard, an intimate body search of a suspect who violently resisted it would have remained an extremely hazardous operation. The demands of both human dignity and safety should have ensured that the

168

SEARCH AND SEIZURE

untutored fumblings of a police constable to retrieve articles from within the private parts of another should in no circumstances have been sanctioned by the law.

It is assumed that where the police wish to search body orifices a suspect is first asked to consent to the search taking place. If the request is put in terms that "if you consent a doctor will do it, if you do not a police officer will," any consent given will hardly be freely obtained. This problem of consent is exacerbated by the fact that a suspect may well have been denied the opportunity to consult with his solicitor prior to the search taking place, bearing in mind that the Act sanctions police denial of access to a solicitor for up to 36 hours in certain classes of cases. Thus the pressure on a suspect to 'consent' to an intimate search is likely to be enormous.

Similar problems of principle are raised by the taking of body samples from suspects in police stations though here the provisions of the Act are more satisfactory. The Act distinguishes between intimate[69] and non-intimate body samples. The former may only be taken where the sample is authorised by a superintendent and the suspect consents to it.[70] In addition, an intimate sample may only be taken where the authorising officer has reasonable grounds to suspect the involvement of the prisoner in a serious arrestable offence and that the sample will tend to confirm or disprove his involvement.[71] The suspect from whom it is proposed to take the sample must be told the reason for it and the sample can only be taken from a person by a medical practitioner unless it is a sample of urine or saliva.[72] The requirement of consent is largely a concession to the practical difficulties inherent in taking such samples in the absence of consent. In the words of the Royal Commission:

> Physical compulsion is unlikely to be
> effective, because it is difficult to
> take such body samples from a person who
> is determined to resist, and the use of
> force is inherently objectionable.[73]

Indeed, the Royal Commission might have added that the taking of certain intimate body fluids would be impossible in the absence of consent.

The requirement that the suspect must consent to the taking of the sample does, of course, give rise to consequential difficulties. In all cases, the

SEARCH AND SEIZURE

need for an intimate body sample will be linked to the investigation of a serious offence, for example, an alleged rape, where a sample of blood or semen from the suspect could help to establish his guilt or innocence. If he refuses his consent the sample cannot be taken. In a case where there is other evidence implicating the suspect in a crime, this might not be of great significance, but it is possible to envisage circumstances where sample evidence could be crucial and in such cases, a guilty suspect might well see his interests best served by a refusal to co-operate. Accordingly, the Act provides that where a suspect refuses to provide an intimate sample without good cause a court may, in subsequent proceedings against him, draw such inferences from the refusal as appear proper and may treat the refusal as corroborating other evidence against him.[74] It is hoped that the courts apply this provision cautiously. In view of the nature of the procedures implicit in the taking of intimate samples, a refusal to co-operate will not necessarily indicate guilt.

We might also note that there is a degree of inconsistency between the approach of the legislation to the taking of intimate samples and its approach to intimate searches. If the major reason for the requirement of consent in the former case is, as suggested by the Royal Commission, the difficulty of taking such a sample from a non-consenting suspect, it surely equally applies to the conducting of an intimate body search upon a suspect who resists it.

With regard to non-intimate body samples - the obvious samples are nail scrapings or samples of hair - the Act provides that they may be taken from a suspect without his consent if (1) he has been arrested and is in police detention; (2) a superintendent authorises the taking of the sample; (3) the authorising officer has reasonable grounds for suspecting the involvement of the suspect in a serious arrestable offence; and (4) he has reasonable grounds for believing that the sample will tend to confirm or disprove his involvement.

The confused state of the common law governing search of private premises upon arrest, together with the recommendations of the Royal Commission were noted earlier. The Act approaches the problem of granting to the police rights to search premises both upon arrest and after arrest. By section 32, a constable may search any premises in which a person was "when arrested or immediately before he

170

SEARCH AND SEIZURE

was arrested for evidence relating to the offence for which he has been arrested," provided that he has reasonable grounds for believing that there is such evidence on the premises. The provision is in terms which are narrower than those adopted by the Divisional Court in Jeffrey v Black though it should be noted that the premises which can be the subject of the search need not necessarily be premises owned by or under the control of the arrestee. The section permits the search of "any premises" and that phrase is unqualified. Thus, where a suspect is arrested in premises which are not his own, those premises may be searched provided, and it is an extremely important proviso, that there are reasonable grounds to believe that evidence of the offence for which the suspect has been arrested will be found on the premises. It is also clear from the provision that a suspect's own premises can only be searched, under section 32, if they are the premises where he was when or immediately before he was arrested. Where premises are searched under this section, the search must be no more extensive than is reasonably required for the purpose of discovering such evidence.[75]

The power to seize evidentiary material found in the course of an authorised search of premises is appended not to section 32, but is found in the general power of seizure contained in section 19 of the Act. Under this, a constable who is lawfully searching any premises may seize anything[76] if he has reasonable grounds for believing that it is evidence of an offence and that it is necessary to seize it in order to prevent its concealment, loss or destruction.

The right to search after arrest is confined to cases where a suspect is in "police detention" for an arrestable offence. The term, "police detention" would appear simply to mean in lawful police custody. Under this power, a suspect arrested for an arrestable offence may have "any premises occupied or controlled" by him searched by a police constable even if he was not arrested at those premises, provided that the constable has reasonable grounds for suspecting that there is evidence on the premises which relates to the offence for which he was arrested or to "some other arrestable offence connected with or similar to that offence."[77] Such searches generally must be authorised by an inspector (and though the Act does not expressly say so, presumably such authorisation can be given prior to the arrest taking place), though a constable may conduct a search of premises under this provision on

171

SEARCH AND SEIZURE

his own authority, before taking the person to a police station, if he decides that this is "necessary for the effective investigation of the offence."[78]

The express limitation that the power "is only a power to search to the extent that is reasonably required for the purpose of discovering such evidence,"[79] is an attempt to control the manner and extensiveness of the search. It will not always be reasonable to search the entire premises, neither will it be reasonable in many cases to lift floor-coverings or floor boards, to inspect private papers or break into locked cupboards. Whether such actions are reasonable in the particular circumstances will be determined ultimately by a court, (provided, of course, that the search is challenged), and as a finding that a search was unreasonably extensive renders it unlawful, the reasonableness requirement is an important limitation upon the manner of the exercise of the power. But, despite this limitation, section 18 remains a wide power because of the ambiguity inherent in the formulation adopted to define the purpose of the search. When is an offence "connected with or similar to" the offence for which the arrest was made? If a suspect is arrested for theft of money, his premises clearly can be searched for evidence of that theft, but if he is in possession of the proceeds of the theft when arrested, can his premises be searched for evidence which implicates another person in that theft or which implicates the arrestee in other arrestable offences? Is an offence "connected with" the offence for which a suspect is arrested, simply because the police believe the suspect to have committed it? In other words, if the only "connection" between a range of totally disparate offences is that the police believe on reasonable grounds that the suspect has committed all of them, can his premises be searched in order to find the evidence which implicates him and third parties in them? The answer is not clear but if it is in the affirmative, then the Act grants a very broad power of search indeed.

(b) Under Warrant

Although a number of Commonwealth countries have for many years possessed legislation containing general powers to issue search warrants for a wide range of criminal offences, until the passing of the Police and Criminal Evidence Act, 1984, English legislation conferred only specific warrant granting powers, that is to say, the power to issue warrants

172

SEARCH AND SEIZURE

was granted on a haphazard basis in specific legislation for specific offences. Unless a statute expressly sanctioned the issuing of a search warrant, one could not be obtained however serious the offence under investigation. An extremely important and controversial consequence of this was the gradual judicial expansion of common law powers of search to fill in the legislative gaps, a process which reached its nadir with the decision of the Court of Appeal in Ghani v Jones.[80]

While the procedures for the obtaining of search warrants were not uniform, the usual model was for a constable to place before a magistrate a written "information" disclosing reasonable grounds for suspecting that particular evidence would be found on specified premises. The issuing of the warrant was thus, an act done by a magistrate in his judicial capacity and the purpose of his involvement in the procedure was (and continues to be), that the detached judgment of an independent officer should determine whether reasonable grounds exist to justify the invasion of personal liberty which the issue of a warrant necessarily entails. It is not surprising, in the light of this, that those statutes which allow a police officer, usually a superintendent, to give written authority for a search should be the subject of criticism.[81] A police officer, however elevated his rank, is hardly neutral or detached from the processes of investigation. But the part played by magistrates in the warrant procedures has also occasionally come under attack. It is sometimes suggested that magistrates do not always bring to bear upon warrant applications an independent judgment: that they give them only a cursory examination and are all too ready to go along with police requests. One consequence of this may be that a magistrate who has shown himself to be diligent in the examination of warrant applications will not be popular with the police and will be avoided by them when warrants are needed.

Nevertheless, it cannot be denied that the prior authorisation of a judicial officer is normally regarded as an important safeguard in the investigation process. The Royal Commission on Criminal Procedure recognised this[82] and recommended that certain improvements should be made to the procedures for the issue of warrants to provide more effective control and monitoring of their use. Most of these have been incorporated into the Police and Criminal Evidence Act which now provides a comprehensive procedural code for the issue of search warrants

173

SEARCH AND SEIZURE

irrespective of the enactment under which the warrant is obtained.[83] Under it, a constable must apply for a warrant in writing specifying the ground on which the application is made, the statutory authority under which the warrant would be issued, the premises to be searched and the articles (or persons) sought.[84] The magistrate or judge to whom the application is made is entitled to question the constable, who will answer any such questions under oath.[85] Where a warrant is issued, it must contain the name of the person who applied for it, the date of issue, the enactment under which it is issued, details of the premises to be searched and the items for which it is proposed to search.[86] When executing it, a constable is entitled to use reasonable force[87] and is required to execute it "at a reasonable hour" unless it appears to the officer concerned that "the purpose of the search will be frustrated on an entry at a reasonable hour."[88] The Act also contains provisions requiring a copy of the warrant to be supplied to the occupier or other person in control of the premises or to be left in a prominent place on the premises where no person appears to be in charge of them.[89] The warrant authorises entry on one occasion only[90] and this must take place within one month of the date of its issue.[91] After execution,[92] it must be returned to the appropriate court authorities,[93] where it will be retained for twelve months and may be inspected at any time during this period by the occupier of the premises to which it relates.[94]

These provisions go a substantial way to meeting the criticisms made about warrants previously, which centred not so much on the extent of warrant granting powers, but upon the manner of their execution and disparate nature. A uniformly applicable procedure has now been introduced which will provide a firmer basis both for evaluating warrant requests and accumulating statistical information about the use of warrants. The combination of these factors should render the monitoring of the use of search warrants by issuing authorities and central institutions alike, more easily achievable. In addition, some of the provisions, particularly those which exhort the execution of the warrant at reasonable hours and that search under warrant should be limited to the extent required for the purpose for which the warrant was issued,[95] may meet, in part, the criticism that "entry under warrant is used as a pretext for the ransacking of premises for any evidence,"[96] though it must be said that the wide

174

SEARCH AND SEIZURE

provisions in the Act relating to seizure during the course of a lawful search,[97] weaken their impact.

Apart from laying down a uniform procedure for the obtaining and execution of warrants, the Act also contains important new warrant granting powers. There is a general power reposed in magistrates to issue search warrants,[98] where on application by a constable, they are satisfied that a serious arrestable offence has been committed and that there is material, on the premises to be searched which is likely to be both relevant evidence[99] and of substantial value to the investigation of the offence. In addition, the issuing magistrate must be satisfied that any of the following conditions apply:[100] that it is not practicable to communicate with any person entitled to grant entry to the premises or access to the evidence; that entry will not be granted unless a warrant is produced; or that the purpose of a search may be frustrated or seriously prejudiced unless a constable arriving at the premises can secure immediate entry to them. Such a power raises important and controversial issues. It will be noted that a warrant can be issued under this provision even though no person has been arrested or charged or indeed, even though there is no suspect as such. It is a power, therefore, which permits a general search of premises for evidence where a serious arrestable offence has been, or is reasonably believed to have been committed. An evidentiary search in these circumstances is vastly different from a search conducted with or without warrant where a suspect has been charged with a specific offence. In the latter case, the enquiry is no longer at large and the police investigation will concentrate on accumulating admissible evidence for production at trial. Where no-one has been arrested or charged, however, and where it may not be certain that any crime has in fact been committed, the granting of a warrant to search for evidence significantly extends the ability of the police to intrude into the private or business lives of citizens. On the other hand, it must be conceded that the pre-existing law in this area gave rise to anomalies, occasionally was a serious impediment to investigations into serious crimes and encouraged the police to resort to subterfuge where the consent of the occupier of premises to a search was not forthcoming. Striking the right balance between the legitimate needs of law enforcement and the protection of individual liberties in circumstances such as these is by no means an easy task and the problem is exacerbated

SEARCH AND SEIZURE

where the items of potential evidential value consist, for instance, of confidential documents.

The Royal Commission on Criminal Procedure recommended that a compulsory power of search for evidence of a confidential nature should be introduced into the law because "where property or information is held on a confidential basis the holders may be unwilling to disclose it for fear of being sued for breach of duty by the person from whom he received it" and "where consent is not immediately forthcoming there may be some temptation for the police to resort to bluff or trickery to obtain the evidence."[101] The Royal Commission further recommended, however, that it should be "a limited power and one subject to stringent safeguards."[102] Accordingly, it suggested a two stage procedure for access to such evidence which would be available only in respect of "grave" offences. The first stage would be an application to a circuit judge for an order of the court addressed to the person in possession of the evidence requiring him to allow access to it. If, following the granting of the order, access should be refused, the second stage would be the issuing of a warrant to search for and seize the evidence. The Police and Criminal Evidence Act builds upon these recommendations and introduces an elaborate new procedure for gaining access to "excluded material" and "special procedure material." By s. 9(1), a constable may only gain access to such material in accordance with the provisions of the Act and s. 9(2) provides that any Act passed before the Police and Criminal Evidence Act which authorised the issue of a search warrant shall cease to have effect so far as it relates to the authorisation of searches for items subject to legal privilege, excluded material or special procedure material. It is clear from section 9, therefore, that "items subject to legal privilege", which the Act defines broadly to include most communications between a professional legal adviser and his client, cannot be searched for under these provisons provided that they are not items held with the intention of furthering a criminal purpose (in which case they would no longer be privileged) and are in the possession of a person entitled to possession of them.[103]

"Excluded material" covers personal records acquired or created in the course of any trade, business profession or occupation and held in confidence; human tissue or tissue fluid held in confidence and taken for the purposes of diagnosis or medical treatment; and journalistic material held in

176

SEARCH AND SEIZURE

confidence.[104] The term "personal records" covers documentary records concerning an individual, who can be identified from them, relating to his mental or physical health, or spiritual or personal welfare.[105] "Journalistic material" means material acquired for the purposes of journalism provided that the material is held in confidence and is in the possession of the person who acquired or created it.[106] It can be seen, then, that the category of excluded material covers a wide range of confidential documentary material of potential evidentiary value including, for instance reports compiled by the probationary or social services, medical records, communications between priests and parishioners, certain kinds of employment records and information communicated to journalists in confidence.

"Special procedure material" is material other than items subject to legal privilege and excluded material, which is held subject to an undertaking to hold it in confidence and which is in the possession of a person who acquired or created it in the course of his trade, business profession or occupation, together with journalistic material which does not fall within the category of excluded material.[107]

Where the police wish to gain access to excluded or special procedure material, they must apply to a circuit judge who must be satisfied that one or other of the sets of "access conditions" is fulfilled. Under the first set, there must be reasonable grounds for believing that a serious arrestable offence has been committed and that there is special procedure material on the premises it is desired to search which is not only likely to be relevant (i.e. admissible) evidence, but also is likely to be of substantial value to the investigation. In addition the judge must be satisfied that other methods of obtaining the special procedure material (for example, by seeking the voluntary co-operation of the person in possession of it) have been tried without success or have not been tried because it appeared that they were bound to fail and that it is in the public interest that the material should be produced.[108] The second set of access conditions relates to the obtaining both of special procedure material and excluded material. They are fulfilled if there are reasonable grounds for believing that there is such material on the premises specified in the application, that a search warrant could have been issued under some other enactment were it not for the provisions of section 9(2), and that the issue of a warrant would have been appropriate.[109]

177

SEARCH AND SEIZURE

Where a judge makes an order under these provisions, its effect is to require the person in possession of the material to allow the police access to it. If the order is not complied with within the specified period (normally seven days) the judge is empowered not only to issue a search warrant[110] but also to deal with the non-compliance as a contempt of court.[111] However, because an application for an access order must be made inter partes, the person against whom the order is sought is entitled to defend the application and argue that the order should not be granted because, for example, the special procedure material will not be relevant evidence or of substantial value to the investigation, or because the public interest does not require the production of the material. It should also be noted that whereas special procedure material can be inspected if either of the sets of access conditions is fulfilled, excluded material can only be ordered to be made available for inspection where the second set of conditions is satisfied. These do not expressly require that the police must suspect that a serious arrestable offence has been committed, although the provision that it must be possible to obtain a search warrant under "an enactment other than this schedule"[112] - for example, the search warrant powers granted by s. 8 of the 1984 Act itself - will tend to mean that for practical pruposes, excluded material will be made available mainly in relation to serious offences.

It is important to emphasise that these access orders do represent a significant extension to police powers. As has already been noted, the pre-existing law did not provide a general power to conduct evidentiary searches in the absence of arrest or charge. The safeguards built into the procedures, particularly the requirement that application must be made inter partes to a circuit judge are, however, considerable and achieve an acceptable balance between the legitimate needs of law enforcement and the protection of individuals from unwarranted intrusions into their private lives.

Seizure

The issue of what goods or items the police may seize when they are lawfully on private premises has long been one of the most perplexing and controversial questions in the law relative to police powers. Early case-law dealing with what may properly be seized under the authority of a search warrant

SEARCH AND SEIZURE

provided a restricted answer - only those items specified in the warrant could be seized.[113] Gradually, however, this strict view was relaxed[114] and in 1968, the Court of Appeal ruled in Chic Fashions (West Wales) v Jones[115] that where the police entered private premises to search for stolen goods, they could lawfully seize not only the items specified in the warrant, but also any other items found during the course of the search which were reasonably believed to be stolen and material evidence in respect of the crime for which they entered. A year later, in Ghani v Jones,[116] Lord Denning MR felt able to "take it as settled law without citing cases" that where police officers entered private premises by virtue of a search warrant or following a lawful arrest they were "entitled to take any goods which they find in the suspect's possession or in his house which they reasonably believe to be material evidence in relation to the crime for which he is arrested or for which they enter. If in the course of their search they come on any other goods which show him to be implicated in some other crime, they may take them provided they act reasonably, and detain them no longer than is necessary."[117]

With this massive extension of the common law under its belt, the Court of Appeal went on to sanction another. Where police officers were lawfully on private premises, even though no search warrant had been granted and no-one had been arrested or charged, they were entitled to seize items from those premises provided that certain conditions were satisfied. Lord Denning MR enumerated the conditions as follows:[118]

1. The police officers must have reasonable grounds to believe that a serious offence has been committed.
2. The police must have reasonable grounds for believing that the article in question is either the fruit of the crime, or is the instrument by which the crime was committed or is material evidence to prove the commission of the crime.
3. The police must have reasonable grounds to believe that the person in possession of it has himself committed the crime or is implicated in it or at any rate his refusal must be quite unreasonable.
4. The police must not keep the item any longer than is reasonably necessary.
5. The lawfulness of the conduct of the police must

179

SEARCH AND SEIZURE

be judged at the time and not by what happens afterwards.

The Court of Appeal had thus contrived in one fell swoop not only virtually to reintroduce the general warrant but had also asserted the entirely novel principle that private property could lawfully be seized by the police in the absence of an arrest or warrant.
The cases following Ghani v Jones tended to endorse Lord Denning's view of the law[119] though in Wershof v Metropolitan Police Commissioner, May J. commented that the guidelines should not be construed "as if they were the words of a statute. They are objective guidelines which a court should follow to assist it in balancing the freedom of the individual against the interests of society..."[120]
Both the guidelines and the sweeping nature of the Court of Appeal's decision were subjected to severe criticism. The decision endangered private property and needlessly extended police powers.[121] It was "unprecedented" and "repellent" and swept away the limitations contained in statutes authorising search warrants.[122] It "connive[d] at trespass and overbearing conduct by police officers."[123] The guidelines were "full of serious uncertainties"[124] and "imprecisely worded and general."[125] The controversy was no less muted in the Commonwealth as some courts endorsed[126] the Ghani v Jones line of reasoning while others resoundingly rejected it.[127] The Royal Commission on Criminal procedure was given an excellent opportunity to recommend that the balance be redressed in favour of individual freedom. It clearly was not oblivious to this storm of criticism because it commented "the risk that premises may be ransacked as soon as a warrant is granted in respect of any offence must be minimised"[128] but the weight of this statement was counter-balanced by the further comment that "it defies common sense to expect the police not to seize...items incidentally found during the course of a search."[129] In the tradition of all the best committees, the Royal Commission accordingly recommended a compromise solution. Where the police enter private premises under the authority of a search warrant, they should be entitled to seize not only the items specified in the warrant but also any other items which are evidence of the commission of a "grave" offence, if they could have obtained a warrant to search for them.[130] A similar approach was recommended with regard to warrantless

180

SEARCH AND SEIZURE

searches.[131]
When we turn to the Police and Criminal Evidence Act, however, we find a general power of seizure granted in terms even wider than those adumbrated by the Court of Appeal in Ghani v Jones. By s. 19(1) of the Act a power of seizure is granted to any constable "who is lawfully on any premises". In other words, the power is available whether the constable is on the premises to execute a search or arrest warrant, to execute an arrest without warrant, or simply on a routine visit with the consent of the occupier. The only requirement is that his presence on the premises, for whatever purposes, should be lawful. Assuming this to be the case, he is entitled to seize "anything which is on the premises if he has reasonable ground for believing that it has has been obtained in consequence of the commission of an offence and that it is necessary to seize it to prevent its concealment, loss, damage, alteration or destruction."[132] This, then, is a power to seize anything which the constable has reasonable grounds to believe to be the fruits or proceeds of any crime committed by anybody. In addition he may seize any other item which he has reasonable grounds for believing to be evidence relating to the offence which he is investigating or any other offence if he reasonably believes such seizure to be necessary to prevent its concealment, loss etc.[133] Again, the breadth of this provision is only apparent when it is realised that the evidentiary material seized need not implicate the occupier of the premises in any crime at all. These seizure powers are "in addition to any powers otherwise conferred".[134] Items subject to legal privilege cannot be seized under these provisions;[135] whether excluded or special procedure material can be is not clear.

Section 9(1) provides that a constable may obtain access to excluded or special procedure material for the purposes of a criminal investigation by making an application under Schedule 1. This obviously means that where a constable wishes to enter premises for the purpose of gaining access to such material, he must make a section 9 application. This view is supported by the wording of section 9 (2), which effectively provides that a warrant to search specifically for special procedure or excluded material cannot be granted under any other enactment. So, where the police have reasonable grounds to suspect that relevant special procedure material is located on private premises, but the occupier will not allow entry on to them and the

181

SEARCH AND SEIZURE

police cannot demand entry because, for example, no offence other than that to which the special procedure material relates appears to have been committed, a section 9 application will have to be made. Suppose, however, that a constable who is lawfully on private premises for other purposes - searching under a warrant issued in connection with completely separate matters or simply there with the consent of the occupier - inadvertently discovers special procedure or excluded material. Is he entitled to seize it under section 19? If the answer is in the affirmative, it renders the section 9 procedure optional and the schedule 1 safeguards nugatory, but on the basis that the section 19 powers are expressly made additional to any power otherwise conferred, it would appear that the answer may well be, yes.

There is no doubt, however, about the effect of section 19 on the other search powers contained in the Act. Section 8, as we have seen, purports to limit what may be seized under a search warrant issued in connection with a serious arrestable offence to material which is likely to be both relevant evidence and of substantial value to the investigation of the offence, i.e. the offence in connection with which the warrant was issued. If, while lawfully searching in accordance with section 8, police officers discover anything which appears either, to have been obtained in consequence of any offence or, which appears to be evidence of any offence, it may be lawfully seized under section 19. The same is true in the case of those provisions in the Act which authorise the search of premises upon or after arrest; they define what may be seized restrictively, but section 19 has the effect of removing the restrictions. The Royal Commission recommendation that items extraneous to the investigation of the crime for which the police entered should be seizable only if a warrant could have been obtained to seize them, has thus been jettisoned. Indeed, it can be argued that section 19 renders the search warrant provisions in the Act largely otiose. There is no need to obtain a warrant at all provided that the police can persuade an occupier voluntarily to grant access to his premises - once lawfully upon them, section 19 appears to authorise seizure of his (or anybody else's) property in very wide terms indeed. The ruling in Ghani v Jones has thus been given the legislative imprimatur, but the much criticised Denning guidelines, which limited its ambit, have

SEARCH AND SEIZURE

not been enacted and police powers of seizure have thereby been considerably extended.

Unlawfully Obtained Evidence and Admissibility

The preceding discussion leads naturally on to the issue of the admissibility of evidence obtained as a result of unlawful police behaviour, because the more widely drawn are police powers to obtain evidence, the more difficult it is to establish that it has been obtained unlawfully. One way of encouraging the police to remain within the four corners of their powers is to adapt a rule which says that where they do not, any evidence obtained as a consequence of their illegitimate actions will automatically be inadmissible in evidence at a subsequent trial. Such a rule has never been embraced by the common law in this country, though in the United States of America, the "exclusionary" rule has a lengthy history.

There it derives from the Constitution, the Fourth amendment of which has been interpreted by the Supreme Court to require the suppression of all evidence obtained in violation of it.[136] The rule is applied strictly and operates to exclude _all_ unlawfully obtained evidence, whatever the nature of the illegality. The purpose of the rule is twofold: to deter unlawful police activity[137] and to preserve judicial integrity. This latter purpose means that the judges cannot be seen to condone, by admitting unlawfully obtained evidence, breaches of the Constitution which it is their duty to uphold.[138] Whether the rule actually deters unlawful police conduct is not clear: violations of the Fourth Amendment are still commonplace in the United States, though, of course, it can be argued that they would be even more prevalent were it not for the exclusionary rule.

In England, the early case-law unequivocally stated that the sole criterion of admissibility was whether the evidence was relevant to guilt or innocence. This attitude was summed up by the uncompromising statement of Crompton, J. in R v Leathem: "It matters not how you get it; if you steal it even, it would be admissible."[139] In more recent times, a series of decisions in the appellate courts asserted the existence of a judicial discretion to exclude otherwise admissible evidence which had been obtained unfairly, oppressively or by trickery.[140] In R v Sang,[141] however, in 1979, the House of Lords denied the existence of any such

183

SEARCH AND SEIZURE

judicial discretion specifically related to the
admissibility of illegally obtained evidence, other
than self-incriminatory statements. The only
discretion which a trial judge possesses in this
regard derives from his duty to ensure that a
defendant has a fair trial. In the performance of
this duty the judge may exclude evidence which would
have "a prejudicial influence on the minds of the
jury that would be out of proportion to its true
evidential value".[142] This is not a rule about
searches and seizures or about unlawfully obtained
evidence. It is a general rule which applies to all
evidence.

The Royal Commission on Criminal Procedure,
perhaps predictably, came down against the automatic
exclusion of unlawfully obtained evidence. After a
brief consideration of the American exclusionary
rule, the Commission concluded that "the United
States experience does not offer an encouraging
prospect of an automatic exclusionary rule achieving
the objectives its proponents set for it here."[143]
It would give rise to an increase in disputes about
the admissibility of evidence and thus increase
trial time and cost and could lead to the patently
guilty going free because of some minor procedural
technicality.[144] Its detailed proposals related to
evidence obtained from a suspect in custody in
breach of the new Code of Practice on the treatment
of suspects in custody and the issue of the admissibility of evidence obtained in consequence of
unlawful police behaviour prior to the time when a
suspect enters police custody was left at large.

The Police and Criminal Evidence Bill, at one
stage on its journey through Parliament, adopted a
"reverse onus exclusionary rule" similar to that
recommended by the Australian Law Reform Commission
in 1975,[145] and operated by Scottish courts since at
least 1950.[146] Under it, evidence (other than
confession evidence) obtained improperly would have
been excluded unless (a) the prosecution proved to
the court beyond reasonable doubt that it was
obtained lawfully; or (b) anything improperly done
in obtaining it was of no material significance in
all the circumstances of the case and ought therefore to be disregarded; or (c) the court is
satisfied that the public interest in the fair
administration of the criminal law required the
evidence to be admitted having regard to its
probative value, the gravity of the offence charged
and the circumstances in which the evidence was
obtained. The result would have been a compromise

184

SEARCH AND SEIZURE

between the extremes of automatic inclusion and automatic exclusion. Before exercising its discretion to admit improperly obtained evidence a court would have been compelled to weigh in the balance a wide range of factors, but the spectre of the patently guilty escaping conviction because of some minor or technical infraction of the law, always a prime argument of opponents of exclusion, would have receded. Regrettably, this clause did not survive the passage of the Bill through Parliament. It was replaced, in the House of Lords, by the provision ultimately enacted as section 78 which provides that evidence (other than confession evidence) may be excluded by a court if "having regard to all the circumstances, including the circumstances in which the evidence was obtained, the admission of the evidence would have such an adverse effect on the fairness of the proceedings that court ought not to admit it." The effect of the provision is essentially to restore the ruling in Sang. Evidence may properly be admitted by a court, however it was obtained, unless to do so would be "unfair" to an accused in all the circumstances. The Act gives no guidance as to how the discretion is to be used or on what unfair means in this context.

Nevertheless, a statutory rule, produced after due consideration in Parliament, is probably preferable to a judicially developed regime in which the wider requirements of public policy may not have been adequately considered. Section 78 is however vague and will almost certainly occasion much litigation, which in turn, will result in a considerable judicial gloss upon its wording. Most seriously of all, it fails to recognise that the search for truth in our criminal justice system ought not to be allowed to overshadow entirely the equally compelling public interest in the protection of the individual against the excesses of the executive.

Notes

1. Polvios G. Polviou, Search and Seizure, (Duckworth, London, 1982), at p. 271.

2. For a good example, see Morris v Beardmore, (1980), 2 A11 E.R. 753.

3. A wide range of public officials are statutorily entitled to enter private premises. See Royal Commission on Criminal Procedure, Law and

SEARCH AND SEIZURE

Procedure, Vol. 1, Appendix 4 (Cmnd. 8092-1), for a full list.

4. (1765), 19 State Trials 1029. See also Leach v Money, (1765), 19 State Trials 1001.

5. Ibid., at p. 1066.

6. Lord Camden's words were described by Salmon L.J. as "both archaic and anachronistic" in Chic Fashions (West Wales) Ltd. v Jones, (1968), 2 Q.B. 299, 319.

7. Though in Inland Revenue Commissioners v Rossminster Ltd., (1980), 1 A11 E.R. 80, the House of Lords did not find "18th century precedents and references to general warrants," helpful. See particularly the speech of Lord Wilberforce at p. 82.

8. A good example is provided by the judgment of Lord Denning MR in Ghani v Jones, (1970), 1 QB 673.

9. Consent having been withdrawn, the officer must be given reasonable time to leave the premises, Robson v Hallett, (1967), 2 A11 E.R. 407. On the general principle, see Davis v Lisle, (1936), 2 KB 434; Kay v Hibbert, (1977), Crim. L.R. 226; R v Waterfield, (1963), 3 A11 E.R. 659; Morris v Beardmore, op. cit.

10. The power to enter to prevent a breach of the peace is particularly associated with the case of Thomas v Sawkins, (1935), 2 KB 249, though it clearly derives from the general duty of police officers to prevent breaches of the peace adumbrated in Humphries v Connor, (1864), 17 Ir. CLR. 1. The judgments of the Divisional Court in Thomas v Sawkins, are both cursory and unclear and have long been the subject of criticism. See, e.g. A.L. Goodhart in (1936-38), CLJ 22 and D.G.T. Williams, Keeping the Peace, (Hutchinson, London, 1967), pp. 142-149.

11. See R v Walker, (1854), Dears CC 358; R v Marsden, (1868), LR 1CCR 131.

12. See Genner v Sparkes, (1704), 1 Salk 79.

13. Burdett v Abbott. (1811), 14 East 1.

14. Report of the Royal Commission on Criminal Procedure, Cmnd. 8092, (Jan. 1981), para 3.38.

15. Police and Criminal Evidence Act, 1984, (hereafter PCE Act 1984), s. 17(6).

16. See Royal Commission on Criminal Procedure, Law and Procedure, Vol. 1, op. cit., Appendix 5.

17. Usually these are issued by magistrates. Exceptionally, they must be obtained from a High Court or Circuit judge. Some statutes permit a police superintendent to grant written authority for a search.

186

SEARCH AND SEIZURE

18. Royal Commission on Criminal Procedure, op. cit., para. 3-35. See also Royal Commission on Criminal Procedure, Law and Procedure, Vol. 1, op. cit., Appendix 7.

19. The Theft Act, 1968 thus places on a statutory basis the ruling in Chic Fashions (West Wales) v Jones, op. cit.

20. Arguably, the right to enter only applies where the wanted person is known to be on the premises. See Lavrock v Brown, (1819), 2 B & Ald. 592, and Royal Commission on Criminal Procedure, Law and Procedure, Vol. 1, op. cit., para. 37.

21. Supra, n. 2.

22. Ibid., at p. 757.

23. PCE Act 1984, ss. 17(1) and (2). The concept of the arrestable offence, originally introduced into the law by the Criminal Law Act 1967, has been expanded by the PCE Act 1984. See the discussion in Chapter 4.

24. Ibid., ss. 8(1), 17(1)(a)(i) and 17(1)(a)(ii) respectively. A warrant of commitment is an order made by a court committing to prison a person who has defaulted on the payment of a sum adjudged to be payable by a court following conviction. The s. 17(1)(a)(ii) power relates to warrants of commitment issued under s. 76 of the Magistrates Courts Act, 1980.

25. Ibid., s. 17(1)(b).

26. The offences specified are offences under s. 1 (prohibition of political uniforms), s.4 (prohibition of offensive weapons at public meetings and processions), s. 5 (prohibition of conduct conducive to breaches of the peace) of the Public Order Act, 1936, and offences under ss. 6, 7, 8, 10 of the Criminal Law Act 1977, (offences relating to entering and remaining on property). See PCE Act 1984, ss. 17(1)(c)(i) and (ii).

27. PCE Act, 1984, s. 17(1)(a).

28. Ibid., s. 17(1)(c).

29. Ibid., s. 18(1).

30. Such searches are not commonplace. A classic example is provided by the American case of Rochin v California, (1952), 342 U.S. 165, where a suspect was taken to hospital and his stomach pumped (against his will) in order to retrieve prohibited drugs swallowed by him immediately prior to his arrest. The Supreme Court held that the evidence so obtained was inadmissible, the method used to obtain it being "close to the rack and the screw".

31. The clearest judicial statement favouring this view is to be found in the weighty New Zealand

SEARCH AND SEIZURE

authority of Barnett and Grant v Campbell, (1902), NZLR 484, 493 per Cooper J.: "The right to a personal search is clearly dependant not upon the right to arrest, but the fact of arrest and that at the time of the search the person is in custodia legis". This is also the position in Scotland, see Adair v McGarry, (1933), JC 72 and McGovern v H.M. Advocate, (1950), JC 33.

32. See e.g. Horridge J. in Elias v Pasmore, (1934), 2 KB 164 at 169.

33. See Leigh v Cole, (1853), 6 Cox C.C. 329, "the searching of a person must depend upon all the circumstances of the case," per Vaughan Williams, J. at p. 332. See also Bessell v Wilson, (1853), 17 JP 52.

34. (1980), 3 WLR 660.

35. Ibid., at p. 665.

36. (1983), 3 A11 E.R. 537.

37. See also R v Naylor, (1979), Crim. L.R. 532, which adopts the same view and refers to the right to search on arrest as "a very limited one".

38. (1947), AC 573.

39. (1970), 1 QB 693.

40. (1978), 1 A11 E.R. 555.

41. Polyvios G. Polyviou, Search and Seizure, supra n. 1 at p. 300. Dr. Polyviou, in his excellent work, concedes, however, that there is no judicial authority for this view.

42. Royal Commission on Criminal Procedure, op. cit., para. 3.117.

43. Ibid., para. 3.118.

44. Ibid.

45. Ibid., para. 3.119.

46. Ibid., para. 3.121.

47. PCE Act, 1984, s. 117.

48. Ibid., ss. 32(8) and (9). Under these powers, a constable may not seize any item subject to legal privilege. By s. 22(1), anything seized may be retained as long as necessary. Where evidence of an offence is seized, it may be retained (a) for use as evidence at a trial, (b) for forensic or other examination, (c) in order to establish its owner, s. 22(2). Any other articles seized in accordance with s. 32 should not be retained where a suspect is no longer in custody or has been released on bail (s. 22(3)).

49. Supra n.4.

50. It is interesting that the list does not include headwear.

51. Or where the arrest takes place in a police station.

188

SEARCH AND SEIZURE

52. PCE Act, 1984, s. 54(1).
53. Ibid., ss. 54(6), (9).
54. With the exception of items subject to legal privilege.
55. PCE Act, 1984, s. 54(3).
56. Ibid., s. 54(4)(a).
57. s. 54(4)(b). Once again, limitations on the right of retention are set out in the Act as are the purposes for which retained items may be used. See s. 22 generally.
58. s. 54(5).
59. This view was expressed by Lord Denning MR in Ghani v Jones, op. cit., at 706.
60. During the House of Commons Committee stages on the first Police and Criminal Evidence Bill, it was suggested that other items, such as listening devices, miniaturised detonators and transmittors could also be orifice concealed.
61. Australian Law Reform Commission, Criminal Investigation, (Report No. 2), 1975 p. 58. The recommendations were implemented in the Customs Amendment Act, 1979.
62. Law Reform Commission of Canada, Working Paper 30 (1983), Search and Seizure in Criminal Law Enforcement, p. 227.
63. Murder, manslaughter, grievous bodily harm, armed robbery, kidnapping, rape, arson, causing explosions, counterfeiting, corruption, burglary, theft and frauds (where large sums of money are involved), the supply, importation or exportation of controlled drugs, perversion of the course of justice, blackmail (and attempts and conspiracies to commit any of the above offences). See Royal Commission on Criminal Procedure, op. cit., para. 3.7.
64. PCE Act, 1984, ss. 55(1), 55(17).
65. Ibid., s. 55(12)(b).
66. Ibid., ss. 55(6), (7).
67. s. 55(5).
68. During the debates on the first Police and Criminal Evidence Bill, the British Medical Association published a statement to the effect that for doctors to carry out coercive body searches would be unethical and that they would be likely to refuse to do so. The B.M.A. has now apparently relaxed this attitude.
69. Intimate sample is defined in the Act as a sample of blood, semen or any other tissue fluid, urine, saliva, pubic hair or a swab taken from the genital or rectal area of a person's body. See. s. 65.

189

SEARCH AND SEIZURE

70. PCE Act, 1984, s. 62(1). Special provision is made for the taking of such a sample from children and young persons. The parents or guardian of a child under the age of fourteen years must consent to the taking of the sample. Between the ages of fourteen and seventeen, the consent of both the young person and the parents or guardian is required. See s. 65.

71. Ibid., s. 62(2). The concept of the serious arrestable offence is discussed in Chapter 4, ante.

72. Ibid., ss. 62(5) and 62(9) respectively.

73. Royal Commission on Criminal Procedure, op. cit., para. 3.135.

74. See s. 62(10). These provisions do not affect the Road Traffic Act 1972 procedures. It is an offence under the Road Traffic legislation unreasonably to refuse to supply a blood or urine sample. The sanction works because the penalty for refusal is broadly in line with that for conviction of a drink/driving offence. In the case of more serious offences, this approach would not work, because the penalty for refusal would have to be the same as for conviction of the substantive offence. In the words of the Royal Commission on Criminal Procedure: "We do not think it feasible or proper to provide sentences up to life imprisonment for mere refusal to give a sample, however unreasonable the refusal may be." (para. 3.136).

75. Special provisions apply where the premises consist of two or more separate dwellings. See s. 32(7).

76. Other than items subject to legal privilege.

77. See s. 18(1).

78. s. 18(4). The Act further provides that in such a case, the constable shall inform an officer of the rank of Inspector or above that he has made the search "as soon as practicable after he has made it," (s. 18(5)), and the Inspector shall make a written record of the grounds of the search and the nature of the evidence sought (s. 18(6)).

79. s. 18(3).

80. Supra n.8.

81. See e.g. D.A. Thomas, The Law of Search and Seizure, (1967), Crim. L.R. 3, 10.

82. "Fairness requires that the issue of a warrant should be a judicial act by the issuing authority". Royal Commission on Criminal Procedure, op. cit., para. 3.46.

83. PCE Act, s. 15(1).

190

SEARCH AND SEIZURE

84. Ibid., s. 15(2).
85. Ibid., s. 15(4).
86. s. 15(6).
87. s. 117.
88. s. 16(4).
89. See ss. 16(5), (6) and (7).
90. s. 15(5).
91. s. 16(3).
92. Or where it has not been executed within the time authorised for its execution.
93. s. 16(10). these will be the relevant clerk to the justices where the warrant was issued by a magistrate, or where it was issued by a judge, the officers of the court from which he issued it. Before returning it, the constable who executed it is required to endorse it stating whether the articles sought were found and whether any other articles were seized. See s. 16(9).
94. See ss. 16(11) and (12) respectively.
95. See s. 16(8).
96. Royal Commission on Criminal Procedure, op. cit., para. 3.37.
97. Particularly s. 19(1). See the discussion ante p. 171, and post p. 182.
98. See generally PCE Act, s. 8.
99. Relevant evidence is defined (s. 8(4)) as "anything that would be admissible in evidence at a trial for the offence".
100. The conditions are set out in s. 8(3).
101. Royal Commission on Criminal Procedure, op. cit., para. 3.41.
102. Ibid.
103. See generally s. 10.
104. See s. 11.
105. See s. 12.
106. See s. 13.
107. See generally s. 14.
108. See Schedule 1, para. 2.
109. Ibid., para. 3.
110. Ibid., para. 12. Certain further conditions may need to be satisfied before a warrant can be issued. See para. 14.
111. Ibid., para. 15(1).
112. Ibid., para. 3(b).
113. See the judgment of Lord Denning MR in Chic Fashions (West Wales) Ltd. v Jones, supra at p.
114. The case-law is sporadic but includes Price v Messenger, (1800), 2 BOS & P. 158; Crozier v Cundey, (1827), 6 B & C 232; Pringle v Bremmer and Stirling, (1867), 5 Macph. 55.

191

SEARCH AND SEIZURE

115. Op. cit. See also Garfunkel v Metropolitan Police Commissioner, (1972), Crim. L.R. 44, Frank Truman Export Ltd. v Metropolitan Police Commissioner, (1977), 3 A11 E.R. 431.

116. (1969), 3 A11 E.R. 1700.

117. Ibid., at p. 1703.

118. Ibid., at p. 1705.

119. See Garfunkel v Metropolitan Police Commissioner, op. cit; Frank Truman Export Ltd. v Metropolitan Police Commissioner, op. cit; Wershof v Metropolitan Police Commissioner, (1978), 3 A11 E.R. 540.

120. Ibid., at p. 552.

121. S.A. deSmith, Constitutional and Administrative Law, (Penguin Books, Harmondsworth, 1981).

122. Leigh, Recent Developments in the Law of Search and Seizure, (1970), 33 MLR 260.

123. Ibid., at p. 279.

124. Leigh, Police Powers in England and Wales, (Butterworths, London, 1975), at p. 196.

125. Polyvios G. Polyviou, Search and Seizure, supra. at p. 309.

126. G.H. Photography Pty. Ltd. v McGarrigle, (1974), 2 NSWLR 635.

127. See e.g. McFarlane v Sharp, (1972) NZLR 838. This case was the subject of extensive comment at the time. See Smillie, McFarlane v Sharp; Affirmation or Extension of Police Powers of Search and Seizure, (1975), 6 NZUL. Rev. 271; Bridge, Search and Seizure: An Antipodean View of Ghani v Jones, (1974), Crim. L.R. 218.

128. Royal Commission on Criminal Procedure, op. cit., para. 3.48.

129. Ibid.

130. Ibid., para. 3.49.

131. Ibid., para. 3.122.

132. PCE Act 1984, s. 19(2).

133. Ibid., s. 19(3).

134. s. 19(5).

135. s. 19(6). The power to seize extends to information stored in a computer, see s. 19(4).

136. The Fourth Amendment provides: "The right of the people to be secure in their persons, homes, papers and effects against unreasonable searches and seizures, shall not be violated and no warrants shall issue, but upon probable cause..." Early American law applied the common law rule that the sole criterion of admissibility should be the relevance of the evidence obtained. It was not until 1914 in Weeks v United States, 232 US 383, that the Supreme Court unequivocally decided that

SEARCH AND SEIZURE

illegally obtained evidence was inadmissible.
Whether the exclusionary rule applied to State as
well as Federal Courts was not finally clarified
until the decision of the Supreme Court in Mapp v
Ohio, 367 US 643 (1961), when by a majority, the
Court decided that it did.

137. See Mapp v Ohio, Ibid., for a clear
statement of this purpose.

138. See e.g. Elkins v United States, 364 US
206 (1960). Recent case-law, particularly United
States v Calundra, 414 US 338 (1974), and United
States v Janis, 428 US 433 (1976), has raised controversy by suggesting that in certain circumstances
the operation of the rule should be relaxed.

139. (1861), 8 Cox C.C, 498, 501.

140. The starting point is the Privy Council
decision in Kuruma v R, (1955), A.C. 197. See also
Callis v Gunn, (1964), 1 QB 495, King v R, (1969),
A.C. 304, Jeffrey v Black, (1978), 1 QB 490.

141. (1979), 2 All E.R. 1220.

142. Ibid., at p. 1229 (per Lord Diplock).
Sang is a confusing decision, however, because the
Law Lords, while purporting to agree with the
leading judgment of Lord Diplock, utter statements
which are in conflict with it. See generally,
Heydon, Unfairly Obtained Evidence in the House of
Lords, (1980), Crim. L.R. 125, who concludes (p.
135): "In the result, Sang's case is not a
conclusive authority in favour of a very narrow view
of the discretion to exclude improperly obtained
evidence."

143. Royal Commission on Criminal Procedure,
op. cit., para. 4.127.

144. Ibid., para. 4.128.

145. Criminal Investigation : Report No. 2, An
Interim Report, Australian Government Publishing
Service, 1975, para. 298.

146. See McGovern v H.M. Advocate (1950), S.C.
(J) 33.

Chapter 7

POLICE QUESTIONING AND SURREPTITIOUS SURVEILLANCE

Police Questioning

Questioning or interrogation of suspects by the
police is commonly regarded as an essential part of
the investigative process. Indeed, one of the
primary reasons why suspects are detained in police
custody is to facilitate the questioning process,
which itself is directed at two main objectives: to
determine whether there is sufficient evidence to
prosecute, and to assemble as strong a case as
possible for the prosecution.[1] Both of these
purposes merge in a third objective of the questioning process - to obtain a confession.[2]
        At one time, questioning a suspect in custody
was prohibited. In Gavin,[3] the court stated that a
suspect in custody must not be questioned, but over
the years, this rule has been substantially relaxed.
In Ibrahim,[4] questioning in custody was stated to be
permissible provided that a suspect was first
cautioned. The Judges' Rules, first formulated in
1916, sanctioned the questioning of a suspect whether
he was in custody or not and in Rice v Connolly,[5]
the Divisional Court emphasised that there was no
limit on the questions which may be put to a suspect
before charge. More recently, the House of Lords
held that it is legitimate to arrest a suspect,
provided of course, that there is reasonable cause
to suspect him of having committed an offence, so
that he can be questioned in a police station.[6]
And, as has been seen, the Police and Criminal
Evidence Act, 1984, now provides explicit statutory
authority to detain a suspect in custody after arrest
for the purpose of obtaining evidence relating to an
offence for which he is under arrest by questioning
him.[7]
        It is against this background of a gradual

194

POLICE QUESTIONING AND SURREPTITIOUS SURVEILLANCE

legal recognition of the centrality of police inter-rogation in the criminal justice process that the fears and doubts expressed about police conduct of interrogations should be considered. The Royal Commission on Criminal Procedure stated that "there can be no adequate substitute for questioning in the investigation and, ultimately, in the prosecut-ion of crime", and that "the police must continue to be allowed to question suspects."[8] However, allega-tions that the police put words into the mouths of suspects, or fabricate damaging admissions which the accused is said to have made orally to them (usually referred to as "verbals"), or bully and cajole suspects into making false confessions, or deny to suspects such "rights" as were accorded to them in custody by the Judges' Rules, have become common-place and are not always groundless. In 1977, for example, the Fisher Inquiry into the Confait case[9] found sufficient cause for concern to recommend the setting up of a Royal Commission to consider, inter alia, questioning and the rights of suspects.

Any discussion of the legal, procedural and professional regimes within which police interrog-ation takes place, or of the wider significance of the right to silence, however, needs to be conducted with an awareness of the fact that our knowledge of police interrogations remains relatively sparse. In what proportion of contested cases is confession evidence the sole evidence against a defendant? In what proportion of cases would a defendant have been convicted irrespective of his confession evidence? How often do suspects at trial retract incriminatory statements made to the police? Are all suspects interviewed by the police irrespective of the crime with which they are subsequently charged? What proportion of suspects is interviewed in a place other than a police station? How often are suspects interviewed more than once by the police? What proportion of interviews takes place during the day and what proportion at night and does the time of the interview have any significant effect upon the progress of the interview? For how long are suspects interrogated and does the length of the interrogation vary according to the nature of the crime suspected? What proportion of suspects is interrogated in the presence of a solicitor or other independent person and how does the presence of such a third party affect the interrogation process?

Recent research helps to provide answers to some, but by no means all, of these questions: even so, the drawing of hard and fast conclusions from it

POLICE QUESTIONING AND SURREPTITIOUS SURVEILLANCE

would be most unwise. It does suggest, however, that confession evidence may not be as important in the detection of crime as is popularly supposed and that the period of time for which suspects generally are questioned is relatively short. Baldwin and McConville found that suspects' statements were of central importance in about thirty per cent of Crown Court Cases[10] and Softley concluded that in most cases there is highly incriminating evidence against suspects apart from that obtained by questioning and that the interrogative process is not usually crucial in the detection of crime.[11] The overwhelming majority of suspects are questioned for less than two hours in total, though, as would be expected, the more serious the crime suspected, the longer the length of the interview.[12] Only five per cent of initial interviews at a police station last for longer than forty five minutes and most suspects are interviewed once.[13] The percentage of suspects who confess to some or all of the charges is high, the research findings ranging from fifty per cent - to seventy six per cent,[14] and the percentage of suspects who, having made a confession are then convicted, is even higher.[15] In the overwhelming majority of cases, no independent third party is present during the interview[16] and only a tiny percentage of suspects exercise their right to remain silent at any stage of the questioning process.[17]

While these statistics may reflect the position prior to the passing of the Police and Criminal Evidence Act, 1984, it cannot be assumed that the general picture which they present will not change, in some respects perhaps, dramatically. As has already been seen, the safe-guards provided for suspects in police detention have been strengthened. Suspects who are better informed at an earlier stage of their rights may choose to exercise them more frequently. Easier access to legal advice may result in fewer incriminatory statements being made. The advent of the tape-recorded and possibly, ultimately, the video-recorded interrogation, may have significant implications for the behaviour of both police and suspects in the interrogation process. The waters are, thus, largely uncharted and it will be some time before the legal and procedural changes will produce reliable statistical effects. A possible consequence may well be, however, that detection and conviction rates will fall.

POLICE QUESTIONING AND SURREPTITIOUS SURVEILLANCE

The Right of Silence

The right of silence or, as it is sometimes referred to, the privilege against self-incrimination, is a concomitant of the accusatorial system of trial which is central to our criminal process. In such a system, the prosecution is required to prove that the defendant is guilty of a specific criminal offence beyond reasonable doubt. The defendant is thus entitled to remain silent throughout the entire proceedings because neither police nor prosecutor are entitled to expect a suspect to assist in the preparation of the case against him. Accordingly, there is no legal duty upon a suspect to respond to questions put to him by the police, though there may be a moral or social duty.[18] Viewed in this way, therefore, the right of silence, along with the presumption of innocence, is a fundamental principle of the accusatorial system. However, it is precisely because the onus of proof rests upon the prosecution that the police need to interrogate suspects. Difficult issues of policy and balance thereby arise.

Thus, the common law developed the rule that in order to be admissible in evidence, statements made by an accused had to be voluntary. The voluntariness of a statement is, of course, conditioned by the circumstances in which it was obtained. In other words, voluntariness has a procedural as well as an evidential dimension. The Judges' Rules, therefore, attempted to provide a procedural framework for the conduct of police interrogations though their impact was weakened by their merely advisory status.

The common law principle of voluntariness is particularly associated with the Privy Council decision in Ibrahim v The King, where in a famous statement, Lord Sumner said:

> It has long been established as a positive rule of English criminal law, that no statement by an accused is admissible in evidence against him unless it is shewn by the prosecution to have been a voluntary statement in the sense that it has not been obtained from him either by fear or prejudice or hope of advantage exercised or held out by a person in authority.[19]

The underlying rationale of the rule was undoubtedly the need to ensure the reliability of confessions, though in Sang, Lord Diplock suggested that its

POLICE QUESTIONING AND SURREPTITIOUS SURVEILLANCE

modern basis is to be found in the maxim "nemo tenetur prodere se ipsum" - no-one shall be compelled to incriminate himself.[20] Lord Sumner's celebrated dictum was not without difficulty: the notion of voluntariness expounded and, in particular, its application by the courts, produced substantial and often conflicting case-law.[21] The problems were exacerbated when in Callis v Gunn,[22] the notion that a confession must not have been obtained by oppression was introduced and in DPP v Ping Lin,[23] where it was held that the issue of admissibility turns not on whether the interviewing police officer did something improper, but whether his words or conduct actually caused the suspect to confess out of hope of advantage or fear of prejudice.

The concept of voluntariness adumbrated by the courts found expression in the Judges' Rules,[24] which set out certain directions to the police on the conduct of interrogations and, in particular, required the police to "caution" a suspect at various stages of the investigative process. The relative ineffectiveness of parts of the Judges' Rules have been commented upon elsewhere in this book.[25] As a whole, however, they suffered from the major defect that they did not possess the force of law and there was no effective sanction against their breach. Courts occasionally asserted the existence of a discretion to exclude evidence obtained in breach of the Rules,[26] but it was infrequently exercised and its existence was sometimes denied altogether.[27]

In 1972, the Criminal Law Revision Committee recommended that it should be possible to draw adverse inferences from a suspect's silence under police questioning. It reported:

> We propose to restrict greatly the so-called 'right of silence' enjoyed by suspects when interrogated by the police ...By the right of silence...we mean the rule that, if the suspect, when being interrogated, omits to mention some fact which would exculpate him, but keeps this back till the trial, the court or jury may not infer that his evidence on this issue at the trial is untrue. Under our proposal, it will be permissible to draw this inference if the circumstances justify it.[28]

Accordingly, the Criminal Law Revision Committee

POLICE QUESTIONING AND SURREPTITIOUS SURVEILLANCE

recommended that the caution should be abolished and replaced with a requirement that a suspect should be warned that his silence "may have a bad effect"[29] on his case in general.

These proposals provoked considerable controversy[30] and, despite support from high ranking judges and police officers alike,[31] were never adopted. The arguments underlying them, however, have continued to be important and were urged with vigour before the Royal Commission on Criminal Procedure. In essence, they amount to an assertion that the criminal process is over protective of the rights of suspects and that the right of silence is a protection only for the guilty and as such, is exploited by "professional" criminals to escape prosecution and conviction. The contrary view, equally strongly argued, is that any abrogation of the right of silence would run counter to a central element of the accusatorial system of trial and would deprive the criminal process of an important safeguard against the risk of false confessions. Indeed, some indication of the strength of feeling on this subject is given by the Royal Commission, which referred to the right of silence as being "one of the areas of sharpest debate in the evidence to the Commission".[32]

In its Report, the Royal Commission supported the maintenance of the right of silence, though the extent to which its support was conditioned by its knowledge that the right is rarely exercised, is a matter for conjecture. It recommended that the content of the Judges' Rules should be reaffirmed, in some places extended, and placed on a statutory basis in the form of a Code of Practice.[33]

The 1984 Act and Code Provisions

(a) The Procedural Framework

The questioning and treatment of suspects in police detention is governed by Part V of the Police and Criminal Evidence Act, 1984 and associated Codes of Practice. Some aspects of the new procedures have been considered in preceding chapters and they will not be discussed again here.

The Draft Code of Practice for the Detention, Treatment and Questioning of Persons by Police Officers restates the principle that all citizens have a duty to help police officers to prevent crime and discover offenders and that a police officer investigating an offence is entitled to question any

POLICE QUESTIONING AND SURREPTITIOUS SURVEILLANCE

person from whom he thinks useful information can be obtained.[34] The duty to assist the police is, as has been seen, a civic rather than a legal duty and the Code also makes this point.

The requirement to administer a caution in the prescribed terms,[35] to a suspect arises as "soon as there are grounds to suspect" him of an offence and an officer proposes to put questions to him for the purpose of obtaining evidence.[36] Two points in particular should be noted about this formulation. First, where questions are put to a suspect for purposes other than obtaining evidence, for example, to establish his identity, he need not be cautioned. Secondly, "grounds to suspect" an individual of an offence may well arise prior to his arrest. Arrest, as has been seen, normally requires the presence of "reasonable suspicion" and this is a stricter standard. Under the Judges' Rules, the obligation to administer a caution did not arise until there were <u>reasonable</u> grounds for suspecting that a person had <u>committed</u> an offence.[37] In practice, the first caution under the new regime is likely to be given at the arrest stage in the majority of cases. Wherever there is a course of questioning prior to arrest, however, the need for an earlier caution is likely to arise.

Where an arrested suspect is taken to a police station, the custody officer is required to inform him orally and in writing of his rights to have someone informed of his arrest, to legal advice, to consult the Codes of Practice and to give him a written notice of the caution.[38] Before any questions are put to him for the purpose of obtaining evidence after arrest, he must be given a further caution or reminded that he is under caution unless the questioning immediately follows the arrest.[39] If there is a break in questioning, there is a similar duty to caution again when the interview resumes.[40] In addition to these cautions, the Code requires further cautions if a suspect is arrested for another offence[41] and when he is charged (or informed that he may be prosecuted).[42]

After charge or after a suspect has been informed that he may be prosecuted, the police may not question him about that offence unless (a) the questions are necessary for the purpose of preventing or minimising harm or loss to some other person or to the public; (b) for clearing up an ambiguity in a previous statement or answer; or (c) where it is in the interests of justice that a suspect should have an opportunity to comment on information which

200

POLICE QUESTIONING AND SURREPTITIOUS SURVEILLANCE

has come to light since he was charged or informed that he may be prosecuted.[43] If they propose to question him, he must be cautioned.[44] He must also be cautioned if at any time after charge the police wish to bring to his attention a statement made by another person (for example, an alleged accomplice) though the Code forbids questioning him about it.[45]

In accordance with the general duty imposed upon the custody officer to oversee all aspects of a suspect's detention, where an investigating officer wishes to interview a detained person, it is for the custody officer to decide whether to deliver him into the custody of the officer and make an appropriate entry in the custody record.[46] Before commencing an interview, the interviewing officer is required to identify himself and any other officers present by name and rank to the interviewee.[47] An accurate record must be made of the interview (whether or not it takes place at a police station), including details of venue, times, breaks in the interview and so on and a written, verbatim record of what was said, or failing this, an accurate summary must also be made either during the course of the interview or as soon as practicable after its completion.[48] The suspect should normally be given an opportunity to read the record and sign it as correct, or indicate the respects in which he considers it inaccurate.[49] If the suspect decides that he wishes to make a statement, it must be made upon the prescribed form and in accordance with the procedure set out in Annex D to the Code. Briefly, this requires that a suspect be given the opportunity to write it down himself and that if he wishes it written down for him, the officer writing it down must take down the exact words spoken. Any questions necessary to clarify it, together with the answers given, must be recorded contemporaneously on the statement form and the suspect must be given the opportunity to correct, alter or add to it. These provisions are virtually identical to those formerly contained in the Judges' Rules.

The effect of the caution requirements is that in the normal case, a suspect will be cautioned: upon arrest; when he is taken to the police station; when the interview commences or recommences after a break; and when he is charged. The fact that the requirement to give a caution now derives from the law should mean that the cautions will be given and as such, the provisions represent both a considerable advance on the Judges' Rules and an important safeguard for suspects. Whether the

201

POLICE QUESTIONING AND SURREPTITIOUS SURVEILLANCE

new procedures will have any significant effect upon the proportion of suspects exercising their right of silence is a matter for conjecture, however, particularly as the effect of the enhanced provisions relating to legal advice remains to be seen. The psychological pressure on suspects to answer police questions is considerable. The circumstances of detention, the style, manner and duration of the interrogation, the time of day or night, the personality of the suspect, together may place an individual under considerable stress and result in a false confession. The requirement that a suspect be reminded of his right to remain silent must be supported, therefore, by further provisions governing the conditions under which questioning is conducted and these are also set out in the Code. They include provisions about the suitability of cells and interview rooms, hygiene facilities, meals and refreshment, exercise, medical treatment, rest and sleep and so on.[50]

Before leaving these issues, two further points should be made. the Code of Practice, like the Judges' Rules before it, does not concern itself in any significant way with the manner of police questioning. The style of questioning employed will depend primarily on the individual officer and his assessment of the suspect. Police officers have traditionally not been systematically trained in interrogation techniques and have been left to develop their own style based on experience and their observation of colleagues. The Royal Commission on Criminal Procedure considered whether the Code should attempt to regulate the content of questioning,[51] but concluded that this would be neither "practicable or desirable".[52] It did emphasise, however, the importance of "training for the police not merely in the skills of interviewing ... but in the psychology of interviewing so that officers can be made more fully aware of its potential to produce false confessions as well as true ones."[53]

Secondly, it must be said that the prominence given to the protection of the right of silence by the Act and Code is belied by the sanctioning in the statute of detention for questioning.[54] The right of silence is particularly hollow for those suspects who can now legitimately be held in police detention for up to ninety six hours for the purpose of obtaining evidence by questioning them.

POLICE QUESTIONING AND SURREPTITIOUS SURVEILLANCE

(b) Admissibility

The link between the voluntariness of a confession or statement and its reliability has already been made. A primary reason for rejecting an involuntary statement or one obtained by oppression is that it is inherently unreliable and it is the reliability aspect of confession evidence which was stressed by the Royal Commission on Criminal Procedure, coupled with the need to provide "workable and enforceable guidelines for the police, criteria that the courts can apply without a feat of imagination that sometimes defies belief and a clear and enforceable statement of the rights and safeguards for the suspect in custody."[55] In 1972, the Criminal Law Revision Committee had similarly emphasised reliability as the basis of its recommended exclusionary rule.[56]

The new regime provided by section 76 of the Police and Criminal Evidence Act, 1984, requires that "where it is represented to a court that a confession has or may have been obtained (a) by oppression of the person who made it or (b) in consequence of anything said or done which was likely in the circumstances arising at the time to render unreliable any confession which might be made by him in consequence thereof, the court shall not allow the confession to be given in evidence against him except in so far as the prosecution proves to the court beyond reasonable doubt that the confession (notwithstanding that it may be true) was not obtained as aforesaid". In addition, a court, of its own volition, may require the prosecution to prove that a confession was not obtained in the manner specified, as a condition of allowing its introduction in evidence.[57] The Act also provides a solution to the thorny problem of the admissibility of facts discovered as a result of an inadmissible confession - referred to in the United States as "the fruit of the forbidden tree." Under the Act, such evidence is admissible, but proof that it was discovered as a result of an inadmissible confession is not admissible, unless evidence that it was so discovered is led by the defendant.[58]

It will be noted that the catechism, "hope of advantage or fear of prejudice exercised or held out by a person in authority", has been jettisoned. It should be noted also, that a court is not solely concerned with whether the confession was obtained in the manner specified, but also with whether it may have been so obtained and this is likely to cause some difficulty, requiring, as it does, from the

203

POLICE QUESTIONING AND SURREPTITIOUS SURVEILLANCE

trial judge an exercise in conjecture and speculation.

A confession which is obtained by oppression is conclusively presumed to be unreliable and hence, inadmissible, unless the prosecution is able to satisfy the court that it was not obtained by oppression. The concept of oppression in the context of confessions was introduced into the law in 1964 and it has proved to be a difficult concept to define with any precision.[59] In <u>Priestly</u>,[60] Sachs J. commented:

> Whether or not there is oppression in an individual case depends upon many elements ...They include such things as the length of time intervening between periods of questioning, whether the accused person had been given proper refreshment or not and the characteristics of the person who makes the statement. What may be oppressive as regards a child, an invalid or an old man or somebody inexperienced in the ways of the world, may turn out not to be oppressive when one finds that the accused person is of a tough character and an experienced man of the world.

The 1984 Act provides a partial definition of oppression. It includes "torture, inhuman or degrading treatment and the use or threat of violence (whether or not amounting to torture)."[61] Deliberate and serious breaches of the Code of Practice governing detention can also amount to oppression, though obviously, it is impossible to draw up hard and fast rules as so much will depend upon the facts and circumstances of the individual case.

A course of conduct or act which does not amount to oppression, may still be sufficient to render a confession unreliable. Section 76 uses the very wide language, "in consequence of anything said or done...likely in the circumstances existing at the time to render unreliable," any confession. Again then, non-compliance with the Act or Codes of Practice <u>may</u> be regarded as rendering a confession unreliable. It should also be noted that the conduct or words alleged to make the confession unreliable need not emanate from the police. The pre-existing case-law on the notion of voluntariness will remain relevant. Its conflicting nature has been pointed out earlier. It has been held to be objectionable, however, for a father to say to his

POLICE QUESTIONING AND SURREPTITIOUS SURVEILLANCE

son in a police officer's presence, "Put your cards on the table. Tell them the lot. If you did not hit him, they cannot hang you."[62]
The new test of reliability is likely to prove as problematic in practice as the test of voluntariness which it replaces. In the short term, at least, challenges to confession evidence are unlikely to diminish. Indeed, now that it is no longer necessary always to demonstrate a causal connection between the challenged words or conduct and the statement made (a court may now consider whether the words or conduct may have induced the confession), they may even increase. In the longer term, however, the advent of the tape-recording of interviews with suspects may have a significant effect, not only upon the conduct of interrogations, but also upon the incidence of challenges to confession evidence.

Tape-Recording

Many of the deficiencies and problems in the interrogation process which have been highlighted in this chapter will, it is argued, disappear when interrogations are tape-recorded as a matter of routine. Allegations that a suspect has been "verballed" or that a confession has been obtained by oppression, trickery or unfair means generally will be dealt with by a trial court listening to a contemporaneous recording of the interrogation. Both suspects and police will thus be better protected.
The debate about tape-recording in this country has been prolonged, notwithstanding that in some foreign jurisdictions, notably the United States and Sweden, it has been a matter of routine for some years. In 1972, the Criminal Law Revision Committee recommended that tape-recording experiments should be conducted[63] and the response of the government was to set up in the mid-seventies a committee to consider the feasibility of a tape-recording experiment.[64] Considerable emphasis has been given by opponents of the scheme to the financial implications and the practical difficulties - the provision of tamper-proof equipment and an adequate number of rooms with an acceptable acoustical standard in police stations, the need to transcribe the tapes, "play-acting" by suspects and so on. The Royal Commission on Criminal procedure, while conceding the existence of practical problems of this kind, concluded that they had been exaggerated[65] and reported that "tape-recording of police interviews

205

POLICE QUESTIONING AND SURREPTITIOUS SURVEILLANCE

at the station is feasible and that it can produce at a not exorbitant cost a more accurate record of important statement evidence."[66] The scheme it recommended, however, was that an oral summary of the interview should be tape-recorded by the officer conducting it, together with the process of taking a written statement.[67] This curious and half-hearted proposal completely missed the point of the desirability of recording the interrogation, of course, and was rightly rejected. The government instead accepted the need to introduce a far more comprehensive scheme.

The Police and Criminal Evidence Act, 1984, by section 60, imposes upon the Home Secretary the duty to issue a Code of Practice in connection with the tape-recording of interviews with suspects held at police stations and to make an order requiring the tape-recording of such interviews. This is a facilitative provision because, as yet, a tape-recording scheme is not nationally operational. Field-trials are, however, being conducted in the Metropolitan Police Area (Holborn and Croydon), Merseyside, Leicestershire, Hampshire and Northumbria. They began in 1984 and will last for two years. The results will then need to be evaluated and in any event, the introduction of a nationwide scheme is likely to be phased. It would be optimistic, therefore, to assume that the scheme will be fully operational before the end of 1988.

The field-trial guidelines indicate that a purpose-built cassette recorder, having only a record function, will be used. A separate machine will be needed for play-back. The interview will be recorded on two tapes simultaneously, one of which will become the master tape which when the interview is completed will be sealed in the suspect's presence and will only be opened with the leave of the court. The other tape will be used and copies taken as required. The machine will record on one channel only; the other will incorporate a coding device to inhibit tampering. The interview will be recorded irrespective of the suspect's consent.

It will be noted that the field trials and the scheme ultimately introduced will be confined to interrogations conducted in police stations. To require interrogations conducted outside police stations to be recorded would cause enormous problems. A similar experiment conducted in Scotland revealed that the number of suspects interviewed during the experiment dropped markedly from the level obtaining in the pre-experiment

206

POLICE QUESTIONING AND SURREPTITIOUS SURVEILLANCE

period and this could only be accounted for by officers interviewing suspects elsewhere than in police stations so as to avoid the requirement to tape-record the interview. It was also found that the average length of interviews fell from thirty nine minutes to around five minutes - in other words, suspects were being questioned for lengthy periods before the tape-recorder was switched on.[68] These clearly are difficulties which the field trials and the monitoring process accompanying them, will be directed towards resolving.

The advent of the routine tape-recording of interrogations will represent a major change in pre-trial criminal procedure involving as it does, the disclosure of aspects of the prosecution case to the defence for the first time in trials before magist-rates. There are still problems to be resolved, however. Among them, is the need to decide for what classes of offences it is appropriate to tape-record the interrogation, because it is highly unlikely that all classes of criminal offences will be comprehended within the scheme. In addition, the equipment has to be proved and it has to be possible to ensure that the police comply fully with the scheme and not circumvent it by conducting a greater proportion of interviews outside the police station. But if these and related problems can be success-fully dealt with, the rights of suspects will be better safeguarded, the police will have some protection against unwarranted allegations of malpractice, the reliability of confession evidence will be easier to determine and "trials within trials" will become more infrequent.

Surreptitious Surveillance

> The use by the police of methods of surreptitious surveillance such as telephone tapping, eavesdropping by electronic means and long range observation may, when it is directed against persons in their own homes or business premises, be regarded as an invasion of privacy akin to a search of the premises.[69]

The extent to which the police utilise sophisticated electronic surveillance devices in the course of criminal investigation is unknown. It is unlikely that there is substantial usage, however, and surveillance of this kind is almost certainly

207

POLICE QUESTIONING AND SURREPTITIOUS SURVEILLANCE

confined to very serious crime. The security services probably utilise these forms of surveillance to a far greater extent than the police, though again, to what precise extent is unknown. It is not surprising in the light of the fact that the use of electronic surveillance is barely acknowledged by the authorities, that there is no legislative basis for it. It is a secret activity over which there is no formal control.

In recent years, events have focussed particular attention upon the interception of communications generally and telephone tapping specifically. The executive has long claimed the power to intercept communications,[70] though its legal basis has never been clear. The usual justification advanced was that it was the exercise of a prerogative of the Crown.[71] An alternative view was that the power lies in a common law right which derives from an inherent power in the Crown to protect the realm against the misuse of postal facilities by ill-disposed persons. Yet a third view was that the power to intercept letters was the result of the creation in 1710 of the General Post Office and that the opening and detaining of letters took place upon the footing that those who entrusted their letters to the post would render them open to inspection at the behest of the Crown.

The legal position since 1710 has been that an officer of the Post Office who opens, delays or detains a postal packet commits an offence unless it is his duty to do so, and it is a defence for him to show that he acted on the authority of the Secretary of State's Warrant.[72] It is important to note, however, that the legislation does not provide the legal justification for the interception of communications under executive warrant: it merely provides a defence to a Post Office employee who complies with the Secretary of State's instructions.

It has been the practice to issue warrants authorising telephone tapping since 1937. Previously the authorities took the view that the power to intercept telephone messages was possessed by any operator of telephones and was not contrary to law. It was decided in 1937, however, that it was undesirable that recordings of telephone conversations should be made by Post Office employees and disclosed to the police or security services without the authority of the Home Secretary.[73] This then is the background of uncertainty and confusion against which the now famous Malone case[74]

POLICE QUESTIONING AND SURREPTITIOUS SURVEILLANCE

and subsequent events, must be examined. In the trial of the plaintiff for handling stolen property, prosecution counsel stated that the plaintiff's telephone conversations had been intercepted by the Post Office on behalf of the police on the authority of a warrant issued by the Secretary of State. Malone claimed declarations (i) that any tapping of his telephone without his consent or disclosure of conversations so heard was unlawful, even if done pursuant to the Home Secretary's warrant, (ii) that he had rights of property, privacy and confidentiality in respect of telephone conversations and that tapping was a breach of those rights and (iii) that the tapping violated Article 8 of the European Convention on Human Rights.

Counsel for the plaintiff argued first, that an individual has property rights in his words as transmitted by the telephone system and thus tapping his telephone without his consent constituted an interference with them. Secondly, even though English law recognises no general right of privacy, it does recognise the right to hold a telephone conversation in the privacy of one's home without molestation. He supported this mainly by reference to the common law offence of eavesdropping and the American case of Katz v United States.[75] Thirdly, he argued that any telephone conversation that was reasonably intended to be private should be treated as a confidential communication and that if there was improper disclosure of the conversation to a third party, an action for breach of confidence would lie. The plaintiff further argued that the European Convention on Human Rights conferred direct rights on citizens of the United Kingdom and should be applied as a guide in interpreting English law. Finally, it was argued that as no power to tap telephones has been given either by statute or common law, the tapping was necessarily unlawful.

All of these arguments were dismissed by the court.[76] There is no property right in words transmitted by telephone, neither is there any right in English law to hold a telephone conversation without interference in one's own home. The offence of eavesdropping, which in any event was abolished by the Criminal Law Act, 1967, did not support this latter contention and neither did Katz which was predicated upon the Fourth Amendment. The Post Office (now British Telecom) and the telephone subscriber do not enter into a contractual arrangement and therefore there could be no implied contractual right that telephone conversations should

209

POLICE QUESTIONING AND SURREPTITIOUS SURVEILLANCE

remain private and free from tapping. No duty of confidentiality lies upon those who overhear a telephone conversation but even if it does, there was "just cause or excuse" in this case for breaking the confidence.[77] The European Convention on Human Rights does not confer direct rights upon individuals enforceable through national courts in this country, because the Convention has not been "transformed" into English law and it is no part of the judicial function to construct the safeguards required to satisfy the Convention - "telephone tapping is essentially a matter for Parliament."[78] Finally, and most importantly of all, in the absence of a clear authoritative statement that telephone tapping is unlawful, the assumption is that it is lawful - "England is not a country where everything is forbidden except what is expressly permitted."[79] Telephone tapping by the Post Office with Post Office equipment or Post Office premises could be carried out without any breach of the law and did not require any statutory or common law power to justify it.

The decision, with its wider implication that anyone can tap a telephone provided no trespass is committed, demonstrated very clearly indeed the weakness of the traditional English approach to the protection of civil liberties. An individual whose telephone was tapped had no reasonable opportunity for protest or objection and no legal remedy. That the issue would go before the European Court of Human Rights, in view of the judge's admission that English law did not satisfy the requirements of the Convention, was a foregone conclusion. Prior to this occurring, however, the government reviewed the whole issue of the interception of communications, but decided not to introduce legislation, commenting: "The interception of communications is, by definition, a practice that depends for its effectiveness and value upon being carried out in secret and cannot, therefore, be subject to the normal processes of parliamentary control."[80] The only significant change in the procedures introduced, was the appointment of a senior member of the judiciary[81] to conduct a continuous independent check to ensure that the interception of communications was being carried out for the established purposes and in accordance with the established procedures. Indeed, not only did the government refuse to take legislative action itself, it resisted all attempts to include in the Telecommunications Act, 1981, provisions which would

POLICE QUESTIONING AND SURREPTITIOUS SURVEILLANCE

have put the interception of communications on a more formal basis. When the Royal Commission on Criminal Procedure reported in favour of statutory control over the interception of communications in late 1981, these proposals too were ignored.[82]

The European Court of Human Rights gave judgment in August 1984,[83] in the knowledge that the U.K. government had quite deliberately failed to take a number of legislative opportunities to remedy the deficiencies in the law. Article 8 of the European Convention provides a qualified right to privacy under which telephone tapping is _prima facie_ unlawful. It states:

> 1. Everyone has the right to respect for his private and family life, his home and his correspondence.
> 2. There shall be no interference by a public authority with the exercise of this right except such as is in accordance with the law and is necessary in a democratic society in the interests of national security, public safety or the economic well-being of the country, for the prevention of disorder or crime, for the protection of health or morals, or for the protection of the rights and freedoms of others.

Predictably, the Court found unanimously that "the law of England and Wales does not indicate with reasonable clarity the scope and manner of exercise of the relevant discretion conferred on the public authorities. To that extent, the minimum degree of legal protection to which citizens are entitled under the rule of law in a democratic society is lacking."[84]

In February, 1985, the government published a White Paper, setting out its proposals for legislation. In it "the properly controlled interception of communications" was justified:

> Major criminals or those engaged in subversive, terrorist or espionage activities should not be free to make use of postal or telecommunications systems to further their activities with immunity from detection. If normal methods of investigation are not available, it is right that means should exist to

POLICE QUESTIONING AND SURREPTITIOUS SURVEILLANCE

> obtain information about such activities
> through the interception of communications,
> so long as this is carried out under clear
> safeguards and strict controls. For many
> years therefore a carefully controlled
> system of ministerially authorised inter-
> ception has existed. Interception has made
> possible the prevention and detection of
> serious crime, including major robberies,
> crimes of violence and drugs offences and
> has led to the prosecution of those
> responsible. It has also been vital in the
> prevention of terrorism and for safeguarding
> the security of the nation.[85]

However, the need for legislation "to provide a
clear statutory framework within which the interception of communications on public systems will be
authorised and controlled",[86] was, at last recognised. The White Paper emphasised that it had not
sought to extend existing practices and the
statistics show that the interception of communications generally operates on a restricted scale. The
average annual number of warrants which are issued
to intercept communications is surprisingly stable
at around six hundred:[87] over 90 per cent of them
authorise telephone tapping. The figures do not
differentiate between those granted to the police in
connection with the investigation of crime and those
granted to other agencies for other purposes. The
majority of the warrants are authorised by the Home
Secretary.[88]
    The legislative scheme envisaged by the govern-
ment was outlined in the White Paper and the Interception of Communications Bill embodying it has
since been introduced into Parliament. The Bill
purports (1) to create a new criminal offence of
unlawfully intercepting communications,[89] (2) to
provide clear statutory authority for the issuance
of interception warrants and (3) to provide a
remedy for those whose communications have been
unlawfully interfered with. Under its provisions,
the Secretary of State will be empowered to issue a
warrant where he believes that the interception of
communications is necessary in the interests of
national security or for the purpose of preventing
or detecting serious crime or for the purpose of
safeguarding the economic well-being of the country.
It must be signed personally by him (except in
emergencies) and will remain valid (unless renewed)
for six months. The discretion conferred on the

212

POLICE QUESTIONING AND SURREPTITIOUS SURVEILLANCE

Secretary of State by this provision is no less broad than that previously exercised by Ministers. In practice, similar administrative guidelines to those currently in use, for example, that normal methods of investigation must have been tried and failed or be unlikely to succeed and that there must be good reason to think that an interception would result in conviction, are likely to continue to be employed and thus confine the discretion to some extent, but it is regrettable that the government has no intention to state criteria of this kind in the legislation.

The major device being employed to harmonise English law and practice with the European Convention requirements, is the creation of a Tribunal of five legally qualified persons to which people will be able to apply if they believe that their communications have been improperly intercepted. It will conduct its proceedings in private and those concerned will be under a statutory duty to provide it with all the information and documentation it requires to fulfil its functions. If, having considered a complaint, the Tribunal finds that a warrant relating to the applicant's communications has been issued in contravention of the Act, it will be empowered to quash the warrant, order any intercepted material to be destroyed and require the government to pay compensation where appropriate. If it finds no breach of the Act, this will be reported to the applicant without it being revealed whether or not interception had taken place. In addition to the Tribunal, the system instituted in 1980, whereby a senior judge keeps under review the operation of the system, will be preserved under the new legislation.

A major criticism of the operation of the executive power to intercept communications has been its obscure legal basis, the secrecy of its application and the lack of any opportunity to challenge it. The powers were in the hands of State officials and exercised in secret for purposes only imprecisely defined and not generally known. The new legislation will provide a firmer legal foundation, but the powers will continue to be exercised by the administration behind closed doors. To an extent this is inevitable and would be acceptable if real controls existed over them. The legislative scheme contains important provisions, but remains the minimum possible concession to the demands of the European Convention. The broad and subjective nature of the discretion to authorise interception

POLICE QUESTIONING AND SURREPTITIOUS SURVEILLANCE

accorded to Ministers under the scheme will ensure
(a) that the exercise of the power is no more
confined than previously and (b) that the Tribunal
will find it difficult to ascertain clear limits
which should not be overstepped. And if, as is
anticipated, the Tribunal upholds the actions of the
executive in most cases, its reasons for so doing,
and thus, the criteria developed by the Tribunal to
assess the justifications for intercepting communications in individual cases, will remain secret.[90]
It would be a mistake, therefore, to place too much
faith in this legislation: in practice, little will
change.

Notes

1. See Softley, Police Interrogation: An
Observational Study in Four Police Stations, Royal
Commission on Criminal Procedure Research Study No.
4, HMSO, 1980.
2. See Irving, Police Interrogation: A Case
Study of Current Practice, Royal Commission on Criminal Procedure Research Study No. 2, HMSO, 1980, who
found that the primary purpose of sixty of the
seventy six interviews he observed in Brighton was
to obtain a confession.
3. (1885), 15 Cox C.C. 656.
4. (1914), A.C. 599.
5. (1966), 2 QB 414.
6. Mohammed-Holgate v Duke, (1984), 1 A11
E.R. 1054.
7. See particularly the discussion in Chapter
4, ante.
8. Report of the Royal Commission on Criminal
Procedure, Cmnd. 8092, (1981), para. 4.1.
9. The Confait Case, Report by the Hon. Sir
Henry Fisher, HC 90, (December 1977).
10. Baldwin and McConville, Confessions in
Crown Court Trials, Royal Commission on Criminal
Procedure Research Study No. 5, HMSO, 1980.
11. Softley, Police Interrogation: An Observational Study in Four Police Stations, op. cit.
12. See Mitchell, Confessions and Police Interrogations of Suspects, (1983), Crim. L.R. 596, who
found that 86 per cent of his sample of four hundred
defendants tried at Worcester Crown Court were questioned for less than two hours.
13. See Softley, op. cit., and Barnes and
Webster, Police Interrogation: Tape Recording, Royal

214

POLICE QUESTIONING AND SURREPTITIOUS SURVEILLANCE

Commission on Criminal Procedure Research Study No. 8, HMSO,1980.

14. Baldwin and McConville, op. cit., found a confession rate of 50 per cent; Mitchell, op. cit., found a confession rate of 70 per cent; Zander, The Investigation of Crime : A Study of Cases tried at the Old Bailey, (1979), Crim. L.R. 203, recorded a confession rate of 76 per cent.

15. Mitchell, op. cit., recorded a figure of 93 per cent.

16. Ibid. In 91 per cent of cases, no third party was present.

17. Zander, op. cit., found that only 4 per cent of suspects in his sample exercised their right to remain silent. Mitchell, op. cit., recorded a very similar figure of 4.3 per cent.

18. See Rice v Connelly, supra. n.5.

19. Supra. n. 4 at 609.

20. (1979), 3 WLR 263, 271.

21. See, for example, R v Reeve and Hancock, (1872), LR 1 C CR 362; R v Gilham, (1828), 168 E.R. 1235; R v Cleary, (1964), 48 Cr. App. R. 116; R v Smith, (1959), 2 QB 35; R v Zaveekas, (1970), 1 A11 E.R. 413; R v Middleton, (1975), QB 191; R v Rennie, (1982), 1 A11 E.R. 385; R v Thompson, The Times, 18 January 1978.

22. (1964), 1 QB 495.

23. (1976), AC 574.

24. Judges' Rules and Administrative Directions to the Police, Home Office Circular No. 89/1978.

25. See particularly, Chapter 4, ante.

26. See e.g. Conway v Hotten, (1976), 2 A11 E.R. 213; R v Elliott, (1977), Crim. L.R. 551; R v Allen, (1977), Crim. L.R. 163; R v Lemsatef, (1977), 2 A11 E.R. 835.

27. In R v Prager, (1972), 1 A11 E.R. 1114, for example, the court ruled that if a confession is voluntary, it is admissible, irrespective of any breach of the Judges' Rules.

28. Criminal Law Revision Committee 11th Report: Evidence (General), Cmnd. 4991 (1972), para. 28.

29. Ibid., para. 44.

30. See e.g. Cross (1975), Crim. L.R. 329; Miller, (1973), Crim. L.R. 343; Zander, (1979), Crim. L.R. 203; Zuckerman, (1973), 36 MLR 509.

31. The Lord Chief Justice at the time, Lord Parker supported them. The police organisations generally were in favour of them and Sir Robert Mark, Metropolitan Police Commissioner at the time, was particularly vociferous in urging their adoption.

32. Report of the Royal Commission on Criminal

215

POLICE QUESTIONING AND SURREPTITIOUS SURVEILLANCE

Procedure, supra. para. 4.40.

33. Ibid., paras. 4.77-4.93.

34. Draft Code of Practice for the Detention, Treatment and Questioning of Persons by Police Officers, Notes for Guidance, 1B.

35. "You do not have to say anything unless you wish to do so, but what you say may be given in evidence." Minor verbal deviations do not constitute a breach of the caution requirement provided that the sense of the caution is preserved. Ibid., section 11.5. A police officer who fails to give a required caution commits a disciplinary offence.

36. Ibid., section 11.1.

37. Judges' Rules and Administrative Directions to the Police, supra. Rule 11. In R v Osbourne and Virtue, (1973), 1 A11 E.R. 649, it was suggested that Rule 11 did not require a caution until there was evidence which could be put before a court, i.e. admissible evidence. The clear implication was that the first caution need not be given, as had been assumed, at the arrest stage, but could be administered at a later stage.

38. Draft Code of Practice, op. cit., section 3.1.

39. Ibid., section 11.4(a).

40. Ibid., section 11.6.

41. Ibid., section 11.4(b).

42. Ibid., section 11.4(c).

43. Ibid., section 17.5.

44. Ibid.

45. Ibid., section 17.4.

46. Ibid., section 12.1.

47. Ibid., section 12.6.

48. Ibid., section 12 generally.

49. Ibid., section 12.12.

50. Ibid., section 8.

51. Report of the Royal Commission on Criminal Procedure, supra. para. 4.112.

52. Ibid., para. 4.113.

53. Ibid.

54. See the discussion of the detention provisions in Chapter 4, ante.

55. Report of the Royal Commission on Criminal Procedure, op. cit., para. 4.75.

56. Criminal Law Revision Committee, 11th Report, Evidence (General), supra. para. 65.

57. Police and Criminal Evidence Act, 1984, (hereafter PCE Act, 1984), s. 76(3).

58. Ibid., ss. 76(4) and (5).

59. See e.g. R v Flynn and Leonard, (1972), 24 NILQ 199; R v McGrath, (1980), N1 91; R v Corr,

216

POLICE QUESTIONING AND SURREPTITIOUS SURVEILLANCE

(1968), N 1 193; R v Prager, (1971), 56 Cr. App. R
151.
    60. (1964), 48 Cr. App. R. 116.
    61. PCE Act, 1984, s. 76(8).
    62. R v Cleary, op. cit. Cf R v Reeve and
Hancock, supra.
    63. Criminal Law Revision Committee, 11th
Report, op. cit., paras. 50, 52.
    64. The Feasibility of an Experiment in the
Tape-Recording of Police Interrogations, Cmnd. 6630
(1976).
    65. Report of the Royal Commission on Criminal
Procedure, op. cit., para. 4.24. The Commission's
conclusions were based on the findings of Barnes and
Webster, Police Interrogation: Tape Recording,
supra. n. 13.
    66. Ibid., para. 4.25.
    67. Ibid., para. 4.27.
    68. See Tape Recording of Police Interviews :
Interim Report - The First 24 Months, Scottish Home
and Health Department (1982), discussed by McConville
and Morrell, Recording the Interrogation: Have the
Police got it Taped?, (1983), Crim. L.R. 158.
    69. Report of the Royal Commission on Criminal
Procedure, op. cit., para. 3.53.
    70. The earliest public reference to the warr-
ant of the Secretary of State authorising the opening of letters is to be found in a Proclamation of
1663.
    71. The Report of the Committee of Privy Coun-
cillors (the Birkett Committee), Interception of Communications, Cmnd. 283 (1957), without deciding the
matter favoured this view (para. 38), though the
leading authority on the prerogative, Chitty's Prer-
ogatives of the Crown, (1820), does not mention it.
    72. See Post Office Act 1953, s. 58(1), Post
Office Act 1969, Schedule 5, and the Telecommunications Act 1984, s. 45.
    73. The Home Secretary authorises interception
at the request of the police, HM Customs and Excise
and the Security Service in England and Wales (the
relevant Secretaries of State exercise these
functions for Scotland and N. Ireland), while the
Foreign Secretary authorises interceptions in
relation to defence and foreign policy when this is
necessary in the interests of national security or
to safeguard the economic well-being of the country.
    74. Malone v Commissioner of Police for the
Metropolis (No. 2), (1979), 2 All E.R. 620.
    75. 389 U.S. 347, (1967).
    76. The application was heard in the Chancery

POLICE QUESTIONING AND SURREPTITIOUS SURVEILLANCE

Division before Sir Robert Megarry, Vice-Chancellor.

77. In Fraser v Evans, (1969), 1 QB 349, 362, Lord Denning MR said: "If certain requirements are satisfied, then I think that there will plainly be just cause or excuse for what is done by and on behalf of the police. These requirements are, first that there should be grounds for suspecting that the tapping of the particular telephone will be of material assistance in...the discharge of the functions of the police in relation to crime. Second, no use should be made of any material obtained except for those purposes. Third, any knowledge...which is not relevant for those purposes should be confined to the minimum number of persons reasonably required to carry out the process of tapping."

78. Malone v Commissioner of Police for the Metropolis (No. 2), op. cit., p. 649.

79. Ibid., p. 638.

80. The Home Secretary in the House of Commons on 1 April 1980. See H.C. Deb 1980, cols. 204-207. The statement coincided with the publication of the White Paper, The Interception of Communications in Great Britain, Cmnd. 7873, (1980).

81. Lord Diplock was given this task in 1980. He expressed himself generally satisfied with the system. See The Interception of Communications in Great Britain : Report by the Rt. Hon. Lord Diplock, Cmnd. 8191, (1981). Since 1982, the review has been carried out by Lord Bridge.

82. Report of the Royal Commission on Criminal Procedure, op. cit., paras. 3.53-3.60.

83. Malone v The United Kingdom, Judgment of 2nd August, 1984, Series A, Vol. 82.

84. Ibid., para. 79. In Klass v Federal Republic of Germany, Judgment of 4th July, 1978, Series A. Vol. 28, the Court had recognised the necessity of legislative powers to intercept communications in strictly defined and limited circumstances.

85. The Interception of Communications in the United Kingdom, Cmnd. 9438 (1985), para. 4.

86. Ibid., para. 7.

87. Ibid., Annex 2. The average is based on the figures for the years 1980-1984 inclusive. The figures for the preceding ten years demonstrate a similar picture - see The Interception of Communications in Great Britain, (1980), op. cit., Appendix 111.

88. Figures for the number of interception warrants authorised by the Secretary of State for

POLICE QUESTIONING AND SURREPTITIOUS SURVEILLANCE

Northern Ireland are not revealed.

    89. The offence will not be committed by a person who intercepts communications in obedience to a warrant issued by the Secretary of State or with the consent of a person occupying the premises to or from which the communication is sent or for purposes connected with the provision of postal or public telecommunication services - Interception of Communications Bill, 1985, Clause 1(1). The looseness of the language in which this provision is couched should be noted.

    90. Under the Bill, for example, the Tribunal can only release information entrusted to it with the consent of the person who gave it. The Bill also includes a provision purporting to exclude appeal or review of a Tribunal decision in the courts.

Appendix

POLICE COMMUNITY LIAISON COMMITTEES

In August/September 1983, the author wrote to the forty one provincial police authorities in England and Wales, together with the Metropolitan Police and Common Council of the City of London enquiring what arrangements had been made in the light of Home Office Circular 54/1982, to implement community consultative schemes. All police authorities responded, as did the Metropolitan Police and the Common Council of the City of London.

The main results of that survey are tabulated below:

POLICE COMMUNITY LIAISON COMMITTEES - TABLE 1

	Liaison Comms. established throughout area	Liaison Comms. established in parts of area	Investigation still taking place	No plans to introduce liaison Comms. in immediate future
COMBINED POLICE AUTHORITIES	Avon & Somerset Dyfed-Powys Northumbria Thames Valley South Wales	Sussex West Mercia	Hampshire North Wales Sussex West Mercia	Devon & Cornwall
COUNTY POLICE AUTHORITIES	Bedfordshire Cambridgeshire Cleveland Cumbria Derbyshire Essex Gloucestershire Hertfordshire Kent Lancashire Northamptonshire South Yorkshire Nottinghamshire Surrey Staffordshire West Midlands Merseyside Norfolk	Cheshire Greater Manchester Humberside Wiltshire Suffolk West Yorkshire	Cheshire Greater Manchester Humberside Wiltshire North Yorkshire Warwickshire West Yorkshire	Dorset Gwent Lincolnshire Durham Leicestershire
LONDON	Metropolitan Police			

POLICE COMMUNITY LIAISON COMMITTEES

Notes on Table 1

(a)   Where Liaison Committees have been established in parts of an area, this has normally been done on an experimental basis so that the results may be monitored by police and police authority before extending the scheme to the entire police authority area. Consequently, some Forces appear in both columns 2 and 3.

(b)   By the Police and Criminal Evidence Act s. 106, all police authorities are now required, in consultation with their chief constables, to set up consultative committees. Those police authorities who at the time of the survey had no plans to introduce consultative committees, will now be under a statutory obligation to do so.

(c)   Devon and Cornwall, at the time of the survey, was in an exceptional position. Community policing, as a policy, had been introduced into the area by the former chief constable of Devon and Cornwall, John Alderson. A network of consultative devices was already in existence prior to the Home Office initiative. Accordingly, no further action was thought to be necessary to implement H.O. Circular 54/1982.

	Liaison Comms. based on Police Divisional Boundaries	Liaison Comms. based on Police Sub-Divisional Boundaries	Liaison Comms. based on Local Authority District Boundary	Other
COMBINED POLICE AUTHOR- ITIES	Thames Valley (7;20-26) South Wales (15; 15)	Avon & Somerset (18;16)	Dyfed-Powys (9;21) Sussex (1)	Northumbria (9;15-20) West Mercia (2)
COUNTY POLICE AUTHOR- ITIES	Cumbria (4; 36) Essex (6; 15-20) Gloucestershire (3;30) Kent (7; 20) Northants. (6; 25) Wiltshire (3; 15-25)	Cleveland (10; 12-21) Gr. Manchester (2; 30) Merseyside[3] (27) Notts. (14; 15-20) Staffs.(15; 20-30) Surrey (11; 15-20) West Yorkshire (5; 50) West Midlands (31;25-30)	Bedfordshire (4; 22) Cambridgeshire (6;16) Cheshire (1; 25) Derbyshire (9; 30-50) Lancashire (14;20-30)	Herts.[1] (9;20-25) Humberside[2] (3;15) Norfolk[4] (5; 12) South Yorkshire[5] Suffolk[6] (1; 14)
LONDON			Metropolitan Police (19; 14-50)	

For each police authority, the number of committees established and the average number of members or range of members, where available appears in brackets after the name.

POLICE COMMUNITY LIAISON COMMITTEES

Notes on Table 2

1. In Hertfordshire, the committees are based on either divisional or sub-divisional boundaries.

2. Based on centres of population.

3. In Merseyside, the arrangements are based on public meetings. There are 27 forums covering all 24 police sub-divisions.

4. In Norfolk, one committee covers the Norwich Divisions, and one committee covers each of the sub-divisions of Great Yarmouth, North Walsham, King's Lynn and Dereham.

5. In South Yorkshire, there is a complex hierarchy of consultative machinery based primarily on police divisions and sub-divisions.

6. In Suffolk, one committee has been established based in Ipswich.

POLICE COMMUNITY LIAISON COMMITTEES

The composition of any committee should closely reflect local needs and circumstances - for example, the number of ethnic minority representatives - but a committee of between twenty and thirty members would typically be constituted as follows:

Police Authority (one of whom would normally be chairman)	3
Police (Divisional/Sub-Divisional Commander and one other)	2
Local Authority (Parish, Town, District councillors)	4
County Probation, Education, Social Services Departments	3
Community/Neighbourhood/Tenants Associations	2
Youth/Sporting Organisations	1
Ethnic Minority Groups	2
Local churches	1
Trades Council	1
Chamber of Commerce	1
Age Concern	1
Crime Prevention Panel	1
Head Teacher/Teacher	1
Local M.P.	1
	24

INDEX

access conditions 177
access order 178
ACPO see Association of
  Chief Police Officers
admissibility
  of confessions and
    statements 203-205
  of unlawfully obtain-
    ed evidence 183-
    185
Advisory Committee on
  Drug Dependence 107,
  144
agents provocateurs 107
Alderson, John 2, 6, 10,
  14
Anderton, James 14, 38,
  71
arrest 94-111
  for arrestable offen-
    ces 98-100
  for breach of the
    peace 95-98
  communication of
    grounds of 108,
    109
  general powers of
    100-102
  by private citizen
    99, 100
  under warrant 94,
    100
  unlawful arrest,
    right to resist
    110

use of force to 109,
  110
requirements of 102-
  111
reasonable suspicion
  to 104-108, 137
for serious arrestable
  offence 122
arrestable offences 96
assault 138, 162
Association of Chief
  Police Officers 2, 66,
  69, 70, 82
Australian Law Reform
  Commission 167, 184

bail 112, 113
Belstead Lord 71
Bow Street Runners 23
breach of the peace
  arrest for 95-98
  on private premises
    159
British Telecom 209
Bristol 15
Brixton disorders 1, 5,
  70

Canada, Law Reform Comm-
  ission of 167
caution 198, 199, 200,
  201
Chadwick, Edwin 25
chief constables 2, 3, 9,
  10, 29, 35, 44-50, 61,
  62, 63

226

INDEX

of Brighton 29
of Cardigan 29
of Devon and
Cornwall 2
of Greater
Manchester 38, 71
of Lancashire 71
of Merseyside 9
of Nottingham 29
of Thames Valley 71
of West Mercia 9
of Worcester 29
circuit judge 176, 177
City of London Police
11, 24, 36, 53
Clothier, Sir Cecil 77
Codes of Practice 112,
114, 117, 120, 126,
151, 200, 206
on Detention, Treat-
ment, Questioning
and Identification
of Persons by the
Police 122, 199,
201, 202, 204
on Stop and Search
147
Commission for Local
Administration 90
Commissioner of Rights
62
Common Council of the
City of London 22,
55
communications, inter-
ception of 208, 210
community liaison
committees, see
liaison committees,
police/community
computer, command and
control 4, 34
Confait, Maxwell 8
confessions 194, 195,
199, 203-205
admissibility of 198,
203-205
reliability of 197,
203, 205
voluntariness of 203,
205

confidence, breach of 210
Constabulary, HM Inspect-
ors of 7, 26, 45, 51,
52, 62, 81, 144
contempt of court 178
County Councils 25
Association of 38
crown prosecutors 12, 50,
72, 73
Criminal Law Revision
Committee 93, 96, 100,
198, 203, 205
custody officers 112,
113, 118, 119, 122,
126, 166, 200, 201
custody record 112, 201

Desborough Committee 27
designated police station
110, 112, 113, 124
detention 111-127
review of 113, 114,
124
for serious arrestable
offences 114-117
treatment of suspects
in 117-122
warrants of further
116
Director of Public Pros-
ecutions 50, 61, 62,
63, 65, 66, 67, 69,
73, 78, 79, 80, 84
district attorney 49
double-jeopardy 63, 66
drugs 144
Class A controlled 168
Duty Solicitor Scheme 120

eavesdropping 207, 209
evidence
admissibility of un-
lawfully obtained
183-185
discretion to exclude
183, 198
exclusion of 126
excluded material 176
exclusionary rule 19,
157, 183, 184, 203

INDEX

false imprisonment 103, 109, 141
Fielding, Henry 23
Fielding, John 23
fingerprinting 121
Force Support Units 5

General Election 1983 75
General Post Office 208
GLC see Greater London Council
Gordon Riots 23
Greater London Council 11, 54

habeas corpus 111
"helping and referral" 13
Home Office Research Unit 143
Home Secretary 8, 11, 23, 28, 50-54, 66, 69, 71, 75, 208
House of Commons, Home Affairs Committee 5, 53, 66, 72, 73, 145
hue and cry 21
Human Rights
European Convention on 209, 210, 213
European Court of 210, 211

Imbert, Peter 71
informers 107
innocence, presumption of 197

Jenkins, Roy 63
journalistic material 177
Judges' Rules 8, 117, 118, 119, 194, 195, 197, 198, 200, 201, 202

Kelly, Jimmy 8, 10

Laugharne, Albert 71
legal advice, access to 119, 196
legal privilege, items subject to 176
liaison committees, police/community 40, 54, 220-225

McNee, Sir David 14
magistrates' court 113, 115, 123, 125
order for fingerprinting 121
Mark, Sir Robert 2
Marshall, Geoffrey 43
medical practitioner 168, 169
Metropolitan Authorities, Association of 14, 38
Metropolitan Police Commissioner 2, 46, 47
Metropolitan Police Force 5, 8, 11, 24, 27, 36, 53, 54, 63, 83, 143
miners' strike 3, 96
Moss-Side 15, 70

National Council for Civil Liberties 18, 66, 144
National Reporting Centre 3
"new police" 20, 23-29, 31
Norman Conquest 21

Operation Countryman 8
Operation Swamp 5
oppression 198, 204, 205
Oxford, Kenneth 14

Parliament 2, 18, 24, 52, 53, 148
Parliamentary Commissioner for Administration 77
Pain, Barry 14
parish constables 22, 23, 26
Peach, Blair 8
personal records 177
Phillips, Sir Cyril 83

228

INDEX

photographing, suspects in custody 121
Plowden, Lord 69
Police Advisory Council 28, 71
police authorities 3, 9, 18, 20, 29, 36-44, 78, 81
   for Merseyside 9, 10
   for South Yorkshire 3, 9, 10
Police Complaints Authority 9, 35, 75-81, 82
Police Complaints Board 9, 35, 63-75, 83, 102
Police Federation 2, 28, 63, 66, 69, 70, 71, 72
Police National Computer 52
police ombudsmen 83-85
police questioning 194-207
Police Staff College 52
Policy Studies Institute 16, 17, 152
policing styles 4, 147
   community policing 6, 7, 10, 54
   reactive policing 5, 7, 33, 34
   saturation policing 5
   Unit Beat policing 4, 34
Post Office 209, 210
prerogative 208
privacy, right to 209, 211
private premises, entry onto 158
Procurator Fiscal 49
prohibited articles 146

recordable offence 121, 122
registered nurse 168
"Release" 144
review officer 114, 122, 124, 126
riot control equipment 6

road-blocks 149-151
road-checks see road-blocks
Royal Commission on Criminal Procedure 7, 12, 49, 72, 73, 93, 98, 100, 101, 107, 112, 114, 119, 121, 123, 126, 143, 145, 150, 159, 164, 167, 168, 173, 176, 180, 182, 184, 195, 199, 202, 203, 205, 211
Royal Commission on the Police 12, 17, 29-30, 36, 45, 61, 93
Royal Commission on Police Powers 12, 17, 32, 61

samples
   intimate 117, 169
   non-intimate 117, 169, 170
Scarman Inquiry 1
Scarman, Lord 5, 7, 9, 18, 40, 44, 54, 70, 71, 83
Scarman Report 6, 7, 39, 41, 44, 54
search 160-177
   at police station 166
   intimate 167, 168
   manner of 165
   of persons following arrest 160-161, 162
   of persons outside police station 165
   of premises following arrest 161, 163, 170
   of premises upon arrest 170
   strip-searching 163, 164
   under warrant 172-178
security services 208
seizure 178-185
self-defence 110
self-incrimination, privilege against 197

229

INDEX

serious arrestable
offences 113, 150,
175, 177
sheriff 22
Shore, Edwin 14
silence, right to 195,
196, 197–199, 202
Simey, Margaret 14
solicitor 114, 115, 117,
195
access to 119
Southall 8
Special Patrol Group 5,
8
special procedure
material 176
SPG see Special Patrol
Group
statements, voluntari-
ness of 197, 203–205
stolen articles 146
stop and search 137–149
for prohibited
articles 145
for prohibited drugs
142
reasonable suspicion
to 147
for stolen property
143, 145
sub-divisional commander
123
summons 94, 100
Superintendents'
Association 69
surveillance 207–214
"sus" laws 145

Tactical Support Groups
5
tape-recording 196, 205–
207
terrorism 124
telephone tapping 207,
208
torture 204
Towers, Liddle 8
Toxteth 15, 70
"trials within trials"
207
tythingman 21

verbals 195, 205
video-recording 196

warrant
of arrest 94, 100
for search 159
of Secretary of State
208, 212, 213
Watch Committees 27, 29,
31
"watch and ward" 21, 26
Williams, Glanville 97

230